About the Author

Journalist KAREN SPEARS ZACHARIAS's commentary has appeared in the *New York Times*, *Newsweek*, and on National Public Radio's *Morning Edition* and *All Things Considered*. She's a popular speaker at universities; civic, literary, and veterans events; and a vocal advocate for our nation's military families. Karen serves on the national advisory board for the Vietnam Women's Memorial, the Vietnam Veterans Memorial Center, and the Virtual Wall. She lives in Oregon and Georgia. You can contact her at www.heromama.org.

After the Flag Has Been Folded

After the Flag Has Been Folded

A DAUGHTER REMEMBERS THE FATHER
SHE LOST TO WAR—AND THE MOTHER
WHO HELD HER FAMILY TOGETHER

Karen Spears Zacharias

HARPER

NEW YORK . LONDON . TORONTO . SYDNEY

HARPER

Previously published in hardcover as *Hero Mama* in 2005 by William Morrow, an imprint of HarperCollins Publishers.

HarperCollins books may be purchased for educational, business, or sales promotional use. For information, please e-mail the Special Markets Department at SPsales@harpercollins.com.

First Harper paperback published 2006.

Designed by Deborah Kerner / Dancing Bears Design

The Library of Congress has catalogued the hardcover edition as follows:

Zacharias, Karen Spears.
    Hero mama: A daughter remembers the father she lost in Vietnam—and the mother who held her family together / by Karen Spears Zacharias.— 1st ed.
      p. cm.
    ISBN 0-06-072148-0
    1. Spears, Shelby Jean. 2. Zacharias, Karen Spears. 3. Spears family.
4. War widows—Tennessee—Biography. 5. Vietnamese Conflict,
1961–1975—Casualties. 6. Tennessee—Biography. I. Title.

CT275.S6147Z33 2005
976.8'95—dc22
[B]

2004054668

ISBN-10: 0-06-072149-9 (pbk.)
ISBN-13: 978-0-06-072149-7 (pbk.)

18 19 20 ❖/RRD 10 9 8 7 6

For

JOHN FRANK SPEARS AND LINDA SPEARS BARNES

AND ALL MY OTHER BROTHERS AND SISTERS AT

SONS AND DAUGHTERS IN TOUCH

TREE OF GRIEF

I came across an awful story the other day. A story of an American soldier. Tim O'Brien tells it in his book, *The Things They Carried*. O'Brien has mastered the art of telling the ghastly tales of the American war in Vietnam.

I'm careful about when I read his stuff. I don't read his prose while eating. I don't read it before bedtime. I don't read it if the kids are around. Simply because his words make my stomach convulse, my heart pound, and the fissures in my soul ooze with confusion and anger. I think Sunday school teachers ought to give their seniors a copy of *The Things They Carried*, instead of those insidious religious books which project a ridiculous Daddy Warbucks image of God. I don't know about you, but I hope the God at my side isn't such a namby-pamby.

I need a powerful God. One who can handle the raw realities of life and death. One who can carry his own weight at the front lines and back me up if I need it. I've been needing that sort of God a lot lately.

Which leads me back to the story O'Brien told about a dead man named Curt Lemon. Here's what O'Brien recalled of his death:

"In the mountains that day, I watched Lemon turn sideways. He laughed and said something to Rat Kiley. Then he took a peculiar half step, moving from shade into bright sunlight, and the booby-trapped 105 round blew him into a tree. The parts were just hanging there, so Dave Jensen and I were ordered to shimmy up and peel him off. The gore was horrible, and stays with me. But what wakes me up twenty years later is Dave Jensen singing 'Lemon Tree' as we threw down the parts."

O'Brien said that you can tell a true war story by the questions it raises: "Somebody tells a story, let's say, and afterward you ask, 'Is it true?' and if the answer matters to you, you've got your answer."

I've been asking lots of people questions about the American War in Vietnam, and about my father.

In a sense, I feel like I've shimmied up a tree to pick through my father's remains. It's an unpleasant task. One that haunts my sleep and startles me throughout the day.

Here's what I know so far: Dad was asleep in his tent when he was hit with shrapnel from a mortar round. He had a wound in his gut and one in his back—the one nobody noticed until he died. The medic who was sleeping in the same tent as Dad got shot in the butt. Forrest Gump didn't make it up. Lots of guys in Vietnam really did get shot in the butt. I wish Dad had gotten his ass blown off. He'd likely have lived through that. But instead, he died, in a muddy LZ, about twenty miles from base camp at Pleiku. It took nearly an hour before he bled to death. Fierce rain pelted the camp all day long. I like to imagine that every soul in heaven, including Almighty God, was weeping for my father. He died July 24, 1966. A Sunday.

On my desk, next to my keyboard, is a picture of my father. He's wearing combat boots, army greens, and a grin so sweet it makes my heart drip with sorrow. Behind him, standing three deep in places, is a row of children. Some are grasping cans of army rations. Others have their hands folded, as if in prayer. All are barefoot. One is wrapped in an army shirt. Others are wrapped in army blankets. Some have bright smiles. One has a gaping, ulcerated sore on his left leg. He's smiling anyway. Behind the kids, stand two soldiers whose names I don't know. And behind them, pointed away from the picture, is a U.S. Army 105 Howitzer.

Sometimes kindly folks tell me I need to get over Vietnam. Just forget about it. Sometimes I wish it myself. But as O'Brien notes in his book: "That's the thing about remembering, you don't forget."

I can't get down out of this tree until I'm sure I've removed every last shred of my father. These remains are all I have left of him to hold on to.

contents

Part III 1971 — 1975:
the years of plenty want

Part IV 1975 — 2003:
the years of apricot skies, rushing
winds, and journey's end

David's Prayer

David went in and sat before the Lord,

and he said: Who am I, O Sovereign Lord,

and what is my family, that you have

brought me this far?

2 SAMUEL 7:18

Losing you ripped

my heart out.

Its phantom aches

daily.

DON'T REMEMBER MAMA CRYING WHEN GRANNY RUTH DIED BUT THE DAY AFTER she gathered together all the pillows in the house and went into the room where her mother's foot-pedaled sewing machine stood silent.

Taking the pair of black-handled scissors, she cut open the tops of Granny's pillows. Aunt Blanche asked Mama what in Jehoshaphat's name did she think she was doing, cutting up all the pillows like that. Mama answered something about finding a crown inside one of those pillows Granny Ruth had fashioned from chicken feathers.

I sat on the floor beside her trying to catch flying feathers.

"Sometimes," she explained, "when a person sleeps on a pillow for a long time the feathers will mold together to make a crown. I don't know why it happens, but Grandma

Louisa had two crowns in her pillow. My aunt kept them in a glass jar."

I stayed in that room all day hoping Granny Ruth had slept on her pillow long enough to earn a crown, but Mama never found any.

She still has the pillows she made from those leftover feathers, but Mama hasn't slept on any of them long enough to form a crown for herself. Ever since that day when the man in the jeep showed up, she's been much too busy to sleep.

Part I • 1965—1966

the year of winter moons

the man in the jeep

a T FIRST I NEVER EVEN NOTICED THE JEEP, WHAT WITH TRYING TO TIE UP THE BULLDOG PUP. GRANDPA HARVE was sitting in a mesh lawn chair nearby, his dead arm slung down between his legs. His good hand flicked a cigarette stub.

"Karen, you hold her," Mama instructed over my shoulder. "Frankie, tie that in a double knot." Daddy's best buddy, Dale Fearnow, had given us a prize bulldog as a gift that day. We were all gathered outside the trailer house trying to figure out where to keep such a creature in a yard that had no grass or fence.

We hadn't lived at Slaughters Trailer Court in Rogersville, Tennessee, very long. It was just a dirt hill with six trailers slapped upside it. One was ours, and one belonged to Uncle Woody, Mama's oldest brother. I'm sure given the situation Mama would have rather not lived in any place named Slaughters.

Folks often laugh when I tell them I grew up a trailer park victim. But when I drive through places like Slaughters, like Lake Forest or Crystal Valley, or any of the other trailer courts I once called home, I ache for the children who live there. And for the circumstances that led their mamas and daddies to make homes between cinder block foundations and dirt yards.

This was late July 1966. Just like any Southern summer, the days steamed and the nights stewed. I found myself missing the ocean breezes of Oahu, where we had last lived with Daddy. We'd left the island just a month before, shortly after I finished third grade. We had family in Rogersville, where both my parents had grown up.

"I knew the minute I saw that jeep," Mama told me later. "There aren't any military bases in East Tennessee."

I don't remember having any premonitions myself. I was used to seeing jeeps. We had lived near military bases all my life. Fort Benning. Fort Campbell. Schofield.

"Shelby Spears?" the soldier asked. He was clutching a white envelope. His fingers trembled.

"Yes?" Mama replied. Her whole face went taut as she clenched her jaw. She turned and handed the pup over to Brother Frankie. Little Linda hid behind Mama, rubbing her bare toes in the dirt. "Finish tying him up," Mama instructed.

Then, pulling down the silver handle of the trailer door, she stepped inside. The soldier followed.

I looked over at Grandpa Harve. His eyes were hidden behind dark sunglasses. A white straw hat shielded his drooping head. Sister Linda followed the soldier. I followed her. Frankie followed me.

For years now, I have tried to remember what happened next. But it's as if somebody threw me up against a concrete wall so violently that my brain refuses to let any of it come back to me. I suppose the pain was so intense my body just can't endure it.

I recall only bits. Crying. Screaming. Hollering like a dog does when a chain is twisted too tightly about its neck.

Frankie was sitting cross-legged on the blue foam cushion that served as the trailer's built-in couch. He pounded the wall with his fists. "Those Charlies killed my Daddy!" he screamed. "Those Charlies killed my Daddy!"

Grasping Mama's hand, Linda buried her face in her thigh.

I was confused. Who was Charlie? Who was this soldier? Why was Mama crying? "What is it?" I asked. "What's happened?"

"Daddy's dead!" Frankie yelled back at me, punching the wall again. "They've kilt our daddy! I'm gonna kill them Charlies!"

I had never seen Mama cry before.

Not even that December night in Hawaii when Daddy left us.

Sister Linda was six years old and was already asleep when Daddy and Mama asked Frankie and me to come into the living room. "We need to talk," Daddy said.

He'd never asked us to talk before. Not officially, like he was calling together his troops or something. Mama sat real quiet beside him on the red vinyl couch. Frankie and I sat on the hardwood floor, dressed in our pajamas, ready for bed.

"Frank, Karen," Daddy said, "I believe you both are old enough now to understand some things."

I was thankful he recognized my maturity. After turning over a whole can of cooking oil on top of my head earlier that evening while helping Mama in the kitchen, I was feeling a bit insecure about my status as the family's oldest daughter. I was nine years old.

"You both know who President Johnson is?"

We nodded in unison.

Daddy continued, "There's a country that needs our help, South Vietnam. President Johnson has asked me to go."

"Where's Vietnam?" Frankie asked.

"Whadda you gonna do there?" I asked.

"It's in Southeast Asia. We'll be helping protect the country from communism."

Tears stung. Not because I understood what communism was, or that Daddy would be in any danger. Simply because my daddy would be leaving me.

"Frank, you're the man of the house now," Daddy said. "I need you to take care of your mama and sisters."

"Yes, sir," Frankie replied, his voice too steady for a boy of just eleven.

"Karen," Daddy said, looking directly at me, "you need to help Mama take care of Linda. Okay?"

I nodded.

I held my tears until after I hugged Mama and Daddy and climbed into bed. Scrunching myself between the cold wall and the edge of my mattress, I began to cry.

A few minutes later Daddy flipped on the light. On the bed next to mine, curled into a ball like a kitten, a sleeping Linda didn't even twitch. "Karen?"

"Yes, sir?" I said as I wiped my nose on the back of my forearm.

"Are you crying?"

"Yes, sir," I replied. I tried to shake the shivers from my neck.

"Why are you crying, honey?" Daddy asked.

"I'm scared," I answered.

"Scared of what?" Daddy walked over and sat down on the edge of my bed.

"That you won't come home!" I wailed. Like monsoon rains, powerful tears rushed forth.

"Karen," Daddy said, smoothing matted hair back from my wet cheeks. "I'll come back. I promise."

Picking me up, he let me cry into his shoulder. He smelled of Old Spice and sweat. "But I need for you to stop your crying, okay? It upsets Mama."

"Okay," I said, sucking back the last sob. I didn't want to upset anyone.

"G'night, Karen."

"G' night, Daddy. I love you."

"I love you too, honey."

He flipped off the light. Grabbing my pillow, I sought to muffle the crying that grown-ups can control but children never can.

Daddy left early the next day, before the sun tiptoed over the horizon. He kissed me good-bye, but I barely woke in the predawn darkness.

FROM VIETNAM, Daddy sent pictures of barefoot children in tattered clothing. He sent Linda a Vietnamese doll wearing a red satin dress, and me one wearing yellow. Vietnamese colors for happiness and luck. And he wrote letters, promising he'd be home soon.

Daddy did return for a short visit. His orders called it an R&R, a rest-and-recuperation trip. The order is dated May 8, 1966. The papers issue Daddy a leave for Manila in the Philippines, effective May 10. Skip a couple of spaces over from "Philippines," and in another type and ink are the words "and Hawii." Later, Daddy swore to Mama he'd gotten ahold of a typewriter and changed his order, just so he could come home to us again. He laughed every time he told Mama about that.

It was pitch-dark outside when Mama locked us inside the house and left to go pick up Daddy. Frankie, Linda, and I sat on the vinyl couch waiting for them to return. I was having a hard time staying awake. Earlier that week Frankie had dared me to stick my hand in a wasp hive in the banana tree out back. I'd done it, trusting, as Frankie claimed, that all the wasps were long gone.

Liar. Liar. Liar. I got stung countless times. My hand swoll up till it looked like a brand-new baseball mitt. The doctor had given me sleeping pills and told Mama that I needed to keep my hand elevated. I'd taken the pills off and on all day long. After a half hour or so, waiting for Daddy, I gave up the struggle and returned to Mama's bed. I was there, asleep, when I heard Daddy's playful voice and Linda's giggles. I was sore that everybody else had been awake to greet Daddy.

"Hey there, Sleepy-head," he said when I stepped into the room.

"Hey, Daddy," I replied, climbing onto his right knee. Linda was sitting on his left one.

"Couldn't wait up for me?" he asked.

"I tried," I said.

"Let me see that hand," he said, taking my right hand into his. He studied the swollen hand. "That must've hurt."

I glared at Frankie. "Yes, sir. It did."

"Guess you won't be sticking your hand into hives again anytime soon."

"No, sir. I sure won't."

Frankie grinned. Mama and Daddy laughed. Linda snuggled closer to Daddy and giggled some more. I continued to glare at Frankie. I couldn't see what everybody thought was so funny.

Daddy had changed since he first left us in December. He was thinner. Malaria, he told Mama. I asked her what malaria was.

"A mosquito disease," she said.

We'd had plenty of mosquitoes in Tennessee. They could leave big welts on a girl's ankles and belly. But I never knew bites could make a person lose weight. Daddy looked awfully thin to me. Like he hadn't had a hot biscuit or plate of gravy in a month of Sundays. Even his hair looked thinner. He had a worrisome look in his eyes, too. Like somebody who spent too much time reading and studying and still couldn't figure out the sum.

I was in the kitchen one afternoon when Daddy told Mama about a little girl he'd seen get blown up by a bomb. That troubled him. It troubled me too, after I heard about it.

Daddy said the girl would come to the camp, and he and the other soldiers gave her C rations, pennies, gum, or candy, whatever they had. Frankie and I liked to get into Daddy's C rations, too. Not because the food tasted good. It was really awful. Most of it smelled and looked like cat food. We just liked the cans because they were painted army green. When we ate from them, we pretended to be soldiers in the jungles, just like Daddy.

Daddy leaned his chair back on two legs as he took a draw from his cigarette. A little bit of the Pet milk he'd poured over his bowl of cobbler earlier had turned the color of peaches.

"The Viet Cong strapped a bomb around her," Daddy said, recalling the moment he'd seen the little girl explode. Mama stood by the kitchen sink, drying a plate, listening to Daddy. She didn't say a word. "She was just a little girl, about Linda's size," Daddy said. "She was always asking me for pennies, for gum. They strap these kids with bombs and send them into our camps. There's nothing we can do."

Daddy took another drag from his cigarette and mashed the end of it into his plate. Mama just kept drying dishes. I studied the sadness on my daddy's face. He looked defeated. Tired. Plumb worn-out. I walked over and wrapped my arms around his neck from behind. He patted my hands. "Hey there, Sissy," he said.

"Hey, Daddy," I replied.

"Wanna go for a ride?" he asked.

"Yes, sir," I said.

"Run go get Linda," he instructed. "She can come with us."

Daddy loved to take Linda and me riding on the moped in between the rows of pineapple fields near our house. He'd found the moped in a ditch one day and brought it home and fixed it up. If something had an engine, Daddy could get it to run. He'd spend hours lying on his back underneath a car, tinkering with its parts. I don't ever remember any car we ever owned breaking down. But Daddy always found some sort of reason to spend his Saturday afternoons underneath the car's hood. The only thing he seemed to love more than fixing car engines was driving cars. Fast. He and Mama shared that, too. Their lead-footed ways.

One day, back in 1957, it had gotten him into a mess of trouble and practically killed Granny Ruth. He had her in the passenger seat beside him when he was broadsided on a highway outside Knoxville. Granny Ruth was hurt real bad. She spent weeks lying in the hospital bed. Mama says Granny Ruth never did fully recover from that wreck. She died from a stroke in 1962, shortly before we left for Hawaii.

Mama didn't like Daddy taking us girls out on the moped. She wouldn't ride it with him except for a time or two, down to the end of the street. And she wouldn't watch as we whizzed in and out of the red dirt roads of Wahiawa's pineapple fields. But Linda and I loved it. We squealed with delight, especially when Daddy revved up the engine.

"Faster, faster!" Linda would scream.

"Yeah, faster, faster!" I'd chime in.

Our hair, hers dark, mine blond, would whip every which way about our heads. Daddy would yell at us, "Hang on tight!"

Linda sat in front between his legs and gripped the bike's handles. Daddy kept one arm around her. I sat on the back, grasping his waist. Sometimes, when he wanted to go really fast, he'd have one of us wait in the fields while he took the other out. "Safer that way," he said.

He wouldn't go far, but he'd go as fast as the bike would take him. It was probably only zero to thirty in five minutes, but Linda and I felt like we were going at the speed of light. It was better than a Scrambler ride at the fair. Plus, we got the extra kick of having Daddy all to ourselves.

During that time he was home in May 1966, Daddy took Linda and me for several rides in the pineapple fields. He took Mama fishing along Oahu's North Shore. And he tossed balls with Frankie in the driveway. He ate hot biscuits and milk gravy that Mama made.

Daddy didn't talk much of war or of Vietnam. Other than the story of the little girl, I never heard him mention it again. He cleaned his gear, shined his boots, and grew sadly quiet as it got closer to the time when he had to return. He didn't make me any more promises. But this time I wasn't worried about his leaving. He'd come home just like he'd said. I figured he'd be home again soon enough. So on May 20, 1966, I barely woke at all when Daddy came in to kiss me good-bye.

"I love you, Karen."

"I love you, too, Daddy," I said. I sat up and gave him a hug. He flipped off the overhead light, and I fell back to sleep, confident that there would be plenty of time for more hugs from Daddy.

In June our family returned to Rogersville in anticipation of that promise. Daddy said he'd be home in time for my tenth birthday on November 12. Perhaps even on Veterans Day.

Daddy kept his promise, in a way. He did come back. Via airmail, in a cargo plane full of caskets.

THE TEARS STREAMING DOWN Mama's face frightened me.

Grandpa Harve didn't rise from his lawn chair until the man in the jeep pulled away. And if he ever hugged or comforted his daughter in any way, I never witnessed it. But tears trickled from beneath his dark glasses throughout the rest of the day. Grandpa Harve loved Daddy as much as any of us.

As I tried to sleep that first night, fear blanketed me. Never warm, it at least wrapped me up real tight. I took refuge in fear's cocoon. Sometimes I still do.

I could hear Mama's cries through the thin panel boards that separated our bedrooms. She had cried all day long. Loud, wailing cries. Bitter water. That day I'd seen Mama raise her head and plead with God Almighty Himself. She kept asking Him the same question over and over. "Why me, God? Why me?"

If God gave her an answer, I never heard it.

I wasn't bold enough to ask God why myself. I figured you had to know Him well enough to ask such a personal question. Still, I prayed each night. Clasping my throat, I prayed the only prayer I knew: "Our Father, who art in Heaven, hallow'd be thy name."

Sometimes I fell asleep before I got to the part about "Forgive us our trespasses, as we forgive those who trespass against us." But not usually. Getting to sleep is hard when you're worried about having your head cut off. It was a notion I obsessed over after I overheard some kinfolk discuss whether somebody had tried to cut off Daddy's head. From that moment on, for years to come, decapitation haunted my slumber. Avoiding dismemberment became my focus early in life.

Prior to Daddy's death, I had never even thought much about my neck before. The only times I ever noticed I had a neck were when

Mama told me there was enough dirt in its creases to grow cotton. But nearly every night hence, I fell into a fitful sleep with my hands resting on my throat. I figured being asleep was too much like being dead. No telling what people do to you when you're dead or asleep.

Once, years later, I slept with a man who didn't understand my fallow fears. While I lay sleeping, he took a pair of scissors and cut off my panties. When I awoke the next morning and found myself nude from the waist down, I was frantic. I couldn't figure out where my favorite pair of underwear had disappeared to. Nor could I recall any particular dream that would have enticed me to discard them. My panic came out in a scream.

I know that poor man never understood the violation of cutting a pair of panties off a woman while she slept. And I tried hard to believe that was the only way I was violated. But when one is asleep, one is never sure what is going on.

I fret that being dead renders the same effect. Perhaps it's different for the dead. Perhaps the dead know what's going on in a way the sleeping don't. But can they really offer any help? Or is it just like those dreams where an intruder climbs into your bedroom window and he's stealthily coming toward you, and you begin to scream for help? Then you wake up and your mouth is open, but there is no sound at all. Just the clock ticking, the refrigerator humming, and dark silence.

I suspect if Daddy really saw how hurt we all were, he would have done something to help us. But he didn't. I hope it's because he couldn't—not because he was so busy rejoicing up in heaven that he didn't care about the hell he'd left us in.

It's hard to explain what losing a father does to a family. Daddy's death is the road marker we kids use to measure our life's journey. Before his death, ours was a home filled with intimacy and devotion. After his death, it was filled with chaos and destruction.

I thought about our family's loss decades later while reading an article published in *The Oregonian*. It was the police account of a young man whose body had surfaced in the Columbia River. Hoping that somebody could help identify the boy, the newspaper ran a photo of the shirt he was wearing. It was a custom-made T-shirt with the picture of a skull on it. Law enforcement officials couldn't identify the boy because his head was missing.

That shirt was his only legacy. And unless someone recognized it, his headless body would be buried in a grave marked "John Doe." Whatever thoughts or memories his soul would carry into the afterlife would literally be cut off forever.

I think that's what losing Daddy did to us. With him gone, we were headless. It was as if somebody came into our home with a machete and in one swift slice decapitated our entire family.

bloodstained souls

bY NIGHTFALL MAMA HAD STOPPED WAILING AND WAS TALKING ON THE PHONE. SHE WAS LISTENING AS HER girlfriend Nita Thorne listed all the reasons why Mama shouldn't just lie down and die herself. "Shelby, think of the children," Nita said, talking Mama through the first of many anguished nights. "What would they do without you? They need you, honey."

Mama wasn't thinking of killing herself or anything like that, but she was frantic. She'd never felt so frayed and torn up in her entire life. Not even when her own mama had died. Back then she'd had Daddy to cry out to. Now she didn't have anyone to hold her and tell her that everything would be okay. The worst kind of stomach flu couldn't have made her gut hurt more than it already did. She could not comprehend that Dave, her beloved, was gone for good.

SHELBY JEAN MAYES and David Paul Spears had fallen in love on a blind date at a county fair in the late summer of 1953. She was sixteen. He was twenty-two.

Daddy was already a seasoned soldier when he met Mama. He'd dropped out of school after the eighth grade and worked as a laborer at Townsend Electrical Company in Greeneville, Tennessee, before enlisting in the Army in August 1951. He did a tour of duty in Korea and was back in Tennessee, working at the steam mill in Persia.

Mama was a schoolgirl, getting ready to start her sophomore year at Rogersville High.

They fell in love from the get-go. Daddy was smitten with Mama's lean, tanned legs, boyish hips, and dark-as-coffee-bean eyes. He liked the way her naturally curly hair cascaded around her neck, and that she didn't have a prissy bone in her shapely body. Mama had grown up with five older brothers. She didn't giggle, gossip, or give a shit what other people thought of her. She was as independent and stubborn as the day is long, and Daddy liked that. It gave him something to laugh about. Shelby Jean Mayes also liked the things he liked most—fishing a riverbank on a sunny day and making love under a tin roof on a rainy night.

In one of the letters he sent Mama from 'Nam, Daddy referred to their first date: "I remember when I took some good-looking girl to the carnival in Kingsport. Do you remember?" The letter arrived shortly after Daddy died. In that same letter, he teased Mama with the following note: "It sounds like Frankie is learning to get around there the same as he does everywhere. Tell him to watch out for those city girls around there for that is where one of them caught me. Ha!"

Mama dropped out of the tenth grade after the first two weeks of school. Five months later, on February 13, 1954, the eve of Valentine's Day, my parents married. Mama was five months pregnant with Frankie.

Daddy had been talking about reenlisting in the Army for months. On January 8, 1954, he signed up for a three-year stint. Daddy was due to report to his station at Fort Campbell, Kentucky, on Valentine's Day. Mama stayed in Rogersville with her parents until Frankie was born on June 16, 1954. Daddy wasn't there for Frankie's birth, but he arrived in Rogersville later that evening. Mama moved to Fort Campbell with Daddy when Frankie was a couple of weeks old.

From that moment on, Mama was a military wife. Her independent streak came in handy whenever she was required to pack up and move kids and caboodle on short notice. She made sure we had up-to-date shots for overseas travel, kept our school records in order, and learned the quickest route for finding new dentists, new friends, and new churches. She mowed the lawn, starched Daddy's uniforms, and made sure Grandpa Harve had an ample supply of cigarettes nearby.

After Granny Ruth died, Grandpa Harve moved in with us. Mama's daddy was disabled. A stroke had rendered his left side useless. He could walk with the aid of a cane, but it was a slow step-shuffle. His speech was equally lopsided. But Daddy always took the time to converse with Grandpa. They were good buddies. They would sit on the porch or under a mimosa tree, drinking cups of black coffee, passing cigarettes and matches and stories between them.

When Daddy got called up for a second tour of duty in Korea, Mama birthed and raised Linda alone for the first fifteen months.

"I called a taxi to take me to the hospital when I went into labor with Linda," Mama recalled. "I didn't have anybody else I could call to help me out."

She left Frankie and me with a girlfriend while she delivered our baby sister without anyone by her bedside. Nobody brought her flowers. Nobody threw her a baby shower. Mama just went about her business, tending to our family's newborn, Frankie, and me.

Mama liked being the soldier's wife. She would dress us up and parade us around base on Armed Forces Day or the Fourth of July. She enjoyed dancing at the NCO club, with Daddy's hands clasped about her waist. It was fine with Mama that other men referred to her as "Sergeant Spears's wife." That's the only title she'd ever envisioned for herself.

All her friends were other military wives. They didn't care who had an uppity education and who didn't. They were focused on raising their kids the best way they could, making sure they didn't miss out on the deals at the commissary, and looking ahead to where their husbands' next assignments might be. They got together to sew school clothes, drink a pot of coffee, and arrange pool parties or the occasional dinner out.

Mama had never been a career woman. She didn't even know any women who were, other than our schoolteachers. She knew some women who worked at diners or Dairy Queens to make ends meet, but if their husbands had made better salaries, they wouldn't have done that. As capable as she was, the thought of providing for her family terrified Mama. She loved Daddy. She needed him. She couldn't imagine life without him. Such a life held no promises, only guaranteed sorrows.

"Nobody really knows how alone I really was then," Mama told me years later.

Perhaps not. But Nita Thorne had some idea of how alone she might feel if she'd been in Mama's shoes. Nita was one of the wives Mama befriended while Daddy was stationed in Hawaii. Nita's husband, Hank, was a good friend of Daddy's. They served in the same unit at Schofield and in Vietnam—Battery B, 2nd Battalion, 9th Artillery, 3rd Brigade, 25th Infantry.

Daddy and Thorne were cannon cockers. Daddy, a staff sergeant, was known as "chief of smoke" because he led the firing battery. Thorne was operating the cannon when Daddy died. Thorne, who was still on active duty in Vietnam, sorely wanted to accompany my father's body home, but his request was turned down. Nita and her two children were living in Alabama.

Mama sat on the edge of the bed, her head downcast, tears streaming down her face as she pressed the black-handled phone against her ear, grasping for the comfort Nita offered her. Nita told Mama she was coming to Tennessee. Mama said it wasn't necessary, but Nita and the kids came anyway, and stayed until after Daddy was buried.

Retreating to my room, I scrawled a note to Mrs. Eye, my former teacher at Helemano Elementary School. The writing helped. I had to quit crying so I could concentrate on my cursive. I think that letter was the first time I used writing as a tool to bring order to chaos. I don't know exactly what I wrote that day, but I know I told Mrs. Eye about my father's death and the bulldog puppy whimpering outside the trailer door. I also told her how Mama's crying frightened me.

After placing the letter in my Bible, I curled up on my bed and wept until I fell asleep. As best as I could figure out, if Daddy was dead, that meant he wouldn't be coming home. Not for my birthday. Not for Christmas. Not ever.

The night before Granny Ruth died in July 1962, Mama opened a box of Toni home-permanent kit and rolled my hair up in scratchy pink curlers with itsy white tissue papers. Then she poured nasty-smelling stuff all over my head. It ran down my face. Thankfully, Mama had given me a washcloth to hold over my eyes. When she took the rollers out, my hair balled up all wiry—like a scouring pad that had been used to clean up the fried-chicken skillet. Daddy chided her: "Little white girls aren't supposed to have hair like that, Shelby."

I hoped Daddy's death wouldn't cause Mama to get out the Toni box again.

THE TOWNSPEOPLE LEARNED of Daddy's death when the local papers ran articles with bold headlines declaring he'd been killed by his own shell. One paper ran a picture of Daddy standing next to a 105 howitzer. He's wearing a white T-shirt, khaki pants, and combat boots covered in mud. The cutline beneath the picture reads: "**Last Picture** – S/Sgt. David Spears, standing by his howitzer, was received by his wife in Rogersville Friday. Two days later she was notified of his death, apparently from one of his own shells."

DEFECTIVE SHELL KILLS ROGERSVILLE GUN CHIEF

ROGERSVILLE • One of his own shells, apparently defective, killed a 35-year-old Army career artilleryman from Rogersville Sunday, his family learned Monday. S-Sgt. David P. Spears was operating a 185 millimeter [sic] howitzer against a hostile force when a round detonated prematurely, the War Department notified his wife. The soldier volunteered for service 15 years ago and served in Korea during that war and again in 1959. He was stationed in Germany in 1955–56 and for the past three years had been stationed in Hawaii. Mrs. Spears and their three children had returned to Rogersville from Hawaii about six weeks ago. Mrs. Spears is the former Shelby Jean Mayes of Rogersville.

That newspaper story always troubled me. I couldn't help but wonder if Daddy had been careless. He was a veteran soldier. I thought he should have been more aware, taken better precautions to keep himself out of harm's way, for our sake. I was distraught by the idea that his own shell killed him.

My own ill-formed concept of good and evil, coupled with the newspaper accounts of Daddy's death, left me wondering if my father was in some way responsible for his own death. Had he done something wrong that caused the cannon to misfire? Was he goofing off, not paying attention? Had he cursed God? Used God's name in vain? For what, in all of heaven and earth, could have caused Daddy to abandon his family this way?

As a child, I considered God to be akin to a senior accountant, with a stash of sharpened number-two pencils and a thick ledger book. His watchful eye never missed a wrongdoing. In my effort to avoid the problem of pain, I searched for suffering's common denominator. I knew being a good girl was mandatory for blessings. And just as surely, I knew that doing something wrong would always result in trouble. I was struggling to figure out what wrongdoing had caused this tragedy to befall our family.

GRANNY LEONA, DADDY'S mama, was a crippled woman. She suffered from bad arthritis and poor circulation. Before we went to Hawaii, she shuffled around the wood floors in her home leaning on crutches or a walker. But during our absence she'd weakened more, so she relied on a makeshift chair attached to four training-type wheels to get around. Her chair would not maneuver through our dirt front yard. And even if she could've managed that, how was she supposed to get into our little trailer house? The steps to the door were too steep for Granny and her walking tools. So she did not come see us when we moved back from the island or on the day we learned that Daddy was dead.

Granny lived in a tin-roofed, clapboard house near the corner of Virginia and Elm Springs Roads in the Lyons Park section of Church Hill, a nearby town. Lyons Park was a community of good-hearted people who feared their fiery preacher. Granny's rental house had a wooden stoop, window screens, and a coal stove in the middle of the living room. Bloody Highway 11-W ran directly behind her house. From the kitchen window at the back of the house, Granny could watch the traffic buzz by or keep count of how many trips the black kids from up the road made to Hurd's or Polson's, the two neighborhood markets along the highway. Sometimes Pap would take Frankie and me to Hurd's to get a Coca-Cola, or as Pap called it, "a dope." Pap was Daddy's father.

His real name was Howard Spears, but nobody called him that. Everybody in the family just called him Pap. People in town called him Red because of his burnished freckles and red mop of hair. Pap was a quiet man, who liked to tease us kids with pinches to our inner thighs or by rubbing his unshaven face up against our tender cheeks. He rolled his own cigarettes with Prince Albert tobacco and filled a lighter with fuel from a blue-and-yellow tin can with a pointy tip. Pap could not write or read anything except his name, and he never drove a car. None of my grandparents did. No reason to learn, since they were all too poor to buy one anyway.

Frankie was old enough to go the store alone. I wasn't. But I was big enough to carry coal in from the heap that sat in the corner of the yard, and I was big enough to go next-door and sit on the porch swing and visit with Mr. and Mrs. Parker and their daughter, Priscilla. Going to Granny's house was usually a lot of fun.

But after the man in the jeep showed up, I felt nervous about going to see Granny Leona. I'd never seen her upset before. The newspaper accounts of my father's death had elevated our family from being part of the town's overlooked and unimportant to people of honor and sacrifice. The war hero's family.

Mama was quiet on the drive out to Granny's. Frankie and I were in the backseat. Linda sat up front. Sister Linda had been at Mama's side, or on her lap, ever since the man in the jeep showed up. She even slept with Mama. I'd heard more than one person remark: "Look at that baby. She won't remember her daddy. I feel so bad for her." Whenever I heard that, I would study Linda. I didn't know exactly what I was looking for. How should grief look on a seven-year-old? I couldn't tell how much she understood. Mostly she'd play quietly with her dollies, or she'd sit and stare at Mama. From time to time she'd reach over and grasp Mama's hand.

I wanted to be next to Mama like that. But I knew that such affection would not be welcome from me or Frankie. We were too old. I'd heard Aunt Gertie make several remarks about Mary Ellen's inappropriate affection for her son. Mary Ellen was Daddy's cousin. She had red hair that I thought made her look just like a movie star. And soft eyes that crinkled like wax paper when she smiled. Mary Ellen was always smiling and always touching folks, especially kids. But I could see Aunt Gertie's point. Mary Ellen's boy was a lean, lanky thing. When he sat in his mama's lap, his legs hung halfway down to her shins and his arms were near about as long as hers. He wasn't as old as Frankie yet, but he looked too old to be hanging on to his mama all the time. I couldn't remember Frankie ever even hugging our mama, much less sitting on her lap. He was far too mature for that.

I tried to be. But in truth, I longed for such comfort. I wished Mary Ellen would pull me onto her lap and hold me, like she did her boy, or Mama did Linda. Most of the time, though, I just pretended my hurt wasn't as big as Linda's because, after all, I was the older sister.

Granny Leona knew better, of course. She didn't tolerate such nonsense. When I walked into her house that day, she stretched out her arms at me, and I ran right for them. I didn't care who saw me. Burying myself in her fragile embrace, I cried and cried like a big ole bawl baby. With nary a word, she comforted me. In her arms, I was able to turn loose all the chaos of the past few days. I didn't have to pretend my hurt wasn't real. I didn't have to hide a thing from Granny Leona. And unlike other folks throughout my life, Granny never ever told me I needed to get over my father's death. I think it's because she knew she never would.

AFTER THE MAN in the jeep came, it seemed our little trailer became the town's social center. Relatives I didn't even know I had turned out. I always suspected some of them came for the fried chicken and pound cake. And I suppose some came to gawk at the widow and her children. I imagined that when they returned to their mountain hovels they said prayers for us and thanked the Lord God Almighty that they didn't have to deal with all of our problems.

I've heard it said that Buddhists believe it's wrong to let a person die hungry. Well, Southern Baptists think it's a sin to let the grieving starve. Aluminum-foil-covered platters and bowls filled our fridge, covered the counters and the dinette table. Even the four chairs held plates of cornbread, pound cake, and banana pudding, pepper-fried pork chops and golden fried chicken. There were glass casserole dishes filled with cheese grits, macaroni and cheese, jelled salads, and piles of baking soda biscuits, yeast rolls, and black walnut bread. There was so much food that when folks came to pay their respects, they didn't have a place to sit. They just stood by the front door, fiddling with the slide in the screen. Mama didn't like us kids playing with the screen door slide, but she never said anything when grown-ups messed with it. I figured it was because Mama would just as soon they not stay too long. The trailer was crowded enough with just us and Grandpa Harve.

Folks usually didn't linger, but they all said the same thing. "I'm so sorry."

Sometimes tears would well up in their eyes and dribble down their chins. I don't believe there is anything more troubling to a kid than to see a roomful of grown-ups cry. I don't think Mama liked it either. She did less crying than some of the women who dropped by.

But worse than the crying to me were those apologies everybody kept making. I didn't know what to say to the kindly folks who'd give me a sideways hug and say how sorry they were about my daddy. It was confusing. When we were little kids, before Linda was born, Mama had forced me to say "sorry" to Frankie after I'd bloodied his nose with a swift kick intended to keep him from knuckle-punching me again. I said it even though I wasn't the least bit sorry. I was proud I'd outdone him for once. Frankie would likely say I was way too smug about it.

Mama had also made me say I was sorry for hoarding three kittens in my bedroom closet in Oahu. But I didn't have to be prodded to say "sorry" when she and Daddy drove by Matsumoto's store in Whitmore Village and saw me shimmy up out of a sewer hole.

New sewer lines were being constructed in the neighborhood. My buddy Bernadette and I would pry open the iron lid and climb down into those dank holes. Then we would wander the shadowy underworld. The cement rounds were spacious, clean, dry, and cool, and in some places, where the sun shone through the sewer lids, full of eerie contours. But what I liked most was the secrecy of what we did. Until, of course, that day my parents drove by.

"Get home now!" Mama shouted at me.

I went straight to the house and pulled out the biggest Bible in the house. The gold-leaf one with the colored picture of a pale, frail Jesus on the front. It took both hands to carry that Bible. Placing it on my bed, I shut my door. Then, kneeling bedside and crying all over that picture, I asked Jesus to protect me from Daddy's belt.

As far back as I could recall, Daddy had never whipped me, but the belt's thickly woven threads and brass buckle left an impression on me nonetheless. I was hoping to never give him cause to use it. "Oh,

Jesus," I cried. "I'm sorry. Please forgive me. I promise to never go in the sewer hole again. Don't let Daddy whip me."

When they got home that afternoon, my parents never even said a word to me about my underworld adventures. I figured God had answered my prayers. There was simply no other explanation for it: Salvation belonged to the truly repentant.

Mama didn't know it yet, but there were other things I was truly sorry for. Terrible secrets far darker than those creepy sewers I'd crawled through.

So right after Daddy's death, whenever some kindly adult would lean over and say to me, "I am so sorry about your daddy," I just wanted to run screaming from the room, yelling, "It's not your fault! It's not your fault!"

Because I sensed all along that it was mine.

I knew it from the moment Frankie slammed his best knuckle punch up against the trailer wall and hollered: "Those Charlies killed my daddy!" I didn't say anything to anybody, but I knew better. Whoever Charlie was, he hadn't killed Daddy—I had.

It seemed reasonable to me that if salvation resulted from repentance, then certainly the reverse was true. The unrepentant would not go unpunished. As Mama went wailing through the house, asking "Why? Why me?" I wanted to cry out, "Because of me, Mama! God took Daddy because I was bad!"

But I couldn't risk losing her. So I didn't.

And although I have told others about my wrongdoing, I have never told Mama that it was all my fault Daddy died. I've only told that secret to people whose love I can afford to live without.

The night before Daddy shipped out to Vietnam, I had been to a Christmas party at church. Our Sunday-school teachers gave Frankie and me each a sack filled with peppermints, peanuts, an apple, an orange, malted milk balls, and, at the very bottom of the brown bag, two chocolate footballs wrapped in gold foil.

Running into the house, I found my father lying on the couch with his head in Mama's lap. "Looky what I got!" I squealed, shoving the bag under his nose.

Taking the sack from me, Daddy began to pluck through the treasures. He took out the apple and placed it on his chest. Then, digging deeper, he found one of the foil-wrapped footballs. "Mmmm, this is the one I want," he said, pinching the tiny football between his thumb and forefinger.

I studied the candy's shiny foil and then looked into Daddy's sky blue eyes. "Oh, no, sir!" I cried. "You can't have that. That's my favorite!"

Then, pulling the bag from him, I fished for a malted milk ball and offered that to him. "But you can have this one, sir."

Shaking his head sideways, Daddy again clutched the bag and held up the shiny football. "Nope. This is my favorite. This is the one I want."

Frankie cozied up beside me. "You can have mine, sir," he said, elbowing me aside.

Then, looking into my face, Daddy reached up and stroked the side of my head and said, "No, it's okay. I was only teasing. I didn't really want any candy. I would like the apple, though."

Reaching into his pants pocket and whisking out his pocketknife, Daddy began whittling away the apple's skin. He always peeled his apples before eating them. He was pretty good at taking off all the skin in one long, red curl.

Placing the chocolate football in my open palm, Daddy grinned. I tore off the candy's foil and popped it into my mouth. Mama smiled at the two of us.

If my father had come home from Vietnam alive, I probably never would have remembered any of this. But as a child I believed the reason he died was because God was teaching me a lesson. A lesson so painful I couldn't tell anyone, not even Granny Leona.

The funny thing was that Granny believed it was her fault Daddy died. She told me this one morning, in the weeks after his death, while she stirred a pan of oatmeal over the stove's gas flame. "I know why God took Dave," she said.

I held my breath. I didn't think there was any way she could have known about the football. I hoped Daddy hadn't told her how selfish I'd been.

"It's all my fault," she continued. I put two bowls on the table and fetched the can of Pet milk out of the fridge. "I was worried about how we was going to put Doug through high school. We didn't have money for school clothes or books. I prayed and asked God for the money. Your mama has signed over part of Dave's Social Security check to me."

Doug was the youngest of Granny's eight kids. He was only a couple years older than Frankie, so he seemed more like a cousin than an uncle to us.

Granny switched off the knob, and the flame died down. "God answered my prayer," she said. "The money from Dave will get Doug through high school. But I'm sure sorry I prayed that prayer."

I wanted to run over and hug Granny. To tell her it wasn't her fault. To tell her how I'd been the one responsible for Daddy's death. Instead, I sat down and topped my oatmeal with a splash of Pet milk, a dab of butter, and two spoonfuls of sugar.

Thereafter, whenever folks stopped by the house to pay their respects and told me how sorry they were about Daddy dying, I wanted to shout out at 'em. I wanted them to know nobody was sorrier Daddy had died than me. And maybe Granny Leona.

His blood stained our souls.

western union

THE MAN IN THE JEEP HAD TOLD MAMA HE DIDN'T KNOW
WHEN DADDY'S BODY MIGHT BE ARRIVING. HE SAID
she'd hear something soon. Over the next few days she received all
sorts of Western Union telegrams. By then I had come to realize that
telegrams were a way of rushing bad news to folks.

This was the telegram the trembling soldier delivered. It was dated
July 25, 1966, at 7:45 P.M.

MRS SHELBY SPEARS.

THE SECRETARY OF THE ARMY HAS ASKED ME TO EXPRESS HIS DEEP RE-
GRET THAT YOUR HUSBAND STAFF SERGEANT DAVID P. SPEARS DIED IN
VIETNAM ON 24 JULY 1966. HE WAS OPERATING A 105 MILLIMETER HOW-
ITZER AGAINST A HOSTILE FORCE WHEN A ROUND DETONATED PREMA-
TURELY. PLEASE ACCEPT MY DEEPEST SYMPATHY. THIS CONFIRMS
OFFICIAL NOTIFICATION MADE BY A REPRESENTATIVE OF THE SECRE-
TARY OF THE ARMY.

JC LAMBERT MAJOR GENERAL USA THE ADJUTANT GENERAL.

Another one arrived the next day. It was dated July 26, 1966,
12:09 P.M.

MRS SHELBY SPEARS

THIS CONCERNS YOUR HUSBAND, STAFF SERGEANT DAVID P. SPEARS. THE
ARMY WILL RETURN YOUR LOVED ONE TO A PORT IN THE UNITED
STATES BY FIRST AVAILABLE MILITARY AIRLIFT. AT THE PORT REMAINS
WILL BE PLACED IN A METAL CASKET AND DELIVERED (ACCOMPANIED BY
A MILITARY ESCORT) BY MOST EXPEDITIOUS MEANS TO ANY FUNERAL
DIRECTOR DESIGNATED BY THE NEXT OF KIN OR TO ANY NATIONAL
CEMETERY IN WHICH THERE IS AVAILABLE GRAVE SPACE. YOU WILL BE
ADVISED BY THE UNITED STATES PORT CONCERNING THE MOVEMENT
AND ARRIVAL TIME AT DESTINATION. FORM ON WHICH TO CLAIM AU-
THORIZED INTERMENT ALLOWANCE WILL ACCOMPANY REMAINS. THIS
ALLOWANCE MAY NOT EXCEED $75 IF CONSIGNMENT IS MADE DIRECTLY
TO THE SUPERINTENDENT OF A NATIONAL CEMETERY. IF CONSIGN-
MENT IS MADE TO A FUNERAL DIRECTOR FOR INTERMENT IN A NA-
TIONAL CEMETERY, THE MAXIMUM ALLOWANCE IS $150. IF BURIAL TAKES
PLACE IN A CIVILIAN CEMETERY, THE MAXIMUM ALLOWANCE IS $300. RE-
QUEST NEXT OF KIN ADVISE BY COLLECT TELEGRAM ADDRESSED: DIS-
POSITION BRANCH, MEMORIAL DIVISION, DEPART OF THE ARMY WUX
MB WASHINGTON, D.C. NAME AND ADDRESS OF FUNERAL DIRECTOR OR
NAME OF NATIONAL CEMETERY SELECTED. IF ADDITIONAL INFORMA-
TION CONCERNING RETURN OF REMAINS IS NEEDED YOU MAY CALL
COLLECT AREA CODE 202 OXFORD 7-7756 OR 5-6553. DISPOSITION
BRANCH MEMORIAL DIVI DEPT OF ARMY.

Mama did not discuss these telegrams with us kids. She didn't
even read them to us, but we knew by the phone calls she made to
Daddy's brothers James and Hugh Lee and her own brothers Carl and
Woody that she was upset. She didn't know when Daddy's remains
would get to town or what condition they might be in. And she
didn't know where to bury him. She could bury him at the town
cemetery in McCloud where Daddy grew up, or at Arlington National Cemetery in Washington, D.C.

Or, given the amount of money she was left with, maybe she

ought to dig a hole in the backyard and stick him there. Mama was crying lots now. Seems like every time a telegram came, she got mad and cried some more, but she had quit yelling at God. Instead she just started cussing out the Army.

"What the hell do they mean by 'returning his remains'?" Mama asked. "How much is left of Dave?"

Hugh Lee didn't have an answer. No one did.

The next telegram was sent on July 27, 1966, at 12:28 P.M.

MRS. SHELBY SPEARS TRAILER COURT WEST BROADWAY ROGERSVILLE TENN REMAINS OF YOUR HUSBAND, DAVID, WILL BE CONSIGNED TO THE NASH-WILSON FUNERAL HOME, ROGERSVILLE, TENNESSEE IN ACCOR-DANCE WITH YOUR REQUEST. PLEASE DO NOT SET DATE OF FUNERAL UNTIL PORT AUTHORITIES NOTIFY YOU AND THE FUNERAL DIRECTOR DATE AND SCHEDULED TIME OF ARRIVAL DESTINATION.

That was followed by one dated July 29.

REMAINS OF S/SGT DAVID P SPEARS ESCORTED BY SFC WILLIE R HUFF DE-PARTING SAN FRANCISCO DELTA FLIGHT NO 806 2:10 A.M. 30 JULY FOR NASH-WILSON FUNERAL HOME ROGERSVILLE TENNESSEE ARRIVING KNOXVILLE TENN VIA DELTA FLIGHT NO 534 7:12 P.M. 30 JULY. REQUEST FUNERAL DIRECTOR RECEIVE REMAINS AND ESCORT AT KNOXVILLE NEAREST TERMINAL TO ROGERSVILLE CG WA MILITARY TRAFFIC MAN-AGEMENT AND TERMINAL SERVICE OAKLAND ARMY BASE OAKLAND CALIF.

Daddy's escort, Willie Huff, wasn't a close friend or anything like that. Mama didn't know him or any of the escorts the Army sent to assist with the funeral. Not even the pallbearers. They were just sol-diers, too, like Daddy, who did their best to carry out their orders. I've often wondered if Willie Huff thought of us over the years. Did he worry about what became of the Widow Spears and her grieving children? Or did he get shipped to Vietnam and come home in a casket, too?

Mama saved the telegrams along with the last few letters that Daddy wrote and the last ones she'd penned that Daddy didn't live long enough to receive. She kept them wrapped with a red ribbon and stuffed into a clear plastic pouch for decades, until December 2001 when she mailed them all to me. I hadn't asked for them, but I suspect she knew how much I would cherish them. Words can breathe life into a dead man and make a daughter remember her father's voice. Words can resurrect time forgotten and love lost. Perhaps it's only for a moment, but for a daughter who has spent a lifetime without her daddy, sometimes that's enough.

Along with the daily telegrams were copies of the local news reports of Daddy's death. The newspapers also told stories on a larger scale, such as the Wisconsin Supreme Court ruling in an antitrust case proposing a move of the Atlanta Braves to Milwaukee. The court threw out the case and ruled that the Braves would remain in Atlanta. Other headline news included that the Holston Army Ammunition plant in Kingsport would add an additional four hundred employees, bringing its total full-time staff to twenty-five hundred. The plant produced RDX, the basic ingredient in mortar rounds like the one that killed my father. And the *Kingsport Times* ran headlines welcoming home the town's newest celebrity, Vicki Hurd, the newly elected Miss Tennessee.

One of the first reports of Daddy's death was stuck in a corner section of the *Rogersville Review.* The headline read: "Rogersville Man Is Killed in Viet Action."

ROGERSVILLE • A Rogersville man was among those listed Tuesday by the Defense Department as killed in action in Viet Nam. Staff Sgt. David Spears was killed during combat with the enemy last Sunday. Spears' wife, of the Sluder [*sic*] Trailer Court in Rogersville, was notified of her husband's death Tuesday. Spears served with the Artillery, 25th Infantry Division.

Uncle James drove Uncle Woody and Mama in his car to Knoxville to meet Daddy's casket. We stayed with Granny Leona. Mama had a car, an old Corvair we had shipped from Hawaii. Frankie and Mama had gone to Virginia to pick it up the week before Daddy died.

Mama wrote this account of that trip on July 24, the same day Daddy was struck by a mortar round that would leave him bleeding to death in a country half a world away:

Dear Darling,

. . . Frankie and I got the bus and went to Norfolk after the car. We rode all night Thursday and got there Friday, picked up the car and started right back. I think we were in Norfolk for one hour and were on our way out. I was scared to death to start driving out of there but we made it just fine and didn't even miss the road one time. We were so tired and sleepy but we didn't have enough money to get a room and it was so hot we couldn't sleep in the car. We came to Rogersville and I wonder really how we did it. We drove 490 miles and stopped three times. We made it in 10 hours and coming through the mountains in Virginia that was really a good time. We bought $6.44 worth of gas and didn't use any oil. . . . One time the car quit and wouldn't start and some men pushed it to a service station for us. They cleaned the battery cable, which was all corroded, and it never give us any more trouble. That noise and the shaking got worse. I'll have to see what is causing that. I was driving through Virginia and keeping up with all the big fine cars. They sure give me some looks when I would pass them. Just like "that damn car won't run like that." Frankie and I came on in and we were so tired we couldn't rest and still feel beat and awful.

I left the girls with your Mom and went after them last night. I have promised them I would take them to Dale's house today to go swimming if they would be good and they sure didn't forget it. I am going to take them over in awhile and they are planning to get that ugly bulldog. I'll probably have to run the kids and that dog off. They are tickled to death about that ugly thing and how can I tell Dale they can't have it? He thinks he is doing something great for them and I guess to the kids it is wonderful, but I can look at that dog and get scared myself. . . . Darling, write to me for I sure need those letters. I am going to get ready and go over to Dale's for awhile. I'll be thinking of you and wishing you were here.

Yours forever,
Shelby

Mama's tears still stain the pages of this letter that my father never received. I can't help but wonder: If she was scared to drive a car through the mountains of Virginia all by herself, how did she ever muster up the courage to face a lifelong journey all alone?

just as i am

MAMA DECIDED TO BURY DADDY AT ANDREW JOHN-SON NATIONAL CEMETERY OVER IN GREENEVILLE, Tennessee. Some of Daddy's kin didn't like that idea; they wanted him buried at McCloud, the town where he'd lived as a boy. To try and make them happy, Mama arranged for the funeral service to be held at McCloud Baptist Church, where Daddy had been baptized. But she made it clear that deciding where to bury Daddy was her decision to make, and the way Mama saw it, country graveyards often get overrun with blackberry brambles.

"Greeneville was a national cemetery and would always be taken care of," Mama told me, explaining her decision when I got curious enough to ask about it. "Country cemeteries are not always taken care of. They become overgrown, run-down, and sometimes graves can't be found years later. I didn't want that to happen." Besides, tending to her husband's grave wasn't something she intended to do. As it turns out, Mama made the right decision. Today, visitors to East Tennessee wouldn't ever be able to find McCloud on the map. The dirt-farm settlement has become part of the town of Persia.

The whole burial thing mystified me. I'd never seen a dead person before, and Daddy was my first one. I hadn't been allowed to go to Granny Ruth's funeral. Instead, I hid behind the vanity in one of the bedrooms and cried. But truth be told, I wasn't grieving as much as

I was just plumb mad—Frankie was doing something I wasn't allowed to do.

Before she brought us to the funeral home to pay our last respects to Daddy, Mama took us shopping. She bought matching linen dresses for Linda and me, a white shirt and clip-on navy tie for Frankie, and cartons of Salem cigarettes for herself.

I hated that dress. It was itchy and too tight, and what's more, I felt ugly in it. I think it also had something to do with the way the lady at Parks-Belk Department Store studied me when Mama told her she was looking for something nice, for a military funeral.

"Oh," the clerk remarked. "Was your husband the one who was killed in Vietnam?"

Looking down, Mama replied softly, "Yes, ma'am."

I had been sticking my hands between the piles of folded shirts and slacks and tapping my foot on the wide-plank floors. But I stopped and looked up at Mama. I couldn't tell what she was feeling, but I felt something like embarrassment or shame. Like we'd all done something wrong for which Daddy had paid the price, and now the whole town of Rogersville was talking about us. Which, of course, they were.

Then the lady said something I will never forget: "Seems like tragedy has come to roost in Rogersville. Did you hear about the accident? Out on Lee Highway? A woman and her two babies were run over by a semi. Her little ole car ran right up underneath that big truck. Killed them all instantly. Her car was all mashed up."

Some folks treat tragedies like jokes. They get on a roll and start telling all the one-liners they know as quickly as they can before they lose their audience.

Mama shook her head. No, she hadn't heard about the wreck. But she didn't look too shocked. After all, there was a reason the menfolk called the two-lane Robert E. Lee Highway the Bloody 11-W. I remembered the photo of the accident that ran in the June 30 copy of the *Rogersville Review*. I'd seen the picture in the newspaper box outside the grocery store. Daddy's cousin Mary Ellen had the newspaper spread out on her kitchen table, opened to that story. The car, crumpled up like notebook paper, was pushed up against the door of a semi with the words "Big Mama" sketched on it. Kimberly Hobbs, two, and her sister Kristi, one, were killed instantly along with their twenty-year-old mother, identified only as Mrs. Glen Hobbs, of Surgoinsville. The article said the car had swerved off the highway and then back into the path of the truck.

I tried to shut out the image of what that mashed-up car looked like. I wondered if the little girls had felt any pain. And if you ran your car up underneath a big ole semi, would it cut your head off? I shuddered. Long trucks had always scared me.

Before moving to Hawaii, we'd lived in Columbus, Georgia, where Daddy trained troops at Fort Benning. Mama had Linda to tend to, so Frankie had to get me to Mrs. Penny's first-grade class at Edgewood Elementary School. He walked me on Morris Road, a main truck route connecting the business districts of Macon Road and Victory Drive. The roar of semi engines silenced the playgrounds at Edgewood School. Layers of asphalt trembled underneath the trucks' unyielding weight. Instead of a sidewalk, Morris Road had a drainage ditch filled with grass. Whenever I heard those trucks coming, I scrambled for the ditch. The first time I did it, Frankie looked at me quizzically. He thought I was diving after something. "What are you doing?" he asked.

"Hiding," I replied.

"From what, stupid?"

Frankie didn't like having to walk to school with a girl. Much less his sister.

"That truck!" I exclaimed. "Those big wheels might suck us right off the road."

"You're so dumb!" he said, walking faster. He didn't even slow down to help me gather my letter-E pages from the ditch.

I didn't say anything else the rest of the way home. No reason to. Frankie was bigger than me. He didn't have to worry about being sucked under the spinning wheels of a semi. But I knew from the way those trucks blew my hair straight up and my skirt sideways that they could mash me good.

Now, while I tried on the funeral dress, I kept thinking about that crumbled car on Bloody Highway 11. Linda's dress was a perfect fit, but mine was too snug across my chest. There wasn't a matching dress in a larger size, and Mama didn't want to fool with it anymore. She needed a smoke. So she paid the lady and turned on her heels. We kids followed close behind.

I was still wondering about the terror those little girls must've felt when the wheels of that semi pressed down over them. I knew any screams for their mama would have gone unheard. I couldn't figure out who I felt sorrier for, them or us. Which was worse? Being mashed or having your head cut off? Either way, I figured the saleslady to be right about one thing—it did look like tragedy had come to roost in Rogersville.

NASH-WILSON FUNERAL HOME sat atop a hill. A low, long brick house surrounded on each side by massive colonial homes with towering white Corinthian columns, it looked like the poor relative. Mama was taking us kids to view Daddy's body. Entering the driveway, we passed through a wrought-iron gate with matching lampposts on each side. I wondered what they looked like at night.

The whole front yard was a parking lot. The first of two cars in the lot was long and as black as my patent leathers. I wondered if someone shined it with butter at night. The other car was white and much shorter. Mama pulled up next to the black car, near the front porch, and parked.

Even though July mornings in Tennessee are hot enough to toast bread on the rooftops, Mama insisted all of us kids dress up. My linen dress itched in spite of my cotton slip. Everything stuck to me, and I had to yank at my anklets to keep them up. Getting out of the backseat, I pulled my slip off my chest, allowing air between my skin and my clothes for a brief moment. I felt sweat trace down to my panties. I let go and once again the slip wrapped me like a warm compress. I so wanted to leave, to go home, put on my shorts, and stand in front of the window air conditioner for a long time.

I looked over at Linda winding her way around the back end of our blue car. Mama held her tiny hand. Linda was sweating. Her dark pixie hair was matted around her face. Her cheeks were flushed pink as rose petals. She stared at her feet.

Frankie slammed the door of the car. His hair would have stuck to him, too, but he didn't have any. The top and sides of his head were shaved so close I could see the freckles on his scalp. He looked funny in a white dress shirt and navy pants, like a tent preacher. Give him a Bible, and he could baptize us all in our own sweat.

Mama nodded quietly at Frankie and me to follow her. We followed Mama and Linda up the three brick steps, walking between tall white pillars. Mama reached for the brass knob of the glossy white double doors. The door on the right opened from the inside. Everything was quiet.

A man wearing a gray suit greeted Mama and welcomed us in a hushed murmur. The first thing I noticed was the air-conditioning. The cool temperature made my dress slip from my body. The itching stopped, but now I had goose bumps and I needed to pee.

Nash-Wilson was fancy, like those big city churches. There was gleaming furniture with puffy seats made of red crushed velvet. The carved wooden legs on the chairs looked like claws. A crystal lamp sat atop an end table with the same claw feet. The lamp gave off the only fake light in the entry. The light reflected off a gold-trimmed mirror mounted behind the man who was whispering to Mama. I could watch him in the mirror without actually staring at him. Mama didn't approve of staring. The walls were papered silver-white. The hallway led only to the left. I noticed a multipaned window with beads of water on each square. I decided not to ask about the bathroom; I'd wait.

Still grasping Linda's hand, Mama headed off after the man. Frankie and I followed them. Mama's spiked black heels sunk into the red carpet that looked like dried blood. I was so busy watching her shoes that I forgot to walk and Frankie had to push me from behind. We passed a closed door on the right and rounded a corner. I heard music, a familiar tune. I was no longer hot, but my hands were sweaty and sticky.

We turned left and went through two doors. I looked up. Little round moons hung from the ceiling. Underneath the moons were rows of pews, like the ones at church, only a lot shorter. Perhaps, I thought, this is a church for little people. Frankie really could preach here. There was a book on a varnished pine podium to my right. An aisle led to a front altar. There was no podium for preaching, but there was a large, lead-colored trunk where it should have been. There was even a cross made from red and white flowers. I wasn't sure what was in the trunk. Mama had never sat us down and explained what we were about to see. I don't think it even occurred to her.

I saw a piano to the right and a small organ to the left. A cross was centered on the wall behind the altar. That's where I'd heard that music before—at church. It was a traditional hymn, sung at the close of nearly every service: "Just as I am without one plea, but that thy blood was shed for me." I had always liked that song. I could sing it all the way through without the book. "Just as I am without one plea, but that thy blood was shed for me, and that Thou bidd'st me come to Thee, O Lamb of God I come, I come."

The man stepped aside to allow Mama access to the aisle. Linda pulled her hand away and stopped four pews from the back. Mama turned and looked at us. Frankie started walking. I followed. Linda stood still, as if she was holding something important, something that would shatter if she moved one inch. Pausing beside her, I challenged her to walk with me. She refused.

Mama was at the center of the altar, by the open trunk. She turned and looked at me. Her thick lips were tautly turned down. Her brown eyes were scolding. They said, "Get down here and leave your sister be!" I walked on by Linda but not quickly. Time seemed to have no hold over the place.

Frankie joined Mama; behind them the trunk sat up high on crossed frames. It was gray and as smooth as Mama's pink nightgown. The cross cast a shadow over it. Turning, I looked at Linda, pleading with her not to abandon me. She saw my plea and looked away, down at her shoes. Angry, I faced forward. I walked faster, my feet moving, my mind shutting down.

Mama walked over to the bench on the right and sat down, looking away from me toward the wall. She refused to see. I wasn't scared, but my heart was beating fast and my petticoat was sticking to me again. Frankie had no expression. He was peering into the top half of the trunk. I touched the trunk's side. It felt cold and wet, like the Popsicle we sometimes got when the ice cream truck circled our neighborhood.

I jerked back. This was no treat. Frankie wouldn't look at me. He stared at the inside of the trunk. The music grew louder: "Just as I am without one plea, but that thy blood was shed for me." Taking a deep breath, I stood on the tips of my patent leathers and looked in.

Who is that? He looked like something from one of those wax museums. Shoot, I think they made a mistake. Put us through all of this and that's not even him. Doesn't look a thing like Daddy. He isn't moving.

I looked at Frankie. He looked mad. Biting his bottom lip, his hands stuffed into his pants pockets, he studied the blue man's face. Frankie had to know. I wanted him to tell me this man wasn't our daddy. Tell me, Frankie, *please* tell me.

With a tissue in hand, Mama bowed her head and wiped her eyes.

Linda was already gone. Aunt Betty, Daddy's oldest sister, had come in. Mama asked Aunt Betty to get her baby out of there, to take her home. I looked again into the trunk. I reached up and touched the Plexiglas that sealed and preserved the dead man for all eternity.

There was a mark under his right eye. Frankie studied the swollen area around the cheek and the nicks and scrapes in the man's forehead. He looked like he could've been in a fistfight. The kind that didn't leave too many marks on a man's face but killed him anyway.

I didn't know this man. I wasn't even sure he was real. Maybe he was a big rag doll. He was awful cold-looking. Someone ought to get him a blanket. Mama? Frankie? I'd never seen anyone that blue. His lips were almost purple.

Nope, that isn't him. I turned away. I felt sorry for that man, and his kids, if he had any. I wondered, what would happen when everyone realized this man is not who they they think?

As we left the parlor, I pulled on Mama's arm and asked a question that she would never be able to answer to my satisfaction: "Why is he so blue?"

Either she didn't hear me or she chose to ignore me. I persisted. Couldn't she see it wasn't him? I was furious at her. I asked again, "Why is he so blue?" Maybe someone should turn off the air conditioner, get that man a blanket.

"Mama, Mama, why is he so blue?" Over and over I begged for an answer.

We got into the car and, slamming the door behind her, Mama turned and yelled: *"Because he's dead!"* She left off the "stupid," although I heard it in her tone anyway. Then, repeating the words quietly to herself, she said, "Because he's dead."

Turning to look out the rear window, she backed out of the lot, leaving behind the long black shiny car and the man in the cold trunk.

Now I was the cold one. Shivers came quickly. I couldn't stop shaking. I needed a blanket. Rocking back and forth, I began humming:

"Just as I am without one plea, but that thy blood was shed for me." I cried for Daddy, for Mama, for Linda, for Frankie, and for me. There are still times when I weep for my father the way I did that day at Nash-Wilson Funeral Home, the day I saw him lying all cold and purple-blue in that casket. Even today Mama is troubled by my tears.

family myths

Once Daddy's body arrived in Tennessee, people came from all over to pay their respects at Nash-Wilson Memorial Chapel in Rogersville. Those who couldn't come sent cards, flowers, or letters. Even the prime minister of Vietnam sent a letter from the embassy in Washington, D.C.:

Dear Mrs. Spears:

I learn with great distress of the death of your husband, Staff. Sgt. David P. Spears, United States Army in Vietnam. He has died a hero to defend this country against Communist aggression at moment when the war enters the decisive phase.

On behalf of the Government and people of Vietnam, I should like to pay heartfelt tribute to you and your husband for his selfless sacrifice. For the noble idea of preserving freedom for Vietnam and happiness for mankind Staff Sergeant David P. Spears left his beloved country and family to join the Vietnamese people in the struggle against a common enemy who seeks to destroy peace and liberty. His name will go down in the history of Vietnam together with those other soldiers from allied countries, who have made the supreme sacrifice for the independence of Vietnam and that of the Free World.

You may rest assured your husband has not died in vain since the Vietnamese people are determined to fight to the last man to crush the

Communist expansionist danger. Please accept the deepest sympathy and sincere gratitude of the people of Vietnam and myself.

Air Vice Marshal, Nguyen Cao Ky, Prime Minister

Mama also received a letter from Captain Frederick Rice, from the 25th Infantry Division, dated August 1966:

Dear Mrs. Spears:

It is very difficult to express my sorrow at learning of the death of your husband. Having served with Sergeant Spears as his Battery Commander from December through June, I admired and respected him as the finest NCO in the Battery, and one of the most outstanding soldiers I have ever met.

He was a very dedicated man who took a great deal of pride in his work, and it showed. His section always stood head and shoulders above the rest, and it was always a pleasure to "show off" his section to visitors.

In gratitude for his fine performance of duty, I wrote a letter recommending him for promotion when I departed the Battery. The high quality of his work can be attested to by the fact that he was the only individual for whom I wrote such a recommendation.

Your great feeling of loss at this sad time is felt by the Army also, since it has lost one of its finest men. The sacrifice which your husband and many brave men like him have made is a difficult one to bear, but their dedication and loyalty will continue on, helping the Free World accomplish its difficult task of remaining free. I extend my deepest sympathy.

Sincerely,
Frederick C. Rice,
Captain, Artillery

Complete strangers sent their condolences, like this lady from Fall Branch, Tennessee:

Dear Mrs. Spears:

I was sorry to read of the loss of your husband. Please accept my prayers and sympathy. My husband is with the 25th Infantry in Viet Nam, too, and I know in a small way how you must feel. I know many people will remember the sacrifice your husband has made for us. God be with you and your family.

Sincerely,

Mrs. James G. Lawson

New York City evangelist A. Gordon sent Mama a note from his West Side apartment, exhorting her to "meditate much on the love of Jesus." And Mrs. Rosamond Christenbery, another lady we didn't know, sent a clipping about Daddy's death from the Knoxville paper with a note attached that read, "Thought you would like the clipping, most folks appreciate kindness." She addressed her letter to "The family of the Late Stf. Sgt. David P. Spears, Church Hill, Tenn. (Please locate)."

Letters also poured in from Hawaii, West Virginia, New York City, Texas, Oklahoma, Alabama, and from Daddy's buddies in Vietnam. There was even one from the White House:

Dear Mrs. Spears:

Mrs. Johnson and I were saddened to learn of the death of your husband, Staff Sergeant David Spears, in Vietnam. Words are inadequate to express our thoughts at times like this, but I hope you find some comfort in the knowledge that your husband's example will survive him. His dedication to the cause of freedom and peace will inspire other men to new appreciation of those great blessings, and a new determination to enjoy them. Please know our prayers are with you and your children in this time of sorrow.

Sincerely,

Lyndon B. Johnson

Mama never talked about these notes, or the people who sent them, not even when the president's letter arrived. She just tied them all up in a red ribbon and stuffed them away in that plastic bag.

I don't know if she ever acknowledged these people and their kindnesses. I suspect she didn't. Mama is a woman of few words and even fewer letters. Besides, with a funeral looming, she had plenty of other business to tend to.

DADDY AND MAMA both came from large extended families, so visiting hours at the funeral chapel were busy all day long and into the early evening. Viewing had lasted the traditional three days; on the third day he was buried.

Daddy was the third-born of eight children, and I'd never seen all his siblings at once. James was the eldest, then came Lynn, Daddy, Betty, Ray, Hugh Lee, Mary Sue, and Doug. Lynn lived up north in Ohio. Ray lived down south in Selma, Alabama. Betty lived in Nashville with her husband, Dode. The rest all lived in East Tennessee.

Hugh Lee, Mary Sue, and Doug weren't finished with their growing-up years yet, so none of them had any kids. But the others had so many, I couldn't remember all my cousins' names. Dode and Betty had six kids. Ray and his wife, Helen, had three. James and his wife, Bon, had two boys. Lynn had kids, but the only one I remember was his daughter, Brenda. She was close to my age.

Mama was the youngest sibling to five brothers—Woody, Tub, Roy, Carl, and Charles. Granny Ruth had given birth to two more girls (one was a fraternal twin to Woody), but Mama was the only daughter who survived childbirth. I'd never seen all Mama's brothers in one place, either. Tub had died years earlier. And Charlie and Roy were living way out in Oregon, so they didn't come to town for Daddy's funeral.

All of Daddy's kin showed up, including his aunts and uncles and cousins from both the Lawson side of the family (Granny Leona's bunch) and the Spears side (Pap's bunch). Granny Leona was always introducing me and Frankie and Linda around to somebody.

"These are Dave's children," she said. "Frankie, Karen, and Linda." All the adults looked the same to me—tall. I cranked my neck all the way back to greet these strangers. And they were always tucking their chins on their chest bone so they could look me straight in the eyes. Nobody ever thought to squat down to a child's level. Granny was the only adult I could see eye-to-eye, and that's because she was an itty-bitty woman anyway and she always was sitting on the edge of her bed, which was in the living room.

My cousins had all been warned within an inch of their lives to be on their very best behavior. So they sat quietly on the arms of the couch or on the floor between their daddies' feet, fiddling with their papas' shoestrings. They would stare in curiosity at Frankie, Linda, and me, with big eyes, like they were afraid they might catch the disease that made us fatherless.

During the days leading up to Daddy's funeral, we kids didn't run outside to climb the coal heap. We didn't play tag-you're-it. We didn't do much of anything but sit around watching the grown-ups drink gallons of coffee and smoke cartons of cigarettes and swap tales of "Remember when" or "Do you suppose."

THE RUMOR THAT DADDY had been decapitated caused some kinfolk to speculate that that was why Mama didn't want an open casket at the funeral. Aunt Mary Sue, Daddy's youngest sister, remembers hearing and even repeating the rumor, although she could not recall where she first heard it or why it got started. "I heard when they first opened the casket, your daddy's head wasn't attached to his body," she told me. "I don't know who all was there when they first opened that casket. Was that the one he was buried in? But whoever it was, they said his head wasn't attached."

Daddy's brother James was there when they first opened the casket, but he wouldn't talk to me about what he saw, and his sister

Mary Sue remembers seeing him lying in his death cradle, his head positioned awkwardly over his right shoulder. Mary Sue is a nurse. She chooses her words carefully and methodically like she's picking through a plate full of cut vegetables, and although she is blunt, she tries hard not to offend. Like Mama, she worries about giving me too much information. I know what they fear is that such information may shatter my soul and all that'll be left of the girl they love will be dangerously jagged edges. I'd be lying if I didn't admit that I'm afraid of the same thing myself.

The decapitation rumor troubled Mary Sue as much as it did me. "It bothered me a lot when I first heard it. But if that's truly how it was, I'm not surprised," she said.

I asked her why.

"Because if a person's blowed up you wouldn't expect him to be all together. I've treated patients who've been shot and are holding their guts in their hands," she said. "If a cannon or big gun blowed Dave up, you wouldn't expect him to be together."

The rumor infuriates Mama, to this day. She curses at the mention of it and is quick to note that Daddy had a military escort from the moment they put his casket on the plane in Vietnam. "Nobody was messing with his body," she said.

From time to time I pull out a photo somebody, maybe Mama, took of Daddy in that casket. Taking pictures of loved ones in their caskets is an unsettling Southern tradition, one of many that give me the heebie-jeebies and make me hope in a merciful God. What I notice first is that Daddy looks too big for the casket. Like a holiday turkey that's been placed in a pan that's too narrow and too shallow. His chest is puffy. A flag is draped over the casket's lower half, its stars evoking an almost festive feel to the photo. But, yes, Daddy's head does look all hinky-kinky. Although dressed in his best military garb, there is nothing uniform about the way he looks. While the three brass buttons line up just beneath the thickly knotted tie, that knot wedges up to the far left corner of his chin, directly under his left eye. Seeing it makes me want to reach in and scooch his head over just a bit.

But what I can't reconcile is that Daddy's face is only slightly marred. There's an abrasion on his right cheek and a few scrapes on his forehead. His eyes are closed, as if in sleep, and his lips are drawn, as if he is in solemn thought. But there is a look of worry about him. Perhaps it's only intense concentration.

I often wonder, what were his last thoughts? Were they of us, his family? Did he know he was mortally wounded? Could he understand how Mama would cry out over the years for the nearness of him? Was he aware of the muffled tears we kids would shed into feather pillows or into piles of folded laundry or over stacks of family photos? Perhaps he knew. Maybe that's why he looks worried.

I didn't care to see another dead person. Especially the blue man in that gray casket. My bones still chill at the sight of open caskets. The person seems almost transparent, like you can see clean through them. Or, if you were to touch them, their chest or forehead would crush under the weight of its own hollowness. There is nothing there.

It's like looking at a June bug's shell. Frankie and I used to find June bug shells clinging to pine trees. We'd mash them between our thumbs and forefingers, and I always wondered where the June bugs went when they left their shells behind. I figured—or maybe I just hoped—they grew into new shells somewhere.

But make no mistake about it, shells, even empty ones, are important to Southerners. *The Atlanta Journal-Constitution* conducted a poll in 2001 that measured the death worries of native Southerners. The article stated that lifelong Southerners think about death a lot. Mostly because they think so much about religion, said Charles Reagan Wilson, director of the University of Mississippi's Center for the Study of Southern Culture. "Southerners have a very literal understanding of heaven and hell," he said. "Death is not abstract. Ministers talk about it, preach about it, 'Are you ready to meet the Lord?'

You drive down the road in the rural South, you see these signs, 'Get right with God.'"

According to the poll, topping the Southerner's list of worries about death is not the soul's destination; 40 percent of the 852 adults polled in thirteen Southern states fretted about whether they'd get the opportunity to say final good-byes. Native Southerners have this uncanny need not only to make things right with God before they die, they've got to make things right with Aunt Ida as well.

Imagine, then, how upset our kinfolk were back in 1966 that they didn't get to say a proper good-bye to Daddy. None of his family had seen him since 1963 when we left for Hawaii. At that time nobody thought about dangers. They were thrilled for our family. Shoot, as far as they were concerned, Daddy had just nabbed an assignment in paradise.

"We were happy for him," Uncle James said. "Everybody thought it was a nice tour of duty for him."

He recalled the last time he saw his brother alive. "The last time I seen him was on Broadway in Rogersville. He was wearing civilian clothes. Shelby was with him. I believe you all were headed to Hawaii. He was happy, and I was happy for him."

Mary Sue recalled that she was living in Nashville with her sister Betty the last time she saw him alive. "Betty's family was there and your family," she said. "It was when you all were going to Hawaii. I don't remember anyone being sad about you all leaving. Nobody thought they wouldn't get to see Dave again."

Aunt Betty and Uncle Dode remember that day as well. They remember what a good mood Daddy had been in. They'd all laughed and carried on over a customer who had been in Dode's shop earlier that day. Daddy was wearing a pair of shorts, and his firm legs had pleased a customer so much the man started flirting with my father. Daddy did have really shapely legs, so I can understand why even a fellow might have been compelled to comment on them. Uncle Dode still laughs every time he tells that story.

Aunt Betty is reminded of Daddy whenever she flours and peppers pork chops, because in July 1966 she was standing over the stove frying up a skillet of chops when she answered a ringing phone and learned that her beloved brother had been killed in Vietnam. For years afterward, just the smell of pork sizzling sent her into a tizzy of tears.

That visit to Nashville, Aunt Betty and Aunt Mary Sue fed us cornbread, fried chicken, and lima beans and told us family stories that made us laugh. They remarked about how big Frankie and I were getting to be and how much bigger we'd be the next time they'd see us. They stroked Linda's brunette hair and said she had the prettiest eyes they'd ever seen. Then Frankie, Linda, and I played hide-and-go-seek in Aunt Betty's backyard with our cousins. And when we tired of that we chased after flickering lightning bugs and swiped at the mosquitoes biting our ankles.

We stayed outside even after twilight settled down around our heels. Darkness didn't scare us then. As children we welcomed the chance to run around obscured from our parents' ever watchful eyes. We weren't even frightened by the spirits of all those dead June bugs stuck to the bark of sap-blotched pine trees.

When it came time for us to leave, we said blithe good-byes because none of us had any idea that the next time we'd all be together would be at Daddy's funeral, mourning our very own war hero.

prophetic gifts

THE FUNERAL SERVICE WAS HELD WEDNESDAY MORNING, AUGUST 3, 1966, AT McCLOUD BAPTIST CHURCH. Mama was up at daybreak. I don't think she'd slept at all the night before. I could hear her trying to move quietly around the trailer, so as not to wake any of us.

Shortly before the sun scrubbed the sky pink, I could hear a pot of coffee percolating. I loved to watch the coffee darken as it thup-thup-thupped through the glass knob on top of the tin pot.

"What are you doing up so early, sis?" Mama asked as I wandered into the kitchen. She was sitting at the dinette table, smoking a cigarette, sipping a cup of black coffee.

"I dunno," I whispered. Frankie was asleep on the couch. I didn't want to wake him. I liked having moments alone with Mama, without my brother or sister intruding. I walked over and stood behind Mama's chair and wrapped my arms around her neck. She patted my hands. We didn't say anything. We just sat there, both wishing that dawn would never break on this awfully sad day.

Uncle Woody and Aunt Gertie and their two girls came over at about 7 A.M. Gertie offered to help Mama get us kids ready for the funeral. Woody was there to tend to Grandpa Harve. Everybody needed a bath. Grandpa would need a shave. Somebody would have to help Linda and me fix our hair. Susie, Woody's oldest daughter, was given the chore of bathing Linda. Susie didn't like being given chores, ever. And Linda was a modest girl who didn't like other people giving her baths, ever. Linda started off the morning sore over that bath.

Gertie fixed us kids a pan of oatmeal. Nobody felt like eating, but we did it anyway. It never occurred to us not to do what we were told. So when Gertie handed us each a bowl of oatmeal and told us to hurry up and eat our breakfast, that's what we did.

After breakfast, we shimmied into cotton slips and those navy blue dresses with the red ties that Mama had bought us at Parks-Belk Department Store. Gertie and Susie worked over our hair. Linda and I both had short pixie cuts. Our fine hair stood straight up in the back if somebody didn't pat it down with Dippity-do gel. Gertie smeared our hair down well, then Susie gave us each a shot of hair spray. We put on our anklet socks, patent-leathers and then the little matching jackets to our dresses.

Once we were dressed, we sat quietly in the living room, watching the black-and-white television waiting on Mama. Frankie was the only one of us kids who'd ever been to a funeral before. He'd gone to Granny Ruth's service. Linda and I didn't know what to expect. Nobody bothered to tell us, and we didn't think to ask.

Mama came out of her bedroom dressed in a navy blue suit, with matching jacket, shoes, nylons, and purse. In one hand she carried a white handkerchief, in the other a pair of white gloves. Mama was a pretty woman, and I loved to see her all dressed up. She was naturally dark but she toasted golden brown during the summer months, so nearly any color looked more vivid on her.

But not on this day. On this day Mama looked pasty pale, the color of mold before it goes green. Pain hooded her dark eyes and drew her lips into a tight line. She had that horrified look cats get when they are tossed into a tub of cold water. I could almost feel her longing to run far, far away, to someplace quiet where she could just shake the day off.

"You ready, Sister?" Woody asked. He always called Mama Sister and always drew out that last syllable. Mama just shook her head, "Yes."

McCLOUD BAPTIST WAS a simple country church, replete with heart-pine floors and varnished pine pews, minus any cushions. It could seat about 150 people comfortably and about 200 if everyone scooted together so that nobody had any elbow room. On a typical Sunday, though, only about 50 people turned out for services and about two hundred dollars were taken up in offering. I know this be-cause on each side of the altar hung scoreboards that listed "Atten-dance Last Sunday" and "Giving Last Sunday" as well as "Attendance Today" and "Giving Today." There was also a clock on the far left wall, behind the podium, so people could time the preacher if he got a little long-winded, as Southern preachers are prone to do.

On the day of Daddy's funeral, those attendance reports were nearly hidden behind the bushels of flowers that lined the altar. I swear every florist in Hawkins and Greene Counties must've run out of flowers that day. Stretching clear from one end of the altar to the other was an arch of pink roses, white carnations, and pink-and-white Stargazer lilies. Tucked into the corners and every empty space around the altar were wreaths fashioned in patriotic colors, red car-nations set off with white lilies and red or navy ribbon. To the left of the altar was a wreath so large it looked like a tree of white roses. A taller bouquet across the altar was made from dozens of yellow roses. Mama always said yellow roses meant good-bye.

A bounty of flowers, from all those country people. I'm sure some families must have spent a month's worth of groceries on their trib-utes to my father. I can't look at the photos of those flowers without weeping over the good-hearted people who sent them.

The most elaborate arrangement of all came from Mama. It was as big as a bush and made of hundreds of long-stemmed red roses and pointy-white spires. In the center was a big red bow. On one side of the bow four white plastic doves took to flight, and on the other side was a flag. Traditional symbols of peace and freedom. But on that particular day, the doves in flight bothered me. We'd always been a family of five. There should've been five doves. Not four. Was this some florist's bad poetry? Had Mama told them to only put four doves on that wreath? I didn't give a care about peace or freedom. I just wanted my daddy back home—alive.

The church pews were packed full. A crowd of people stood at the back of the church and flowed out into the foyer, over the steps and into the yard. It looked like the Red Sea parted, only this sea was made of my father and my mother's people. Tivus Spears was there. He was my Grandfather Pap's brother. A bunch of Louvenia Kincer's kids showed up. Louvenia was Granny Leona's sister. Dale Fearnow, Daddy's best childhood bud, and his wife, Ruby, were there. There were townspeople whose names I didn't know from Church Hill, Rogersville, Persia, and Kingsport. Linda sat on one side of Mama, Frankie on the other. I sat next to Linda. Grandpa Harve sat beside Uncle Woody and his family.

Six young soldiers—four of them white, two of them black— carried my father's flag-draped coffin into the church. They were dressed in heavily starched khakis, red neck scarves, and green hats with brass insignias. A contingency of other soldiers stood at attention and saluted my father's coffin as it was carried past.

There were no fancy choirs in robes or special solos. Daddy's beloved cousin Mary Ellen, the lady with the beautiful red hair, played the organ. She must've played the music from memory, because she couldn't have seen any sheet music through her own tears. Mama grasped Linda's hand in her gloved one while the congregation sang "Rock of Ages." She kept reaching up, wiping away tears, but Mama wasn't sobbing in hysterics or anything like that. Nobody was. There was simply a constant sound of muffled weeping from throughout the church. I can't remember anything Preacher Jinks or anybody else said about Daddy at the funeral.

Echoes from the battlefields of Vietnam's Central Highlands settled into the foothills of Tennessee's Smoky Mountains that morning. It was the sound of a shattered, shell-shocked people wandering helplessly, hopelessly, searching for a comfort that could not, would not be found. I didn't know it then, but my father's death had intricately linked the mountain people of these two countries together in a spiritual way that had nothing to do with churches and preachers and traditional hymns but had everything to do with blood sacrifice.

Shortly after the congregation opened up their hymnals and sang "In the Garden," Granny Leona passed out. She was sitting behind us, so I didn't see her collapse, but I heard the commotion. A couple of people gasped. Somebody said, "I've got her." Linda, Frankie, and I turned to see someone carrying Granny out of the church. For the rest of the day her sons carried her, lifting her by the elbows or scooping her up into their arms. The family could see that Granny was really sick and needed medical attention, but she absolutely refused to go to the hospital, and everybody knew better than to try and argue with her. There was no sense upsetting her further, so they put her in the car for the trip to Greeneville.

THE FUNERAL PROCESSION from McCloud Baptist Church to Andrew Johnson National Cemetery in Greeneville was grueling for everyone. The two-lane road was nothing but S curves snapped together. Greeneville was a good piece up the road from McCloud, about forty minutes if you're driving regular speeds, much longer when police escort is leading you along. Mama, Frankie, Linda, and I rode in one of Nash-Wilson's long shiny black cars, following the hearse that held Daddy's casket. Ahead of the hearse were the flashing lights of police cars and military escorts, and following behind us were long, long miles of cars and trucks, every single one of them with their headlights switched on.

Linda got violently sick on the ride. Without any forewarning, she bent over the floor of the limo and threw up that oatmeal Aunt Gertie had fixed for breakfast. When she leaned back against the seat, her bangs were matted into sharp pencils across her forehead. Her face was white as a summer cloud, and her dark eyes looked like sinker holes. Mama pulled a handful of Kleenex out of her pocketbook, placed a couple over the upchuck on the floorboard, and began to wipe Linda's face with the others. "This is too much for her," Mama said to no one in particular.

Frankie and I didn't dare say a word. We just looked at each other in that knowing way siblings do when they realize the whole world has gone topsy-turvy. Mama reached over and rolled the windows down halfway, hoping the fresh air would ease Linda's tummy ache.

Looking out, we saw farmers standing over hoes in their tobacco fields remove their straw or felt hats and place them over their hearts out of respect for our daddy. Black boys pushing grocery carts and women with kerchiefs tied around their heads chasing after toddlers stopped flat in their steps and bowed their heads for us. Old men and old women sitting in front-porch rockers rose to their feet and stared at us as if we were royalty come to pay them an unexpected visit. Merchants came out of their five-and-dimes and stood under the flags hanging outside their doors. Some saluted as we rode by. Even the cattle and horses seemed to be staring at us. There was no sound, just the rush of wind as we passed by a world that had stopped living for a moment, in a show of respect for a fallen soldier and his griev-ing family.

The fresh air didn't help Linda much. Mama instructed the driver to pull over. The narrow roadway didn't have much of a shoulder, but he pulled off anyway, and the cars behind us followed suit. Mama opened the door and, taking Linda by the hand, helped her lean out. Linda threw up again and again and again. Uncle Woody ran up to the car to see if he could help. "Is she carsick?" Woody asked Mama.

"I don't know," Mama said.

"Poor thing," Woody said, offering Mama his handkerchief.

And thus the slow trip to Greeneville was made even more nerve-wracking as the limo driver made several more stops along the route so Linda could heave up a bowl of oatmeal that seemed to keep replicating itself the way the loaves and fishes did when Jesus fed the multitudes.

Finally, as the noon sun blistered the sky and boiled the sap in the pine trees, we pulled past the wrought-iron gates of Andrew Johnson National Cemetery. On the crest of the hill, a flag the size of a couch throw flapped in the hot breeze. Off to the left of the flagpole stood a half dozen soldiers with guns strapped to their shoulders. They had on white gloves and patent-leather shoes.

A set of stairs led down the hill, past row after row of granite tombstones, each one arched at the top and many with crosses etched in them. About halfway down the stairs, a tent was pitched over a big earthen hole that looked ever so much like one of those fire pits our Filipino neighbors used to roast pigs in on Oahu.

The man who was assigned to be Mama's military escort led her by the elbow down the stairs. Linda was walking beside Mama. Frankie and I followed close behind. Then came Uncle Woody and his family. Grandpa Harve didn't come to the grave service; he couldn't have walked all those stairs. Somebody brought Granny Leona in and sat her in one of the folding chairs. Pap was there, too, right beside her. The preacher waited until all the people were gathered on the hillside, and the soldiers heaved Daddy's flag-draped coffin onto a makeshift frame hovering over the pit before he cracked open his Bible and began reading.

I don't have a clue what Scriptures the preacher read. I never looked up at him. My eyes were down as I stared at the hole at my feet, scared to death and so very, very sad that these soldiers were about to plop my daddy into the bowels of the earth. Frankie was crying. Mama put her arm around his shoulders. Seeing the tears fall from Frankie's chin made me cry all the more, but I tried to remember what Daddy said about not upsetting Mama, so I wept quietly, trying my best to swallow as much bitter water as I could. Mama was constantly wiping at her own tears.

Linda had stopped throwing up, but she looked downright pitiful. Her pixie cut was like molten wax on her scalp. Her sunken eyes were pools of muddy water, and steady streams ran down her face. She kept wiping her nose with the back of her hand. All three of us kids shuddered when the soldiers standing on the hill behind us fired off their 21-gun salute. I got chicken skin, goose bumps all over, and my stomach ached clear through to my backbone. I scrunched in closer to Mama. She was gnawing on her lower lip, a nervous habit she still indulges whenever she's pondering a troubling situation.

I watched as the soldiers picked up the flag off Daddy's coffin and meticulously snapped it into a taut triangle; then, with a salute, they handed it over to Mama. She clutched it to her breast like a newborn baby. I half expected her to fall over into the pit, screaming for Daddy. But she didn't. She just stood there, head bowed, weeping so softly only the angels could hear her.

As the bugler played the mournful taps, a desperate urge to bolt surged up from somewhere deep in my belly. Perhaps if I were somewhere else, running through sewer holes with Bernadette or racing across pineapple fields in Hawaii, then none of this would be happening. Without me there, they couldn't bury Daddy. If I had the powers to transport myself back in time, I could save Daddy and put an end to all this hurt.

But I didn't have any powers. I didn't even have any prayers. I felt empty inside. That achy, hot burn that had been in my gut since the day the man in the jeep arrived was fading. I was plumb worn out. I wanted to curl up in that coffin right beside the cold, blue man that everyone said was my daddy and just fall asleep, forever.

I don't remember the ride back to Rogersville, or much of anything else that day, except the dream I had that afternoon.

Mama said we should all lie down. Frankie protested. He was too old for naps. He wanted to go biking with a buddy.

"Awright then," Mama said. "Go on. But change your clothes first."

Linda crawled into bed with Mama, who didn't even take her dress clothes off. I curled up on the twin bed in the adjoining room. As Frankie headed out the door, I fell asleep crying softly, so as not to upset Mama.

I was awakened by a dream in which I saw Frankie at the front door, covered head to toe with blood. I wasn't sure it was Frankie, so I just closed my eyes again, a reverse blink. It was.

As I sat up in bed, wide awake, the phone in Mama's bedroom rang. I ran to grab it, but Mama had already picked up the black-handled receiver. She motioned for me to hand her her glasses. I did.

It was Daddy's cousin Mary Ellen.

"Frankie's been in an accident," Mary Ellen said. "He's banged up pretty bad."

"Where is he?" Mama asked, sitting up on the edge of her bed, fumbling with a cigarette and lighter.

"I think somebody's taken him to the hospital," Mary Ellen said. "You'd better get on down there."

"Okay," Mama said, hanging up the phone. She took a drag from the cigarette she'd managed to light. "Shit fire, save matches."

Linda and I just looked at her. We had no idea what "Shit fire, save matches" meant, but Mama said it a lot.

I didn't have time to tell Mama about my dream. Somebody was pounding at the trailer's front door. Linda and I followed Mama down the narrow hallway into the kitchen. Mama opened the door and there stood Frankie, covered from head to toe with blood, just like he'd been in my dream. Mary Ellen's information was wrong. They'd brought Frankie to the house instead of the hospital.

Frankie had taken a spill on his bike and gone head over tail over the handlebars. With a neighbor's help, Mama rushed him to the hospital. He had a busted nose and a broken arm.

The gift of knowing things unseen is defined as faith in the Scriptures. I didn't know it that day, but God had anointed me with the spirit of Mamaw Molly, Daddy's paternal grandmother. Folks around town said that Mamaw Molly was a certified witch, a fortune-teller. She had wispy hair the color of talc powder, which she kept pulled back in a net at the nape of her long neck. She wore cable-knit sweaters, even in August. And her limbs were long, like a weeping willow. They draped or swayed depending on whether she was sitting still or moving about. She died long before Daddy got his papers for Hawaii.

I never bought into all those stories about her being a witch, but I couldn't dismiss Mamaw Molly's prophetic gift altogether because I'd heard the stories about how she had warned Aunt Mary Sue about the dangerous man she'd marry. And I'd heard how Grandma Molly wouldn't reveal Mama and Daddy's future.

I'm sure Mama had pretty much forgotten about Mamaw's mute prophecy until the man in the jeep pulled up. But by then it was too late. Others in the family would eventually mention it.

Unlike Mamaw, however, I have never been able to read palms, but I can sense things, troubling things, before they happen. They are most often revealed to me in dreams. These visitations always leave a fire in my belly. I know that if I don't do whatever the spirit is urging, I will regret it. Sometimes I'm led to pray, sometimes to caution others. And sometimes the spirit tells me to sit still and pay close attention. Many a family member and friend have wished that spirit had simply rendered me mute.

I never told Frankie, but that day the spirit told me the road ahead of him was going to be more hazardous than a mountain pass slathered in black ice. For many years I wasn't sure if he would be able to maneuver his way clear of the hazards that awaited him. Of all my loved ones, I've prayed for him the most.

I clung to the gift of faith that told me what I could not see. That someday, somehow, we'd all be okay. By God's grace, we'd figure something out. And maybe Daddy's death would eventually make sense.

THE DAY AFTER Frankie's arm was put into a cast and Daddy was laid to rest, the Kingsport newspaper ran a story that would confuse and upset me for years to come:

SGT. SPEARS KILLED BY HIS OWN SHELL
IN VIETNAM

— Full military honors were accorded S.Sgt. David P. Spears when he was laid to rest in the Andrew Johnson National Cemetery in Greeneville Wednesday morning. S.Sgt. Spears, a Rogersville man who early in life chose the Army as a career, was a Vietnam casualty. His service of 15 years to his country ended Sunday, July 24 when he was killed by one of his own shells, which was apparently defective.

S.Sgt. Spears was operating a 105-millimeter howitzer against a hostile force when a round detonated prematurely, the War Department notified his wife. . . . A military escort accompanied the body here on Saturday afternoon and remained until after the funeral which was held at 10 a.m. Wednesday morning at the McCloud Baptist Church. The Rev. Lee Jinks and the Rev. C.V. Brown officiated. Only the wife was permitted to view the body and this was for identification purposes.

I hated the headline on that story, and even worse I hated the possibility that my father, a career soldier, was somehow at fault for his own death. Something told me that there was more to the story than what was reported in the newspaper. A letter Mama received from Daddy's commanding officer (CO) in September 1966 seemed to support the idea that what was being reported in the newspaper wasn't the truth. I wouldn't read that letter for many years, but when I did I knew there was more to my misgivings than just a child's nagging hunch.

It was the second of two letters Captain John Osborne mailed to Mama from Vietnam. He'd initially sent her a form letter, typed and dated August 19, 1966. It was the standard stuff: Sorry about the death of your husband; he made the supreme sacrifice; he served his country well; please accept the sympathies of the Battery.

Upset by the dismissive letter, Mama immediately sat down and fired off a letter to the captain, demanding to know exactly how Daddy died. The next letter Captain Osborne sent Mama was written in his own script. It was dated August 30, 1966. According to Osborne, my father was nowhere near his howitzer when he was killed:

> Sgt. Spears was not only one of the finest NCO's that I have ever known but as a man he was a close and dear personal friend. So it is with great difficulty on my part that I relate to you now the details of his death.
>
> Sgt. Spears was the acting chief of firing battery and was sleeping in my tent, along with myself and my medic, a Sp. 4 Riddle. At about 5:30 a.m. there was a single explosion which woke me up. Sp. 4 Riddle informed me that he was hit and as Sgt. Spears was not yet awake, I immediately checked him.
>
> He was, of course, hit and unconscious. Sp. 4 Riddle, although wounded in the hip, and myself, both immediately rendered first aid to your husband and within five minutes there were also a doctor and three senior medics in attendance to him.
>
> My ExO, Lt. Duffy and at least nine other men in my battery gave blood for immediate transfusions. In all everything humanly possible was done but your husband's wounds were too great and he died shortly without having ever regained consciousness.

Osborne admitted in the letter there had been some confusion about the exact source of the explosion.

> After a complete check, it is my opinion and the opinion of the Army that he was killed by a single, incoming, enemy mortar round. It was thought at first that it could have been a muzzle burst from one of our

*own guns. But after a complete investigation, I am firmly convinced
that it was not.*

And he even made an attempt to answer the question that Mama had
cried out the moment she heard word of Daddy's death—"Why me,
God? Why me?"

*You asked me the age old question of why he was killed. I only wish
I had an answer for you. I can only give you this advice. God wanted
Sgt. Spears and we all know that God makes no mistakes.*

Now, I can't speak for Mama, or Captain Osborne, but it has never
made any sense to me that God needed my daddy more than I did. The
suggestion of an omnipotent power willy-nilly orchestrating who died
and who didn't in wars festered an ache in my soul. However, Osborne
did make one comment that I appreciated wholeheartedly: *"I don't
think he ever knew what hit him."* If that was true, Daddy was lucky—all
the rest of us were reeling from the impact.

THE ARMY'S OFFICIAL ESCORT dropped by the trailer that day to
see if there was anything more he could do for Mama. Mama said she
didn't think so. It was time for her to sort through things on her own,
to figure out how best to care for her invalid father and her three fatherless children. There was plenty of paperwork to finish, so she could
collect Daddy's death benefits and begin receiving his Social Security.
Meanwhile, she needed to find us a home. School was starting in just a
couple of weeks.

the kirby

Y THE TIME SCHOOL OPENED, MAMA HAD MOVED US FROM THE TRAILER AT SLAUGHTERS TO A HOUSE ON Rogersville's Clay Street. Our furniture had arrived from Hawaii, and we needed someplace to put it. The trailer was too cramped.

The white rental house was smack-dab at the end of the street, banked up next to the railway tracks. Waxy hardwood covered all the floors except in the kitchen, which had a sheet of beige linoleum over it. French doors led to the bedroom where Linda and I both lay sick with a bad case of mumps while Mama, Frankie, and Uncle Woody set up house.

Mama and Aunt Gertie both ordered me to not get out of bed for any reason other than to go pee. They warned me that if my "mumps fell," it would render me sterile, and walking around the house or motion of any sort just might do the deed. I had no idea what being sterile meant, so I asked my cousin Linda, Woody's youngest daughter. She told me that meant I wouldn't be able to have any kids when I grew up. Having kids when I got older wasn't even on my agenda as a nine-year-old, so I was put out by the rigid constraints. After all, my sister had the mumps and she was allowed to roam about as she pleased. But when I pointed out this discrepancy to Mama, she had a perfectly good explanation for it. "Linda isn't as old as you are," she said. "If her mumps fall, it won't hurt her."

Nobody dared broach the word *puberty*, so Mama's reasoning still made no sense to me. Tired of hearing my whining, Mama finally mollified me with bowls of ice cream. Lying around eating ice cream greatly improved my disposition and slowly helped restore my body. But Linda didn't seem to be recovering as quickly as Mama expected. She had never really regained her strength from the day of Daddy's funeral when she'd thrown up so much. She wouldn't eat ice cream or anything else. The first day of school came and went with the two of us still at home on the mend.

One afternoon, shortly after we moved into the house, Linda and I watched as a door-to-door salesman offered the Widow Spears his condolences. Then he asked Mama if he could have a moment of her time. Mama opened the screen door and let the fellow in. Without any further prompting from Mama, the man began to show her how a made-of-stainless-steel Kirby vacuum cleaner could be her knight in shining armor.

Like a magician at center stage, he flipped nozzles and switches, sucking up dust balls and marbles. I couldn't tell if Mama was mesmerized by his antics or just wanted him to get the hell out of her house. Either way, she didn't dare argue that a good Kirby would be more reliable than a man. So she plunked down money she could ill afford and bought a machine that weighed more than a wheelbarrow full of coal. Always a clumsy contraption, it became a constant source of anger and frustration for me, like the grief I could never quite get a handle on.

Most of the time I could shove both the Kirby and Daddy's ghost into a dark closet and walk away. But once I opened that door, I had to face an unwieldy monster. Taking care to unwrap the stiff electric cord, I tried my best to steer the Kirby clear of sharp corners. But inevitably, I wound up dinging the corner of the sofa or coffee table or ran the darn thing over my bare toes on a backward pull. Then, yanking the cord from its plug, I'd wind it, noose-fashion, around the Kirby's neck and kick it back into the closet.

Over and over, again and again, day after day, I would vacuum the floors of our homes. Sometimes I would pull out a nozzle and suck up the goobers and lint between the sofa cushions. And a couple times a year I'd lift the grates on the heating vents and stick the nozzles down those holes to clean up gunk-encrusted pennies and dust balls. But each time, I cursed that Kirby salesman because I came to realize he was the first of a long string of men to take advantage of the Widow Spears. And I hated most of them. Not because they were awful, but simply because they weren't Daddy. I began to feel like one of those discarded pennies that had fallen between the vent grate. I felt like my core was becoming encrusted with all sorts of gunk.

AFTER MY SWOLLEN JAWS shrank down to a suitable size, Mama enrolled me at Rogersville Elementary School, the same school she'd attended as a young girl. Everybody was real nice to me, but I felt out of place all the same. Some of it was because I was late getting enrolled, but mostly I was troubled by the look in my teacher's eyes when she greeted me that first day with a comment about being so sorry about my father's death. I didn't want to be the object of other people's sympathy. I didn't like being singled out as the only girl in fifth grade whose father was killed in war. I didn't want to be fatherless at all, but if I had to be, I didn't want other kids to know about it.

I don't remember talking to any other kid in the entire school other than Frankie. He was always watching out for me, and during those first few weeks at Rogersville Elementary he was extra attentive. He no longer complained about having to walk with me to and from school, the way he had back when we lived in Columbus, Georgia. It was as if he'd taken to heart Daddy's last instructions to him: "Frankie, you're the man of the house now. Take care of your mama and sisters."

We'd been close pals before Daddy's death, but now Frankie and I were inseparable. We did our homework at the kitchen table without complaint and played on the train tracks beside the house until suppertime. We answered "Yes, ma'am" to everything our mama asked us to do, which wasn't very much. We even both got baptized during the same late-summer evening at the First Baptist Church in Rogersville. I can't speak for Frankie, but the reason I answered salvation's call was pure-tee-white-knuckle paranoia. I was afraid of dying and spending eternity without Daddy. If water baptism could assure me eternity with Daddy, then praise the Lord and dunk me quick!

Mama accepted her assignment as the war hero's widow with unwavering reserve. It was her duty, her obligation, and one she fulfilled with headstrong determination and very little emotion. There was never a moment in the days, weeks, or months following Daddy's death when Mama sat us kids down and tried to explain anything to us, and it never occurred to us to ask. From the get-go, we did not discuss Daddy—not with Mama, not among ourselves. It was almost as if our entire history as a family of five had been erased from the chalkboard of our memory. But of course, it hadn't. Daddy's absence was emblazoned across our hearts, like that telling letter *A* the adulteress Hester Prynne was forced to wear in Nathaniel Hawthorne's *Scarlet Letter.* It felt as though each one of us had been marked and marred for life.

I recoiled from the recognition that accompanies a brave soldier's death. I suspected Mama did, too. On September 11, 1966, in front of a crowd of aging World War I and II veterans at the VFW Post 9543 in Rogersville, Army officials awarded Daddy the Purple Heart.

Mama laid out the funeral clothes across our beds. It was the last time Linda and I put on the itchy navy dresses with the red ties and look-alike jackets. I'd never been to a VFW hall. I thought it was some sort of uppity joint for members only, like the country club. I had no idea what a Purple Heart was or why Daddy needed a heart at all, now that he was dead. Frankie told me it was a medal of great distinction—the sort only really good soldiers received.

"Oh, one of those," I said. I was saddened that Daddy wasn't around to enjoy this honor himself, since he was, after all, the one who'd earned it. I was learning rapidly that there are a lot more reasons to be sad than proud when a daddy dies a war hero.

The VFW hall was just outside of town, high on a hill. Woody and Gertie were the only other family members that I remember being there that day. I don't think Granny Leona or Pap were there, or any of Daddy's siblings. Maybe Mama hadn't told them about it. Or maybe because back then, with that troublesome two-lane stretch of road connecting the mountain towns, Church Hill and Rogersville seemed too far apart for them to make the trip.

Mama was greeted by a group of men wearing blue hats that looked like envelopes made of felt. They were decorated with all sorts of gold and silver doodads—pins and monograms—and the men wore them cocked to the right, so that the VFW 3543 insignia was just above their bushy white eyebrows. In addition to the VFW members, a couple of soldiers dressed in their best khaki suits greeted us.

Even though it was afternoon outside, it was dark as the dickens inside. Red, blue, and purple spots flashed as my eyes adjusted to the lack of light. The place smelled like a tray of half-smoked cigarettes. The walls were paneled, like the walls of the trailer we'd just moved out of, only with a darker veneer. Multicolored linoleum squares covered the floor. Folding chairs, the kind the music teacher used for choir lessons, were uniformly lined up across the room. There were enough seats for a hundred people, but they could've managed just fine with about two dozen. An air conditioner hummed in the background.

Somebody brought over plastic boxes with enormous white-carnation corsages for Mama, Linda, and me. Linda and I had never had corsages before. We made funny faces at each other while Aunt Gertie pinned them on us. We felt ridiculous. The corner of the linen jackets kept folding beneath the weight of the puffy flowers. Frankie was grinning at us. I could tell he was glad he didn't have to wear one.

One of the soldiers led us to seats in the front row. Woody and Gertie sat in the row beside us. As the flags were presented, we all stood up, with our hands over our hearts, and recited the Pledge of Allegiance. This was something we did every single day at school, so I knew the words without thinking about them, but the whole recitation seemed different to me now that I was the daughter of a soldier killed in action. I couldn't say "with liberty and justice for all" without considering the price of such a pledge.

After that, one of the soldiers asked us to join him and some of the VFW men at the front of the room. They were standing next to a cafeteria-like table where a black Bible and gold-embossed certificate were placed, along with a box holding Daddy's Purple Heart. We did as we were asked and stood next to Mama at the table as Captain John Ammon spoke to the crowd. Mama gnawed on her lower lip and fought back tears. Her right hand rested protectively on Linda's shoulder. We stared at the gold-and-purple medal on the table before us, as Captain Ammon told the smattering of people gathered there: "Sergeant Spears gave all he could possibly give—his life."

The next day the newspaper reported the event and noted that it was the first Purple Heart to be presented in Rogersville since World War II. But, as we were busy discovering, such medals of distinction are of little comfort to widows and children in the middle of the long nights that always follow a soldier's death.

IN ONE OF HER last letters to Daddy, dated Sunday, July 17, Mama made it clear that she had no intentions of staying in Rogersville for any extended period of time. "I'll tell you one thing," she wrote, "you'll never get me to live back here and you can be looking for another lake or river to do your fishing in. If we get away from here I don't think I will ever come back here."

Mama noted in the same letter that Frankie and I talked about Columbus, Georgia, where we had lived before Daddy was transferred to Hawaii, all the time. We had good memories of Columbus. Our home had bordered a park with an active recreation center. When we weren't in school we were at that park playing baseball, tetherball, or dodgeball, or, on rainy days, playing board games in the rec center. It was the one place stateside that Frankie and I considered home.

For much of my life, I couldn't understand why my mother wanted to leave the town where she had grown up. This was the place where she and Daddy fell in love. The place where she'd birthed Frankie and Linda. (She'd been in Germany when I was born.) It was home to some of her family and Daddy's. Wouldn't she need their help to look after us? But according to Mama, none of them were ever much help. Her brothers didn't offer Mama any help caring for their daddy. Before Daddy's death and afterward, they left that chore to their wives. "I'm not impressed with anyone's grief," Mama recalled. "Not a one of them came to me and asked me, 'What can we do to be of help to you?' "

IN THAT SAME LETTER, Mama mentioned that she had nearly run herself ragged: "I had an infection in my side and have been to the doctor twice. He said I was pushing myself a little too far and was headed for trouble if I didn't slow down and rest. He was talking about the worry and upset of moving here, worrying about finding a place here and trying to get settled, plus trying to work and take care of the family, also worrying about you over there."

Mama had found a job in the weeks just prior to Daddy's death. She wanted to save money to buy a house, which wasn't easy to do on Daddy's pay of three hundred dollars a month. She started working at a plastics plant, while we kids stayed home with Grandpa Harve. Formal child care was out of the question. Nobody had heard of day care centers in that part of Tennessee. Besides, Frankie was twelve and I was almost ten, plenty old enough to fend for ourselves and see to our sister by the standards of hardscrabble mountain people. And Aunt Gertie was just two trailers up if any emergencies arose. That whole situation never really developed into a routine; Daddy's death threw a wrench into everything.

The plant was holding Mama's job for her. She could go back to it if she wanted, and she might have done that if Linda hadn't fallen sick. First at the funeral, then with the mumps, and then with some illness that kept her running a low-grade fever and feeling punk. During the month of September Linda spent as much time home sick as she did in school.

Mama took Linda to the doctor in Rogersville, who then sent her on to a doctor in Kingsport. They took all sorts of X-rays and blood tests. Finally, the doctor in Kingsport told Mama that Linda was likely suffering from a blood disease called leukemia.

That was all the reason Mama needed to make that move to Columbus, Georgia. Linda was going to need lots of medical attention, and she could get it for free at Fort Benning's Martin Army Hospital. So in October 1966 Mama bought a twelve-foot-by-sixty-foot three-bedroom trailer on wheels and had it moved by semi-trailer to Columbus.

I don't know why Mama bought a trailer home in Tennessee and then had it hauled all the way to Georgia, rather than just buying one in Georgia. Her fiscal decisions have often been a source of confusion to me. Mama said that before she bought it she asked the folks if they would move it, and they said they would. She didn't bother to tell them until after she paid for it how far she intended it to go.

a premonition and a promise

MAMA'S BROTHERS WERE MUCH OLDER THAN HER, WITH FAMILIES OF THEIR OWN TO PROVIDE FOR, so she didn't ask any of them for help. Since Granny Ruth was dead, there wasn't anyone else around to offer Mama the salve of consolation or sage advice. I know she didn't seek any from Grandpa Harve. Since his stroke, he simply wasn't capable of dispensing comfort or fatherly wisdom.

Of Mama's five brothers, one was dead already. According to the family rumors, Uncle Tub had been poisoned by his second wife, Ollie. In fact, Tub died of scleroderma, a disease that hardens the body's internal organs. But no one ever made mention of the disease that killed Tub, insisting instead that he'd been done in.

Tub had gotten his nickname from Uncle Roy. "I always called him Tubhead," Roy explained. "Tubhead was for the big head. He was always watching over us younger kids, telling us what to do." Decades earlier, Uncle Tub, Uncle Roy, and Uncle Charlie had all moved out to Oregon. Mama was just entering her teens at the time. We'd lived with Uncle Charlie and Aunt Joyce in Medford while waiting for Daddy's papers for Hawaii to come through. Uncle Roy got Daddy a temporary job at the Kinzua Lumber Mill. After supper the adults would sit at the dinette table, playing cards and smoking cigarettes until well after midnight.

Frankie, Cousin Barb, and I would stay awake for as long as we could listening to the grown-ups talk. Sometimes in those late hours, our parents spoke of how Uncle Tub got up one morning, ate his bowl of oatmeal, walked out in the backyard, and dropped over dead. Just like that.

Had to be poison, they concluded. How else could you explain the rigor mortis that had set in before the doctor could get to him? And why else did his wife, Ollie, have him cremated, unless she was trying to hide something? She probably deserved that spray of bullets that boy gave her years later. He obviously hadn't wanted her to marry his daddy, or maybe he just didn't like her cornbread.

Uncle Charlie never whispered anything, so we kids were hardly eavesdropping when we heard him tell our folks about how Aunt Ollie and her new husband, Dan Swanson, were murdered in their trailer home in Madras, Oregon. "Ollie was sitting on the sofa," Uncle Charlie said, "and Dan was sitting at the table working on a fly reel. His boy was outside when he just started shooting up the place. The windows, the walls, everything was riddled with bullets. Crazy boy."

Uncle Charlie had his own bouts of irrational behavior. He once told me he came to Oregon because he was running from the Tennessee law. Family legend has it that Uncle Charlie attempted to rob a drugstore in Rogersville. Rather than face a jail term, he ran off across the country. Years earlier, Uncle Tub had supposedly done the same thing when he got caught robbing a store at Christian Bend.

"When I got to Oregon, I sent that sheriff a postcard," Uncle Charlie bragged. "It said, 'Here I am. Catch me if you can.'"

I didn't know what to think. Charlie was always full of tall tales. I had a hard time imagining Mama's brothers doing anything to attract the attention of a lawman. And I had an even more difficult time understanding how come Mama's brothers would be given over to trouble when their own daddy had been a policeman.

Grandpa Harve served as Rogersville's patrolman for years. Well liked, he was urged to run for sheriff, but he wouldn't do it. Uncle Roy said it was because he couldn't drive. Grandpa Harve insisted it was because he didn't want to run against his good buddy John Hale. Because it was true that he didn't know how to drive, Grandpa did all his patrolling by foot, doing his part to keep the streets of Rogersville clear of illegally parked cars, suspicious-looking characters, and would-be vandals.

Uncle Tub was the first of the Mayes boys to leave Tennessee and migrate west. Tub and his first wife, Bea, were having marital disputes. He was in the service, but he left his military post so he could come home and tend to the kids that Bea had gone off and left. That absent-without-leave status was Tub's first run-in with the law. Things just escalated from there. Finally, tired of the marital upheaval and ensuing legal battles and financial woes, Tub reportedly broke into a store, where the store owner caught him rifling through the cash register. The owner put a gun to Tub's head and told him to get the hell out. Tub took the fellow's advice and moved away, far away.

Eventually, Roy moved out to Oregon, too, leaving his seventeen-year-old wife, Katherine, and the couple's children in Rogersville. As soon as he got a job, he promised to send her money to join him, and that's how Uncle Charlie ended up in Oregon.

"I couldn't have made that trip without Charlie," Katherine said. Charlie, who would never father children of his own, helped Katherine get her kids, Wanda, a toddler, and Eddy, an infant, to Oregon via the train. The trip took three nights. Charlie entertained Eddy the entire way.

Charlie was always good with kids; it was authority figures he couldn't handle. Kinfolks hesitant to talk about Charlie's run-in with the law are quick to note, "He was a real renegade."

I don't know what Grandpa Harve thought of his boys. He never said much, but I figured he didn't like their wild ways none. And even though James was Daddy's brother and not Grandpa Harve's son, I reckoned that if Grandpa's dead hand had worked, he might have used it to knock the meanness outta James, after my uncle robbed that bank shortly after Daddy died. Instead, Grandpa Harve just sat in that mesh lawn chair most every day, smoking one Pall Mall after another, never saying a word.

JAMES IS DADDY'S oldest brother, the one he depended on for help. In May 1966, Daddy called James from Hawaii and asked him to promise that if anything happened to him overseas, James would take good care of Mama and us kids.

"Dave called me on the telephone from Hawaii," James said. "I believe it was after he'd already been to Vietnam. Didn't he come home again for an R&R? I believe it was while he was home for that R&R.

"Dave said he was going back over there and he said, 'Who knows? Maybe I won't come back. If anything happens to me, you look after my family. Help 'em any way you can.' He let me know it was a tough deal over there. That there was a good chance he might not survive. I told him I'd do whatever I could."

There was a long pause while James pondered Daddy's last request again.

"I think when he called he had a premonition he wasn't coming back," he said. "I didn't see it then because your daddy had served in Korea. He was a good soldier. He was on Heartbreak Ridge when it was shut off. He'd managed to survive that. But he didn't make it back from Vietnam."

At first Uncle James tried to help his brother's widow.

"I went to Knoxville to the airport with Shelby to get your daddy's body," James said. "I took her there in a 1966 Chrysler Newport. There was a soldier with your daddy's casket. Yes, your mother did have to identify the body. I was right there with her the whole time. Even when they opened the casket. But I try not to think about all that. If I get to thinking about it, it bothers me."

Mama hoped Uncle James would keep his word to Daddy. She trusted he'd be there to help us. He was one of the first people she called after she found out she was a widow woman. But Uncle James seemed to have his hands full with all sorts of problems of his own making.

James had married a crazy woman. At least that's what everybody said about Aunt Bon. She was the sister of his cousin Mary Ellen's husband, Paul. I don't think I ever heard Aunt Bon's name mentioned without somebody tacking on the crazy label. But James insisted Bon wasn't crazy, just plumb nuts. Crazy is something you're born with. Nuts is what happens to folks when life knocks them around a few times.

Family members continue to banter about who was more nuts—James or Bon. At any rate, when they first married, Uncle James was a man of ideas. He owned his own TV-repair shop. By 1965, he said he had obtained the exclusive franchise rights to provide cable TV to Church Hill and Mount Carmel. More communities than towns, they neighbored the larger metropolis of Kingsport, home of Kodak's gargantuan Eastman plant and one of the Army's largest munitions plants.

James went door-to-door selling cable systems for five dollars each, no installation fee. Some families paid for three connections per household. James drafted the entire cable system from scratch, and he tried to raise cash for the project. But when the power-company people got wind of it, they hiked their rates from a dollar a pole to five dollars. Eventually, Intermountain Telephone Company bought James out of the cable business for thirty thousand dollars and a guarantee of a job, plus he could keep the money he'd already collected.

By family standards, James was a man of means and a man of his word. I didn't know all this as a kid, of course. I only knew that his boys, cousins Roger and Bill, had their own televisions in their bedrooms. I figured they must be rich.

Yet, despite his seeming successes, on Monday, November 21, 1966—four short months after Daddy was buried—James took a gun and robbed a branch of Kingsport National Bank.

Folks at the barbershop and around town were saying the robber made off with thirty thousand dollars. But later news reports said the lone suspect had pocketed an estimated nine thousand dollars. According to the *Kingsport Times-News*, this was the first robbery of a Kingsport bank in modern history. It made headline news that very afternoon:

COLONIAL HEIGHTS BANK ROBBED: LONE GUNMAN FLED WITH $9,000 CASH

A lone gunman quietly robbed the Colonial Heights Branch of the Kingsport National Bank of an estimated $9,000 in cash this morning and fled on foot. Two tellers didn't see the gunman who went behind a teller's cage, pulled a pistol with his right hand and scooped up a drawerful of bills with his left. Federal, state, county and Kingsport law enforcement officers converged on the scene within minutes of the holdup at 10:09 a.m. And began an immediate search of the area around the bank branch. First descriptions of the robber said he was in his late 30s, a white male, five-feet 10 inches, weighing about 170 pounds, having crew-cut hair and wearing a gray jacket, a blue work shirt and light trousers.

The physical description alone was probably enough to tip off the local police. The menfolk on the Spears side of the family are creatures of habit. I never saw Pap in anything other than gray slacks, gray work shirt, and gray felt hat. His clothes were always clean and heavily starched. Pap was a trim and good-looking man, so he looked handsome in his outfit, but it never, ever changed. By the same token, James wore the same navy blue work shirt, light gray trousers, and jacket to match every single day. And he had kept his blondish red hair in a flattop buzz cut since he was old enough to pay for haircuts.

The newspaper story humorously noted that the robbery occurred on the first day on the job for Colonial Heights bank president W. R. Teague. There was no word on whether Mr. Teague was amused.

The bank teller, Mrs. Allison, stood next to an empty cash drawer and told everyone who would listen how the lone gunman walked into the bank shaking like a Gospel Mission drunk. A friendly soul, Mrs. Allison commented on the cold weather. The stranger mumbled a response. She went on about her business, writing out bank notices, and then stepping up to the teller window, she offered the fellow some help.

Lifting a pistol with his right hand, and with a steady but urgent voice, the man demanded the teller's cash. "I want your money," he said. "I want every bit of it. This is no joke."

Mrs. Allison knew better than to question a gunman's intention. His fingers were gripped around the trigger, and the barrel was pointed in her direction. "Come on around and he'p yourself," she replied. As the bandit approached the cash drawer, Mrs. Allison didn't bother trying to dissuade him in any way. She opened the drawer all the way and stepped back. "I didn't want to be a dead hero," she said.

The man never took his eyes off her as he reached into the wooden drawer and with his left hand scooped up all the bills—$9,157 total—and shoved them into the neck of his shirt. A lone dollar bill flitted out. He didn't stop to retrieve it. He issued a warning to Mrs. Allison: "Don't move. Don't try to follow me. Don't stick your head out the door or I'll blow it off!"

Then the man walked out, more at ease than when he'd first entered the bank. Mrs. Allison watched as he walked swiftly past the post office next-door, and again as he paused at the nearby shrubbery and looked back at her. His eyes were piercing, threatening, as if to say: "Remember what I told you now."

The other two tellers in the bank were totally oblivious that a robbery had just occurred right under their noses.

With a tremor in her voice, Mrs. Allison announced, "Girls, we've been robbed!" Then she turned the key, locked the bank's front door, and called the main office and then the police. Law enforcement officials were swarming the place within minutes.

Mrs. Allison figured they were dealing with an amateur. "Otherwise, he would have gone for the bigger cash in the vault," she said.

What she didn't know is that the gunman wasn't interested in money so much as he was just trying to find a way to break free from a marriage gone sour. He'd been begging for a divorce. Bon kept refusing him. James was seeing another woman. They were both aggravated as hungry hornets.

Earlier that day, James and Bon had gotten into a row over money. James ordered Bon out of his repair shop. When she didn't budge, he stormed into his office. Bon chased after him. Then, without a second thought, he whipped out a pistol.

"I didn't mean to do anything but threaten her," James recalled. "But when I swung that pistol around, it was in her mouth. I told her, 'If you don't leave right now, I'll blow your damn head off.' She left. But that upset me, her messing with my business that way. She was griping about me not making my support payments, but then she was messing with my livelihood."

Later that day James got a call from the sheriff.

"He told me I needed to get over to the courthouse and take care of business because Bon had gotten a warrant out for my arrest."

The sheriff was a friend. "He never would arrest me," James said. "He'd just tell me about the warrants. I was on my way to Rogersville to the courthouse when I thought, 'Hell, I'll just go rob a bank.' "

He didn't put any forethought or planning into the robbery. He just grabbed his gun and sauntered into the Colonial Heights bank. After he left the bank, he put the stolen money into a lunch box and swam the Holston River to a nearby town, where he bought a car and headed out-of-town.

By the time our family showed up at Granny's for Thanksgiving, Daddy's death had been relegated to the list of things our families didn't talk about anymore. All the hushed murmuring taking place that weekend focused on whether Uncle James had been the one who robbed the bank in Kingsport. The local rumor mill had pegged him as the prime suspect. Granny Leona said she didn't believe for one minute that James had robbed that bank. "I asked James to his face if he stole that money," she told me. "I could tell by looking into his eyes, he hadn't done it. He didn't say that. He just didn't say nothing. But I could tell he hadn't."

But of course, he had.

From the moment James disappeared, FBI agents began watching most of Dad's brothers and sisters. They even harassed Mama that first year. They showed up at the door of our trailer house in Georgia, dressed in dark suits, narrow ties, white shirts, and butter-shined shoes.

"Is your mother home?" the taller of the two asked.

"Just a minute. I'll get her," I said, not bothering to invite these strange-looking fellows inside. Mama didn't invite them in either.

"Mrs. Shelby Spears?"

"Yes," Mama said.

"We are agents with the Federal Bureau of Investigation. We are looking for James Spears. We understand he's your brother in-law."

"So?" Mama replied.

"Do you have any idea where he might be? We have reason to believe he may have robbed a bank in Tennessee."

"I don't have any idea where James is," Mama said.

The fellow wrote down a phone number and handed it to Mama. "Would you give us a call if you hear from him?" he asked.

"No," Mama said. "I don't know where James is. But even if I did, I wouldn't tell you. I'm not telling you anything Ma'am doesn't want me to."

Ma'am was the name all the adults in the family called Granny Leona. Mama may not have gotten along all that well with Granny Leona, but there was no way she was going to purposely cross her. Granny wasn't in the best of health. Understandably, Mama didn't want to upset her any more than Daddy's death and James's disappearance already had.

So, throughout 1966 and 1967, I would come home from time to time and find men, dressed in black, sitting in a car, watching our trailer house. But nobody in our family heard from James again until he was behind bars.

Federal agents finally tracked James down in Colorado a year later. By then he'd spent every nickel of the money he'd made off with. That was the same year Intermountain Telephone Company sold that cable franchise they'd bought from James. They reportedly got a million dollars for the system they'd paid thirty thousand for. A couple of years later it was sold again—for a reported three million dollars. If he'd made wiser choices, James could've been sitting on a beach drinking rum instead of learning to knit at the Atlanta Federal Penitentiary or, as James called it, the University of Atlanta.

He had a lot of time to sit and ponder whether he really would've shot Aunt Bon or the bank teller that day. He still isn't sure. "Maybe," he said. "It scares me when I think about it."

The jury sentenced James to forty years. He served nearly seven years, until February 1975. From the time I was eleven until I was eighteen.

"That's where I goofed up," James said. "I wasn't able to do what I told Dave I would do."

He knows he not only broke a promise to his dead brother, but he also failed his own two boys. "It's weighed heavy on me for years what I done to them two boys and the rest of the family," he said.

Still, he has no regrets about Aunt Bon. "I never regretted putting her ass out on the streets," he said with a chuckle.

There's no question that James put our family and his family through a lot of misery and aggravation. Sometimes, on the rare occasions when he allows himself to think about it, he weeps over his actions. "It's bothered me for years I wasn't able to do what Dave asked me to do," James said. "But look where I ended up. How could I help you all when I was in the Atlanta penitentiary? I had my own problems."

It's an awful thing to say, but in some ways I'm glad Daddy didn't live long enough to see James go to prison. Daddy looked up to his older brother; he would've been troubled by James's plight. I suspect if he knew about it, Daddy would be royally pissed that James didn't keep his promise to help care for us.

Ironically, right next to the *Kingsport Times-News* headline article about the bank robbery was a story about the 25th Infantry Division retaliating for a massacre that had taken place days earlier in the Central Highlands. It was all part of the same ongoing military operation, known as Paul Revere, that Daddy had been involved in during the months leading up to his death:

GIs REVENGE TRAGIC LOSSES

— Two companies of the U.S. 25th Division returned today to the scene of a Saturday tragedy and killed 11 more North Vietnamese in one of a series of sharp clashes that broke out in the Central Highlands jungles near the Cambodian border. The 25th killed 166 in the clash only a few miles from the spot where hundreds of North Vietnamese troops overran an American 1st Air Cavalry Division platoon Monday and virtually wiped it out. That battleground is some 240 miles north of Saigon. Today's action brought to 711 the number of Communists who have been killed in Operation Paul Revere IV, since it opened on Oct. 18. Over-all American casualties were reported light although the three platoons of the 1st Cavalry involved in Monday's fight suffered heavily . . . (The surrounded platoon of 21 men was overrun by 400 North Vietnamese. Only 3 Americans survived.) In one of the new actions, a company—up to 200 men—of the U.S. 25th Infantry Division's 3rd Brigade fought a Communist force of unknown size about 12 miles west-southeast of Plei Djereng.

Uncle James hasn't talked much about Daddy over the years, but I'd bet there isn't a day that goes by that he isn't tortured by his broken promise to his brother.

It seems to me there are two kinds of problems in life: the kind we create for ourselves, and the kind others create for us. Unlike James's, Mama's problems weren't of her own making, not at first anyway.

Looking back, it's hard to tell which of our family's problems were the result of Daddy's death and which were the result of our own sorry choices. Truth is, after Daddy died, none of us could think too clearly anymore.

Part II • 1967 — 1970

the years of violent storms

taking
care of business

I T HAD BEEN TWO YEARS SINCE THE MAN IN THE JEEP
DROVE AROUND THE S-CURVED ROADWAYS OF HAWKINS
County to tell the Widow Spears that her husband had bled to death
in Vietnam's Ia Drang Valley. Two years since doctors told the Widow
Spears they thought her youngest child had leukemia and might be
dying. Two years since the Widow Spears called Elmer White, a former neighbor on Morris Road in Columbus, Georgia, and asked him
to find her a place to park our new home. Two years since some man
hitched a twelve-by-sixty-foot trailer to a rig and hauled the Widow
Spears and her children all the way to Georgia.

Linda was treated by military doctors at Fort Benning's Martin
Army Hospital. It was the very same hospital Daddy had carried me
into in 1961 when I'd tumbled willy-nilly from my bunk bed and
busted my chin wide open. The front of my cotton slip had been
covered with blood, and I'd hollered for Mama the entire time as
Daddy sped down Victory Drive toward the hospital. "It took five
stitches," Daddy told Mama when he delivered me safely back home.
Like the blood on my slip, my tears had all dried up.

Daddy had made me and everybody else in the emergency room
laugh when he said I looked like a prizefighter. Making other people
laugh was easy for him.

In the aftermath of my father's death, I couldn't remember the last

time Mama had laughed or smiled. She may have breathed a sigh of relief when the doctors at Martin Army said Linda didn't have leukemia,
just a severe kidney infection and a heart murmur. But such relief
passed as quickly as an afternoon cloudburst, so common to Georgia. It
did little to diminish the constant burn in her soul.

Leslie was the first friend I made at Lake Forest Trailer Court. She
was a year younger than me. I was in sixth grade; she was in the fifth.
We met at the pool. She was wearing a black-and-white one-piece
bathing suit and was among a group of kids diving from the sides of
the deep end of the oval-shaped pool, strands of blond hair clumped
together around her shoulders. She didn't have freckles like me. Her
arms and legs were the color of caramel candy. Across her back was a
smattering of small, dark moles. She was having a difficult time keeping her ample chest tucked into the zip front of her suit.

Her older brother, James, didn't look at all like her. With freckles
and a shock of coarse red hair, he looked as though somebody had
given him a good dusting from a box of cayenne. His legs, arms, and
shoulders were thick, like a linebacker's.

The pool was the first thing Mama had pointed out to us when
we arrived at the trailer court. A chain link fence was the only border
between the pool and the stream of traffic running north-south along
Morris Road. Lake Forest was about a mile down the road from the
house we'd lived in before Daddy got his orders to Hawaii. The
neighborhood seemed familiar. I recognized the school yard at Edgewood Elementary where I had built miniature houses from pine
straw with my classmates during recess. Across the street from the
school was the grocery store where Mama bought milk and eggs.
Even the brick house we'd called home before moving to Hawaii appeared the same. There was the cement stoop where Mama sat after
tying a string to my loose tooth and telling me to walk toward the pine
towering over the front yard. Ball games were still played in the dusty
diamond where Frankie and I had played catch with Daddy before
supper each night. But I didn't recognize the car parked in the

driveway where Daddy used to hop off the back of an Army truck after a couple of days in the field.

And I didn't notice it right away, but somewhere between where Edgewood Road turned into Morris Road, a crevasse appeared. Often ignored but not the least bit invisible, the divide separated North Columbus from the south side, the haves from the have-nots, the city's privileged children from the underprivileged.

Kids in North Columbus lived in brick homes with backyard patios, oval-shaped pools, and gas barbecues. Lawn companies hired men from South Columbus to keep the sweeping lawns of North Columbus green and clipped. In South Columbus, kids lived in trailers or housing projects. They swam in snake-infested creeks or dashed through sprinkler hoses to cool off. They played ball in dirt streets and built forts in dusty yards.

Before Daddy's death, we had lived north of that divide. Now we lived south, just across the railroad tracks and down the road apiece from the projects. Or as I more often than not heard the large complex referred to, "that place where all them niggers live."

I did not return to Edgewood Elementary. Instead I attended Tillinghurst, a school for white kids in what was primarily a black neighborhood. School was already in full swing by the time we arrived in October.

Even before we moved to Hawaii in 1963, Mama had tired of the sporadic waitress jobs she held whenever Daddy needed help making ends meet. She decided that maybe she'd study to become a nurse. Nursing would give her a regular paycheck, one that Daddy couldn't gamble away. An avid poker player, my father often won big, but once in a while he lost big, too. "He'd lose whole paychecks at a time," Mama recalled.

When Daddy was stationed at Fort Benning, before we moved to Hawaii, Mama had began her nursing studies at the Medical Center in Columbus.

"I had a girlfriend, Ivy, who came to live with us in Columbus,"

Mama said. "She wanted to get out of Rogersville, and I wanted to go to school. It worked out pretty good for a few weeks, until Ivy decided to return to Tennessee." Ivy didn't stick around long enough for Mama to earn any credits, just long enough for Mama to get a glimpse of higher education.

In the fall of 1966, after enrolling Linda and me at Tillinghurst and Frank at Eddy Junior High, Mama signed up for classes through the Manpower Program. Enacted in 1962, the Manpower Development and Training Act instituted a major federal job-training program designed specifically to provide work incentives for disadvantaged families like ours. It would take Mama a little over a year to earn her certification as a licensed practical nurse. Manpower gave her a small stipend, about fifty dollars a month.

She still had about $2,500 left of the $10,000 serviceman's insurance provided for us. The trailer had cost her $5,700, and she had bought some new furniture. Beds mostly. The living room furniture was the same set my folks had bought in Hawaii: a couch crafted from ornately carved Koa wood, holding six plump but unforgiving cushions, and a matching chair and coffee table. I don't know what possessed my folks to buy such an ensemble, but it wasn't comfort.

Social Security and veterans' benefits also helped Mama pay the bills. But she had made Granny Leona one of Daddy's dependents so she could turn over a portion of his benefits to her. This was a generous move, considering that Mama had no idea how she was going to support three kids once her remaining twenty-five hundred dollars ran out.

Mama doesn't talk about why she signed that money over to Granny. She simply says that Granny needed it. I'm not even sure any of my relatives knew what Mama had done. Honestly, I don't think many folks, kin or otherwise, ever gave a second thought to how Mama would pay the bills. Most of our kin were living hand-to-mouth themselves. With the exception of Uncle James, who'd robbed the bank, the only family member with any change to spare was Uncle

Carl, who had made a comfortable life for himself in Clinton, a town that made money from Tennessee's Oak Ridge nuclear-weapons plant, proud producers of the atomic bomb. Out of all the Mayes boys, Carl did the best job of carving out a middle-class life for himself and his family. In his later years, he was a generous man, but early on, selfishness marred him. Mama had referred to her brother's flaw in a letter Daddy never got, dated July 17, 1966:

> *Carl and Blanche came up yesterday and stayed for a couple of hours. Blanche cried and talked and I guess she thought I would say everything was okay, but I sure did not. I told her how I felt. She told Carl I said they were less than nothing to me. I told him I didn't say those exact words but I felt pretty much that way. I told them I don't get over things like that in a few days.*

I asked Mama to explain why she was so upset with her brother at the time. Carl and Blanche had taken my mother in when she was fourteen. Granny Ruth had left Mama with Grandpa Harve while she made a trek to Oregon to see her sons, and she ended up staying gone for a couple of years. Mama told me Granny Ruth had likely tired of Grandpa Harve's mean ways, so she just up and left, leaving Mama to fend for herself. Carl and Blanche stepped in as surrogate parents. Carl once told me he took Mama in because she was running the streets, becoming way too familiar with boys. Blanche treated Mama just like a daughter, making sure she had clothes for school and keeping a tight rein on her. I couldn't imagine what had transpired between them in 1966 that upset Mama so.

"When we were getting ready to leave Hawaii, I wrote to Roy, Carl, Charlie, and Woody and asked them to send me money so I could get Dad a plane ticket home," Mama explained. "Charlie wrote back and said he didn't have any money, but I could send Dad to Long Beach and he and Joyce would pick him up there and care for him until I got there.

"Roy sent some money. I can't remember what Woody did, but Carl sent me a letter. He said if I wanted money I could get it the same way he did—go to the bank and borrow it. I finally went to Schofield and asked somebody there to help, and they did. The Army paid for Dad's plane ticket. Charlie took care of Dad until we arrived in the States a couple weeks later.

"I was mad, so I didn't tell Blanche and Carl that I was back in Tennessee. When they found out I was there, they drove over to see us, and that's what I wrote your Daddy about. I told Carl that I would never forgive him for what he did. I told him, 'You didn't just do this to me or Dad. You did this to my husband. I won't forgive you for that.' "

But Mama and Carl eventually patched things up. And in the later years of his life, Carl was generous to us. He loaned me a thousand dollars to buy my first home. I paid him back one hundred dollars a month until the loan was paid in full. For years I kept the letters we exchanged during that time. Carl and I became great friends in the process.

After we moved back to Georgia, Mama managed to care for us and her stroke-smitten father on her own. She even scraped together enough money to hire a woman to come in and care for us. For five dollars a day, Thelma did the washing, ironing, cleaning, and scolding.

Thelma taught me how to make a bed, wash a plate, and fry a chicken. "Don't just wash the front of that plate," she said. "It's got a back, too!" Bending over the corner of Mama's bed, Thelma would lift a section of sheet and fold it into a triangle, like the back of an envelope. "Now tuck that up under the mattress," Thelma said, explaining how to make a flat sheet fit snug on a bed. "That's called a hospital corner."

Thelma could be firm, but she was never cross or mean. She and Grandpa Harve liked to spend their afternoons sipping peach brandy and watching the soaps or ball games. Thelma was the first black person I felt the freedom to love or be loved by. She took good care of us kids in that first year after Daddy died.

Mama doesn't recall those first few years after Daddy's death as being all that difficult, financially or any other way, and it angers her that I do. A fiercely proud woman, she insists that our family did not suffer any financial consequences due to Daddy's death.

"I don't recall you going hungry at any point," she said. "You had a roof over your head and clothes to wear. I don't know where you get this idea that we were poor. We lived in a brand-new trailer. We even had a maid!"

"You paid her five dollars a day."

"It was the going rate," she said. "We were never underclass."

"Okay, so we were obviously better off than Thelma," I said. "But you honestly don't remember having to struggle after Daddy died?"

"No, I don't," Mama said. "The only poverty that existed exists in your mind."

If there is one thing Mama can't tolerate, it is the suggestion that our trailer-park existence made us disadvantaged or "underclass." She abhors the idea that outsiders might have considered us trailer trash, or white trash, just because of our lifestyle and our socioeconomic standing.

When Mama carries on this way, I am reminded of why Daddy found her stubborn streak amusing. Mama chain-smoked, drank her coffee black, and preferred her beer straight from the can. She danced with men whose names I never knew and bedded more than a couple of them. In a five-year span, the trailer was moved four times. We never stayed in one lot long enough to remove the rubber tires or to warrant a porch. To this day I think of wooden porches as a sign of stability. I'm a sucker for a home with a wraparound porch. After Daddy died, Mama wasn't up for the kind of commitment a wooden porch required; so for the first three years, cinder blocks were piled outside the front and back doors of the trailer so we could step in or out of the house. Cinder blocks could be loaded in a hurry.

But on the chance that I was wrong about my memory of our economic and social standing following Daddy's death, I called my sister and asked her about her remembrances. We had a good chuckle about the symbolism of a front porch. "Do you remember doing without after Daddy died?" I asked.

"Yes," Linda said. "I remember we got clothes once a year, right before school started. Usually it was just a couple of outfits and one pair of shoes. I remember never having money for lunch. If I could scrape together twenty-five cents, I would try and get somebody in the lunch line to buy me an ice cream sandwich. They wouldn't let you buy the ice cream without the lunch, and there weren't free lunch programs in those days."

"Did you consider us poor?" I asked.

"Yes," she said. "But not the same kind of poor Mama grew up with."

Mama's definition of poverty is much more austere. For good reason. She has memories of growing up impoverished among the stately manor homes that belonged to the wealthy families in Rogersville. Grandpa Harve and Grandma Ruth's house didn't have a bathtub or shower. Baths were given in an aluminum tub in the kitchen, with water heated in kettles atop the woodstove and shared among the kids. The last person to bathe usually did so in cold, dirty water. There were no light fixtures, only bulbs on a string. Grandma Ruth took in other people's washing to help make ends meet.

"Do you know who had to deliver those clothes?" Mama asked me. "I did. I would carry baskets of laundry to the back doors of those big fine homes. Do you have any idea what that made me feel like? I couldn't wait to move out of Rogersville. After growing up that way, I can see why kids who are taunted kill other kids. People looked down on me. They treated me like I was shit. Like I was nothing because I was poor. Your daddy's family was poor, too. They lived in a two-room house in McCloud, and they ate nothing but beans and corn-bread every day of their lives growing up. Every day. It never varied.

"You've had a much easier life," Mama told me. "You have never realized in your life how far I've come."

Mama's wrong about that. It's by remembering these things that I can measure how far our family has come, over the years, mostly due to her efforts. Neither Linda nor I have forgotten how many lonely nights we spent in that trailer crying, wishing and praying that Daddy would come back and that God would bless Mama with an easier life. I suspect Mama's own childhood had created a hunger in her to improve her lot in life long before Daddy died. His death was simply the impetus for her to do that.

what mama didn't know

YING ON THE FLOOR AT THE FOOT OF MAMA'S BED I COULD BARELY FEEL JAMES'S STUBBY FINGERS STROKE MY breasts. I pressed my face into his neck. He smelled of sweat. It wasn't the sour kind men boast of after mowing grass in the noonday sun. Rather it was sweet, like honeysuckle, like the sweat that drips from a toddler's brow during a summer nap.

James was sprawled plumb atop me. This fondling was awkward for twelve-year-old kids like us. I was downright uncomfortable, but James didn't seem to be. He was struggling to find his way underneath the layers of the white negligee of Mama's that I was wearing. There wasn't much need for me to resist. Frank was less than a foot away, making out with Leslie, James's younger sister, on Mama's bed.

I could tell James was far more excited about this moment than I was. His erection was prominent, although not much bigger than his index finger. Pressing into my right thigh, he sought to inch over on top of me. My ankles weren't crossed, but they might as well have been.

I was a good girl, not a slut.

I'd been raised to say "Yes, ma'am" and "No, sir" to all my elders. I called grown-ups by their proper names—Mr. and Mrs. I didn't backtalk much for fear of being slapped silly. I didn't smoke like James's and Leslie's older sister, Beth. I didn't drink like Frank. And

I never, ever said swearwords. To be honest, I was afraid to be near folks who took God's name in vain.

Mama tried her best to raise me and Frank and Linda up right. When we were really little, she used to read Bible stories to us from a big red book every night after supper. She'd pay us a dime if we could correctly answer questions like "What color was Jacob's robe?" or "How many days did the rains that flooded the earth fall?"

Usually, Frank called out the answer before I'd had time to hear the question. He's always been smart, even though he hasn't always been the quickest study.

But Mama hadn't had much time for anything or anyone since we moved to Georgia. When she wasn't in school, studying, or working, she was hanging out with Juanita, the next-door neighbor, who was also a nursing student.

While we were holding our make-out sessions in Mama's bedroom, Linda was usually watching cartoons in the living room or playing with that overstuffed Thumbelina doll of hers. Linda had been a chatterbox, but once Daddy died, she mostly sat by herself on the cement patio or the front stoop's cinder blocks. She'd sit sucking her bottom lip, dressing and undressing that baby doll of hers, ignoring Frank and me, like we did her.

It was Frank who first coerced me into kissing a boy. No, not him. His buddy Joe. Joe and his sister Mary Jane were hanging at our trailer house one afternoon. Frank wanted to put the move on Mary Jane, but he was hindered by the presence of me and Joe. The solution seemed simple enough. If Frank could get me and Joe out of the room, he'd have a chance with Mary Jane.

"Why don't you and Joe go to the other room?" Frank asked as he stroked Mary Jane's waist-length golden locks.

"Why?" I asked.

"Y'all can make out or something," he replied.

Joe took me by the hand and led me into my brother's bedroom. "I've never kissed anyone before," I said, giggling nervously.

"That's okay," Joe said. "It's not hard. I'm going to put my mouth over yours. You have to leave yours open a little bit. There's nothing to it."

Joe was not a particularly good-looking fellow. He had expressive eyes, a great tan, and the ugliest set of teeth. Sharp fangs grew out over his eyeteeth. Two sets of teeth were shoved into one very crowded mouth. I couldn't help but stare at Joe's mouth as he leaned in for a kiss. I had visions of Dracula Barnabas Collins from *Dark Shadows* leaning in for a lusty bite.

Then, SLAP! BAM! A bookcase full of *New World Encyclopedias* tumbled over behind me. I tripped and fell into Joe. He caught me but not before slamming his forehead up against the wall above the bookcase.

Frank and Mary Jane came running. "What's going on?" Frank yelled.

I was doubled over, laughing. Stunned, Joe rubbed his forehead. "I was trying to kiss your sister," he said, laughing too.

Frank took one look at all the books sprawled about our feet and shook his head. "That must've been some kiss," he said.

Pushing James off the top of me, I stood up. Frank poked his head up from the bed. "I'm done," I said.

James picked himself up from the floor. Frank climbed over Leslie and off Mama's bed. Leslie stood and pulled her shirt down and tucked it back into her shorts.

I slid open the door to Mama's room and marched down the hallway to the living room. Sitting in a corner, in a half-circle, were a bunch of scraggly kids. My good friend Mary Jane, and Joe, and Frank's good buddy Joe Kirkland. I don't remember if Opie was there that night or not. Joe K. was spinning a Coke bottle, waiting for his chance with Leslie. Flipping his blond locks away from his forehead, he looked up at Frank and grinned.

This is how we spent our Friday and Saturday nights—playing

spin the bottle or post office—groping each other in the darkest corners we could find. Sometimes we'd spread a blanket over the pine needles behind an empty trailer. Other times, if our parents weren't home, we'd conduct our explorations in their beds. Sex was like boxed cereal. It could be poured out and devoured at a moment's notice. Sometimes it was sweet, but it was nearly always colder than the real affection we'd once known as a family.

Mama didn't know anything about our nocturnal activities. She didn't like leaving us kids alone at night. Grandpa Harve was there, but he didn't offer us much supervision. Sometimes, when he was really upset, he'd beat the floor or the walls with his cane, telling us kids to quiet down or yelling for Frank to hurry up and empty the coffee can Grandpa kept under his bed for peeing in. But Grandpa Harve was as much a burden as a help to Mama. His right hand, the one on his dead arm, hung heavy at his side or between his legs when he was sitting. Unable to will it to move, Grandpa Harve would fling it around with his one good hand. He had to have help buttoning his shirts, hooking his pants, tying his shoes, and opening his pack of cigarettes. He couldn't even pick at his own sores.

"Karen, c'mere and help me with this," Grandpa said whenever the eczema scab covering the elbow of his good arm got too thick. Flexing his arm up, he'd nod toward the white crusty scab.

"Peel that back, would ya?" he asked.

Kneeling by his chair, I'd start picking at the outer edges of the sore. As I peeled back the meringuelike layer, very little blood seeped out. The scab covered a dry spot that had grown callous from years of picking. Still, the skin underneath was as red as rib-eye steak. I knew it must pain Grandpa, although he never once winced or scolded me.

I hated picking Grandpa's sores; I didn't have the stomach for it. But it troubled me even more that Grandpa couldn't do such a simple task for himself. And I knew it discouraged him. The ritual was performed every six weeks or so in an almost reverential silence.

Grandpa Harve and I never talked about much of anything. We didn't speak of his days as a deputy or his life with Granny Ruth. We didn't talk about his boys, or his daughter, my mother. And we never ever talked about Vietnam or the Army or my father's death. Sometimes, he'd give me a pat on the head or a quick grin, but mostly he just sat smoking his Pall Mall cigarettes, one right after the other, and thinking about things I knew nothing about. If Grandpa Harve was worried about the company Frank and I were keeping, he never said.

The kids we ran around with weren't really bad kids. We were just mostly unsupervised. James and Leslie's parents, Mr. and Mrs. Williams, held the tightest parental reins, but they managed a business—Shipley's Donuts, out on Wynnton Road—that demanded their attention. They were up long before the crack of dawn, tossing flour and sprinkling powdered sugar for the hundreds of orders they filled each day. When they got home, they would plop down in recliners in front of the television set and tune the world out.

They were always polite and always made me feel welcome in their home. Mrs. Williams was a big wrestling fan. Sometimes she'd invite me to join the family for the wrestling events at the Columbus Coliseum. I only went a couple of times, but I was there one of the nights Mr. Wrestling was cheered on. Tim "Mr. Wrestling" Woods was a favorite among the Columbus crowd. Just like the Mr. Clean fellow in the laundry commercials, Mr. Wrestling always wore white. White boots. White briefs. White mask. That's how we all knew he was the good guy—his attire was white as snow, like the souls of those saved by the blood of the Lamb. But it was that white mask that Woods wore that kept the crowd mesmerized. I sat on the edge of my seat that night, just hoping his opponent would rip it off. Like a lot of girls, I wanted to know if Mr. Wrestling had a face as handsome as the rest of his anatomy.

I'd never seen Mrs. Williams get too riled up. She was a fairly even-tempered woman, not prone to hollering at her kids or her husband, so I was dumbstruck to see her get all worked up over a man in polyester briefs. When Mr. Wrestling climbed through the ropes and waved to the crowd, Mrs. Williams was perspiring and hooting like a schoolgirl at a pep rally. I could tell she really favored him. But then, so did the rest of the crowd. You'd have thought Elvis had just walked onstage the way everybody was clapping and screaming.

That same crowd was ready to lynch Mr. Wrestling's opponent later that evening when blood squirted from beneath the white gloves Mr. Wrestling wore. The jerk had chomped down on Mr. Wrestling's finger so hard, he liked to bit it in two. Blood dripped down Mr. Wrestling's hand, down his forearm, down his elbow. Only a low-down scoundrel would wrestle that way, Mrs. Williams said. Following the match, we maneuvered our way through the crowds and down the stairs to the parking lot. Everybody was fuming mad at the dawg who bit Mr. Wrestling.

On other occasions, Mrs. Williams took Leslie and me to watch Leslie's sister, Beth, in modeling shows. Beth was a tall, skinny thing, like that famous fashion model Twiggy. She didn't have an ounce of fat on her body, which I always thought odd because Mrs. Williams was the plumpest mother in the neighborhood. Beth had red hair, like her brother James, but not as many freckles. She took modeling classes under the guidance of Miss Mable Bailey at Mable Bailey's School of Charm and Modeling. For several decades, taking a course from Mable Bailey was nearly a rite of passage for many Columbus girls. Even those of us who lived in trailer parks. Mama tried to sign me up when I got older, but I refused to go. I probably needed it more than the average girl, but I knew it'd take a legion of well-heeled women to make me over.

Besides, Mable Bailey scared me. She had an air of strictness about her, like a librarian schooled in the Dewey Decimal system. Or a Sunday school teacher whose favorite book of the Bible was Leviticus. Her black hair was backcombed and piled high atop her head. She must've used a can of "Extra Hold" Aqua Net to keep it in place because she never had frizzes or wispies falling down around her forehead. Her lips were ruby red, all the time. And she wore a girdle, even though she didn't need one.

Mable Bailey taught thousands of gangly schoolgirls how to walk confidently down a runway while wearing stilettos. Leslie and I marveled over Beth and her charm-school friends, but we suspected that we weren't cut from the same cloth. For one thing, Leslie was much too busty for button-down blouses and smocked jumpers. And me?

Well, I'd dropped out of Brownies after the first two meetings because uniformity made me nervous. I didn't like PE classes at school because all the girls had to wear the exact same navy blue gym shorts that snapped up the side, like a toddler's romper. So if belonging to the in crowd required me to wear a Brownie sash or Playtex girdle, well then, I was a confirmed misfit.

Beth knew my weaknesses, and for some reason or another, she loved to prod my sore spots. I think it was mostly because of her own sibling rivalry with Leslie. Although Beth was the trained model, Leslie was the natural beauty. She looked more womanly than her stick-figure sister. The boys swarmed to be near Leslie whenever we played spin the bottle or any of our other make-out games.

Beth's closest friend was a trashy gal named Evelyn. She didn't live in the same trailer park as the rest of us, but sometimes Evelyn rode the bus home with Beth. Evelyn had peroxide-dyed hair, even at fourteen. And big boobs. D cups. Bigger than Leslie's, even. She wore so much eyeliner, she favored a raccoon. Like Beth, she smoked, cursed, and flirted with older men. Including the school bus driver.

I kept my distance from all three of them—Beth, Evelyn, and the bus driver. I hadn't liked him since he chided me one morning while en route to Eddy Junior High.

"That gum you're chewing is going to heaven," the driver said, glancing up at the mirror above his head. That's how he kept track of us kids, watching us through the mirror.

"I'm sorry, sir," I said. We weren't supposed to chew gum on the school bus. I must've looked as uncomfortable as I felt.

"I said that gum you're chewing is going to heaven 'cause you're chewing the hell out of it now," he said with a laugh.

I immediately swallowed the peppermint wad.

But that driver never said a word to Beth or Evelyn when they chewed gum. He even supplied them with cigarettes from time to time. Whenever Evelyn was on the bus, he was downright attentive, always studying the mirror to see what she and Beth were up to in the backseat—and laughing right along with them.

One day Evelyn got on the bus and told everybody within earshot that as soon as the bus stopped she was going to whup my ass. I don't know what prompted her threat. I was sitting in my usual spot at the front, trying to avoid her and Beth and everybody else. All the boys on the bus thought that'd be a dandy thing to watch, Evelyn kicking Karen's ass. And they told her so.

I'd never been in a fight with anyone other than Frank or Linda. The one thing I knew for sure: I wouldn't run from one. I was pretty sure Evelyn could do just what she threatened, but I was going to go down like Mr. Wrestling, fighting with all my might.

Sure enough, as soon as we got off the bus, Evelyn walked up to me. "I don't like you," she said.

"Tough shit," I replied, mustering up some of Mama's attitude.

Evelyn hauled off and slapped me across the cheek. My books fell out of my arms. The boys—James, Joe K., Joe C., and some others—formed a circle around us and began egging Evelyn on. "Kick her ass!" someone screamed.

Evelyn reached up and yanked a handful of my hair. I balled up a fist and punched her left D cup.

That pissed her off royally. She pushed me to the ground, climbed atop my chest, and began to beat at my face. I flung my arms at her, grabbed a handful of her bleached blond hair, and pulled out a gob. She kept wailing on my face. I ran my nails down her cheek, scratching as deep as my weak nails would go. The boys kept hollering. "You little bitch!" Evelyn screamed.

"Fat ass!" I cried back.

She slapped me again. I pushed her off and scrambled to my feet.

"Crybaby!" one of the boys yelled at me.

"SHUT UP!" I yelled back, bending to pick up the schoolbooks strewn about the dirt road.

Evelyn patted down her skirt, her hair. "Don't mess with me anymore, girl, you hear me?" she ordered.

I shoved past her, through the circle of gawkers, and took off running for the trailer house. I was still crying when I got there. Grandpa was sitting in the living room, watching a ball game. He never asked me why I was crying, or why my face was covered in dirt. I think he figured the less he talked, the less bother he'd be to any of us. Unlike Mama, he knew what no-good things us kids were up to. But he didn't really know how to put a stop to it. I imagine Grandpa Harve spent many a lonely night in that trailer praying that God would send Daddy back or grant Mama an easier life.

i take it back

f RANK AND I WEREN'T THE ONLY ONES WHO TURNED TO SEX FOR CONSOLATION DURING THE CHAOTIC AFtermath of Daddy's death. Mama observed her first year as a widow in the custom of that day. All her dresses were black, her demeanor reserved. But by early 1968, she'd discarded her widow's cloak and invested in a wardrobe of hot pants, baby-doll dresses, and miniskirts short enough to make Jeannie C. Riley blush. Men shot through that twelve-by-sixty-foot trailer house like paper airplanes on a breezy day. They'd start their evenings in the living room but frequently end their nights in Mama's bedroom.

Years later, Mama asked me if I could name all the men who had been her lovers. I recalled the construction worker that she married, oh so briefly; a young soldier named Delmer, whom we called Floyd (he moved in with us for a short while); Uncle Hugh Lee, one of Daddy's younger brothers; a burly guy whose name I couldn't remember who sold fire insurance; and Lewis, the architect she loved but was too afraid to marry.

Mama grinned when I finished ticking off the names. "Is that all?" she asked.

"Were there more?" I replied. Her gleeful eyes told me there were. "Maybe a few one-nighters?" I asked.

"Maybe," she said, refusing any more information.

The widow Spears married a construction worker named Auld, on New Year's Day in 1968. By that time, she'd already earned her LPN certification. Uncle Ray, one of Daddy's brothers, had introduced Mama to his friend Auld. I think it was Ray's way of trying to take care of us. Auld worked construction in Alabama. He was a big guy, well over six feet tall and 230 pounds. He had a ready smile that seemed all the more brilliant against his tanned face. He didn't talk much to us kids. He was only around on the weekends. Even then, I don't remember him being out of Mama's bedroom much.

The wedding was small. Just us kids and Uncle Ray and Aunt Helen from Selma, Alabama. The church was somewhere out Victory Drive, a red-brick structure with white posts, not pillars. Mama wore a pale pink dress. Her thick black hair was piled extra high atop her head in a beehive. I remember her being more scared than elated.

Following the brief ceremony, we pulled out of the church's gravel drive and headed for the reception at a hotel on Manchester Highway. Mama smiled nervously at her new husband as she laughed a jittery laugh and began to sing the lyrics of a country song: "I take it back, I didn't mean it. I must've been outta my mind."

The small reception had all the trimmings—cake and dancing and toasts—but six weeks later, Mama called the whole thing off.

"I don't know what I was thinking when I married him," Mama said. "Your uncle Ray and aunt Helen and the Spears family thought it was a good idea."

When she told Auld she wanted to end the marriage, he didn't seem too shaken. "The only thing he said was would I be wanting any money out of him for support," Mama recalled. She told him no; she just wanted out.

The marriage was annulled, and Mama never, ever married again. And it was decades before she would step foot in a church again.

Shortly after Mama married Auld, I had the first of what would become a reoccurring lifelong dream. It starts with Daddy suddenly appearing at the front door of our trailer. He doesn't knock. He just

walks in with that "Honey-I'm-home" welcome of his. I run to
him, and he embraces me. "Where's your mama?" he asks.

My stomach knots. I try to avoid his question. "I love you, Daddy.
Why have you been gone so long? We thought you died. They told
us you died."

He laughs. "They had the wrong guy," he replies. "It wasn't me."

With tears streaming down my cheeks, I bury my face in the
crook of his neck. "I knew it! I knew it!" I cry. "I knew it wasn't
you. I kept telling Frank it wasn't you."

"Where's your mama?" Daddy asks again, taking me by the hand
and walking from room to room. "Shelby Jean? Shelby Jean?"

Finally, I blurt out: "She's not here, Daddy. Mama's not here."

"Where is she?" he asks.

"She's out with another man. She didn't know. She thought you
were dead."

That's when I wake up, and I never find out what Daddy thinks
about Mama being with another man.

The dream leaves me feeling horrible. I'm angry with Daddy for
dying and leaving us. And I'm angry with Mama for being unfaithful
to my father.

Mama has had her own troubling dream, over and over again. She
dreams Daddy comes home from Vietnam, but he won't come live
with us. Instead, he lives with another family. He makes love to another woman. When Mama wakes up she feels awful, too.

MAMA'S NEXT BOYFRIEND MOVED in with us. Juanita, our next-
door neighbor and Mama's girlfriend, introduced her to the soldier
boy named Delmer Floyd. We always called him Floyd, the name
printed in black above the pocket of his Army greens. He had a twin
brother named Elmer, and they came from a family of nine kids. They
weren't Mormons, or Catholics, just Baptists without birth control.
There was another set of twins, a boy named Lester Lavelle and a girl
named Janelle. Floyd's family was from Arkansas. That explains that.

Floyd was such a nice guy that I didn't even mind that he and Mama were living in sin. He was always real sweet to us kids, perhaps because he was such a kid himself. He was twenty-four, Mama thirty-one. He was built more like Daddy than Auld had been. Lean and muscular. His sandy-colored hair was shorn clean off except for the bristle right on the top of his head. He wasn't tall enough to tower over folks, but he could reach the glasses on the top shelf without having to stand on his tiptoes.

Floyd never did anything abruptly. He spoke in that same deliberate tone that history and Latin teachers use. Never yelling, never demeaning. He was always willing to explain one more thing, one more time. He seemed to have an innate understanding that some folks are just born slow-witted. Out of all the men Mama danced with, I liked Floyd the best. He filled that trailer with so much life that there was no place for grief to linger. Sometimes I would catch Mama humming along to a Buck Owens tune: "No more loneliness, only happiness. Love's gonna live here again." When Floyd was around, Mama wasn't so lonely.

I used to pray that Mama would marry him. I think he was praying for the same thing. Mama invited Floyd to move in with us just a few months after her marriage to Auld was annulled. She was working as a licensed practical nurse. She wasn't even considering college yet. Nor was she ready for another long-term love.

Floyd had been living off base with an older brother, Bobby, who was also stationed at Fort Benning. Floyd had joined the Army in 1965. He signed up purposely, in an attempt to avoid being sent to Vietnam. At that time there was the notion that soldiers who volunteered had more options about where they served than those who were drafted. Sometimes it worked in a soldier's favor, sometimes not. In Floyd's case, it worked. He served with the 507 Engineer Corps, building roads and bridges. By the time he met Mama, Floyd had already finished a tour of duty in Thailand. His older and younger brothers had both done tours in Vietnam. Much to his and Mama's delight, Floyd wouldn't be headed there. Mama was understandably fearful that she'd get into a relationship with another man headed off to war.

When Bobby was discharged in spring of 1968, Army brass wanted Floyd to move back into the barracks. He wiggled his way out of that by moving in with us. When Floyd lived with us, life seemed almost normal again. The dreams of Daddy continued, but there was something about Floyd's presence that made me feel safe. And I didn't worry so much about Mama. Floyd made her laugh like Daddy used to do.

GRANDPA HARVE HAD moved back to Tennessee to live with Aunt Cil, Granny Ruth's sister, just outside Church Hill. Mama had sent him there because she had to have surgery to remove uterine cysts during the summer of 1967 and couldn't care for Grandpa while she was recuperating. Grandpa Harve was happy to return to Tennessee. He liked Aunt Cil, and he especially liked being back in the foothills of the Smokies. Grandpa never cared much for Georgia. Too hot, too flat, too many flies.

Aunt Sue and Thelma made sure we were looked after while Mama healed. Spurred by my concern for Mama, I took a jar and went door-to-door throughout Lake Forest, collecting nickels, dimes, and pennies.

"Do you have change you could spare?" I asked one man who answered the rap on the door.

"What's this for?" he asked.

"We're buying flowers for a lady who had to have surgery," I replied. My friend Leslie was standing beside me, not saying a word.

"Which lady? Which lot is she in?" the man inquired, pressing me for details, suspicious, I suppose.

"Shelby Spears," I said. "She's my mama."

The fellow studied me for a moment longer before dropping a dollar in the jelly jar cupped in my hands. The memory of going door-to-door collecting money to buy Mama flowers shames me in ways I can't explain. I was only ten. I knew no other way to earn money to do the things for Mama that I knew Daddy would do if he was around, like buy her flowers when she went to the hospital. In those early years after Daddy died, I tried hard to be our family's caretaker, to ease Mama's life just a bit.

Mama's workday didn't end until 4 P.M., and she often didn't get home until five or later. Once she finished school, she'd let Thelma go. All the insurance money was gone, and Mama needed every penny she made to pay the bills. For women like her, child care was a luxury. Besides, at age thirteen, Frank was plenty old enough to watch over us girls.

I hated having Frank in charge of me. He was stupid and mean. Always bossing and knuckle-punching if he didn't get his way. We fought over the television constantly. I liked to watch *Dark Shadows,* a Dracula-themed soap opera. Since I walked to school and he rode the bus, I usually got home before he did. So, there I'd be, tuned to Barnabas Collins the vampire and some peroxide-blond victim with blood dripping from snakelike puncture marks on her neck; and Frank would drop his books and flip the channel. I'd scream. He'd punch. I'd yell louder. He'd ignore me. Then, just for spite I'd decide it was a good time to do chores. Yanking that Kirby out of the closet, I'd plug it in and run it right up between Frank and the television. Over and over again. That section of green shag carpet between where Frank sat cross-legged about a foot away from the television was the cleanest in the whole house.

When Floyd moved in, the bickering between Frank and me subsided. Floyd stepped into the paternal role as easily as he did his lace-up boots. Because he usually got home before school was out, Floyd would watch for Linda and me. He'd stand at the corner where the entrance of Lake Forest joined Morris Road and smoke a cigarette. It was pretty much a straight shot down Morris Road to Tillinghurst Elementary. Floyd would count the cars and kids going by until he saw Linda and me. Then he'd mosey down the dirt path a bit and take Linda by the hand and chat with us all the way back home about our day.

"You kids were like my first kids," Floyd said years later. "I loved your mother, and I loved all you kids, too. I remember waiting for you to get home from school. I worried about kids before the world got crazy." I was touched by his remark. During a time when childhood abductions were uncommon and when he was barely more than a boy himself, Floyd worried about our safety.

After school, Floyd would fix us a snack. A bologna sandwich on white bread with mayo for me, and a mayo-only sandwich for Linda. And he'd pour a glass of iced tea or cup of milk for us while he talked about what we should have for supper. Floyd was a good cook. He liked to grill and bake. He gave me my first cooking lesson. Teaching me how to make cookies one afternoon, Floyd gently chided me when I nervously attempted to stick a pan of cookies into a hot oven with one very shaky and outstretched arm.

"Here," he said, taking the cookie sheet between two gloved hands. "Don't be afraid of it, Karen. Remember, in the kitchen, you're the boss." Then he confidently slid the pan onto the oven rack without once burning himself. Floyd was the first man I ever met who knew his way around a kitchen. The only thing Frank knew how to make was fried-bologna sandwiches, and they weren't even really fried. He'd put a slice of bologna on top of a piece of Little Miss Sunshine bread, and, not bothering to use a cookie sheet or biscuit pan, he'd place that directly on the oven's top rack. Then he'd switch the knob up to broil, and as soon as the bologna started to sizzle and the sides of the meat curled up, Frank's sandwich was done. He never offered to make Linda or me one. If we were hungry, Frank would tell us to fix our own.

SHORTLY AFTER FLOYD MOVED in, all hell broke loose in Georgia, when Daddy's sister and her baby moved in with us. Mama didn't care how crowded the trailer was or how chaotic our lives were; Aunt Mary Sue needed a safe place for her and Baby Melissa, so Mama gave her one.

Mary Sue's husband, Uncle Joe, was a mean fellow. Especially when he was drinking firewater, which he did just about all the time. Joe was an ex-con. He'd been jailed twice on attempted-murder charges after he nearly strangled his first wife to death. He wasn't really our uncle, because he and Mary Sue had never gotten married. But that's what we were told to call him, so we did.

Joe picked up his taste for alcohol at an early age. Mary Sue told me that his father was a well-known bootlegger in the Kingsport area. Part Native American, Joe might have had a genetic propensity for becoming an alcoholic. It didn't help matters that he was only a boy of two when his daddy gave him his first sip of beer.

Mary Sue and Joe were dating when we moved back to Tennessee from Hawaii. Mama didn't approve of Joe from the moment she met him. Mary Sue was only nineteen, several years younger than Joe. I'm sure Mama was worried that Joe was taking advantage of Daddy's little sister. But mostly she didn't like him because of the way he acted. Mama had even told Daddy all about her feelings in a letter dated Sunday, July 17, 1966:

> *Mary Sue and Joe came down here Thursday, and I was off from work that day to go to the doctor. When I come back from the doctor's they were here. He was drinking and they were fussing and carrying on here all day. About 4:30 in the afternoon I finally told him he had better get out of my house for he was saying things in front of the kids that no one should listen to. I couldn't stand him at first sight and he just got worse all day. He wanted me to borrow Hugh Lee's car to take him and Mary somewhere and I told him I wasn't about to and he got mad. Your mother probably won't like me telling them to get out but she won't let him stay up there either. He is the sorriest thing I've run across in years.*

Hugh Lee was born ten years after Daddy. They weren't very close as brothers, but Mama and Aunt Mary Sue repeatedly turned to Hugh Lee whenever they really needed help. He was never too busy to give a ride and never too broke to lend a dollar. And Uncle Joe was selfish and arrogant enough to demand both of him and anybody else who crossed his path.

But Uncle Joe could be charming when he wanted. Complete strangers would stop him on the street and tell him how much he looked like that movie star Robert Mitchum. He had a head full of hair that was black as soot, thick-lidded eyes that made him look as though he was only half awake, and a slow grin above his cleft chin. Mary Sue was seduced by Joe's looks. Unsure of herself and raised with a religious code that honored perseverance, she tolerated Joe's alcoholic and abusive ways for far too long.

After Melissa was born, Mama took us kids up to Atlanta where Mary Sue and Joe were living. Mama made the trip during the day when she figured Uncle Joe wouldn't be home. Mary Sue had called and told Mama that Uncle Joe had beat the holy shit out of her.

Driving that little white Corvair of hers, Mama found the rental house in Atlanta without much trouble. Mary Sue was standing at the gas stove stirring a pan of oatmeal when we arrived. Coffee was percolating in a tin pot on the back burner. Mary Sue turned the flames down, reached for a thick-glass cup, and poured Mama some coffee.

"You okay?" Mama asked, gingerly taking the steaming cup from Mary Sue.

"Yeah," she replied.

Mama eyed the nasty bruise on the fleshy part of Mary Sue's arm. It was as big as a softball. "Ye Lawdy, Mary Sue," Mama said.

"I know," she replied. Baby Melissa stirred. I walked over to the bassinet sitting next to the doorway to the expansive kitchen and peered at her. Her skin was pearly white. Like a bride's gown, it captured light and dazzled onlookers. A crop of fox hair, orange and fuzzy, covered her head. God had fashioned Melissa from heaven's raiments and Satan's flames.

"What time is he getting home?" Mama asked.

"I don't know," Mary Sue replied. "He's working construction. He might show up for lunch."

"Are you packed?"

"Won't take long," Mary Sue said.

"Well, let's get going," Mama said. She pushed aside her cup of coffee and stubbed out her cigarette in a saucer. That marked the first of many times that Mary Sue and Melissa would come to live with us over the next few years.

It's hard to remember who slept where once Mary Sue moved in. I think Mary Sue and Melissa took my bed, which was in the middle of the trailer's narrow hallway. I moved into Frank's room with Linda, She took the bottom bunk; I took the top one. Floyd and Mama had the back room, and Frank slept on the couch. It was always crowded and full of noise—a television blaring, a baby squalling, kids arguing, grown-ups yapping.

It wasn't long, maybe a week or two after Mary Sue and Melissa moved in, that Uncle Joe showed up at the house. It was after dark on a school night. Linda and I were already in bed, our bunk beds pushed up against the same quarter-inch plywood wall that the television was pushed up against in the adjoining living room. I could hear every word from the television and nearly every word that was spoken in the other room.

I heard Uncle Joe before I saw him. He showed up at the door, asking for Mary Sue. Nobody invited him in, but he stepped inside anyway. He'd been drinking. "I've come here to take you home," Joe said to Mary Sue.

"I ain't going nowhere with you," Mary Sue replied.

"Like hell you ain't!" he hollered.

Mama was standing next to Mary Sue, who was holding Baby Melissa.

"Gimme that baby! That's my baby!"

"Leave them alone and get the hell outta my house!" Mama yelled back.

Then I heard Mama scream. Uncle Joe kicked her in the gut, sending her flying across the kitchen floor.

Disturbed by all the commotion, I climbed out of bed and was standing at the edge of the hallway. Terrified, I didn't know what to do. I wanted to run for Mama, but Floyd and Frank were headed my way. I hustled back to bed, crying.

Floyd and Frank ran down the hallway toward Mama's room. I started screaming bloody murder as I heard them scrambling for the handgun Mama kept in her bedside dresser. Frank heard my cries and came to calm me down. Climbing on the rail of Linda's bed, he slapped me fiercely across the face. "Shut up!" he said.

I sat there weeping, one palm pressed over my hot cheek. Floyd ran down the hallway with the pistol in hand. Mary Sue grabbed Melissa and ran in the opposite direction. When Uncle Joe saw the pistol, he took off out the door, toward his car. Floyd took off after him, firing one shot, then another. Either mechanics at Fort Benning aren't taught how to shoot to kill, or Floyd wasn't really trying to hit Joe. One bullet struck Uncle Joe's car as he sped away, and the other must've landed in a pine tree somewhere.

Mama was on the floor, trying to catch her breath. Her slight frame—120 pounds, five feet five inches—was doubled over in pain. Holding my palm over my red-hot cheek and crying ever so softly, I crawled out of the bed again and was hiding in the shadows of the hallway, watching as the drama continued to unfold.

"Mama, Mama, are you all right?" Frank asked. He searched for signs of blood.

With one arm grasping at her lower abdomen and the other

reaching for the corner of the kitchen table, Mama rose to her knees. Then she pulled herself up. "Aw, shit!" she groaned.

Floyd placed the pistol on the kitchen counter and rushed over to help her.

"I'm all right," Mama said as Floyd gently led her to the couch. Then, eyeing me in the shadows, she said, "Get to bed, Karen."

I crawled over Linda to the top bunk and pulled the ribbed-cotton covers up over my head.

"What's going on?" Linda asked.

"Uncle Joe kicked Mama," I replied. "Floyd shot him."

Linda didn't ask me anything else.

I fell asleep crying and praying: "Please, God, send Daddy back home."

It wasn't long after that that Floyd left us, too.

dead man's daughter

MY SIXTH-GRADE YEAR WAS MARRED NOT ONLY BY MY VIOLENT UNCLE AND THE ON-AGAIN, OFF-again relationship between Floyd and Mama but by a virulent outbreak of pus-filled boils on my arms and legs. I cleaned them every night with Phisoderm lotion per Mama's instructions, but the sores wouldn't go away.

I had one especially bad boil on my left shin, about the size of a nickel. The sores might have healed sooner if I'd been willing to forgo hosiery. But in 1968 fishnet stockings were all the rage, and it was the first year Mama gave me permission to shave my legs or wear stockings. So even though the threading of the fishnet hose made an X directly across the top of the nastiest boil, I refused to go bare-legged to school. Since girls weren't allowed to wear anything other than a dress or skirt, I wore fishnets almost every day. After lunch, I would sit in my homeroom class and gently pull threads away from the boil's bloody crust. An hour later, I'd do it again.

"What is wrong with your leg?" one boy asked after observing my afternoon ritual.

"Infantigo," I replied.

"What's that?" he asked.

"Beats me," I responded.

A typically quiet girl, sitting nearby, piped up. "It's im-pe-ti-go, not infantigo," she said snootily. "Dirty kids get it. My mama says."

I was not a dirty kid. Different, yes. Dirty, no.

But I wasn't the only different person at school. Our science and reading teacher had Raggedy Ann legs. They hung limp from her hips, unable to support her, even though she didn't appear to weigh much more than any of us students. She told us it was the result of the polio that struck her as a child. Mostly she stayed put behind a desk. But whenever she needed to tend to something, she grabbed hold of the walker beside her chair. She'd lift its rubber-tipped corners one at a time, in a heel-toe, heel-toe rhythm, her feet dragging beneath her. I would hold my breath and pray she wouldn't fall. Sometimes she'd stumble awkwardly. She'd pause, flash us a smile. Then, grasping the walker tighter, she'd move on.

Smile and move on. Even as a child I recognized that it takes a certain amount of humility and a generous amount of grace to be able to do that. I lacked both. I was keenly aware that not having a father around was a handicap. While not as obvious a deformity as my science teacher's, sometimes it was just as debilitating.

A classmate who came home with me for an afternoon inquired about my parents.

"Mama's a nurse. And I don't have a daddy," I replied.

After my friend went home, Mama called me aside. "Why did you tell that girl that you don't have a daddy?" Mama asked.

"I dunno," I said, suddenly aware that Mama didn't approve of my answer. "I don't have a daddy, you know."

"Yes, you do," she said. "You have a daddy, Karen."

"Well, he ain't here. What am I supposed to tell my friends?"

"You tell them that your daddy's deceased," Mama answered.

"Deceased? What does that mean?"

"It means he's dead," Mama said.

Dead. Dead. Dead.

I despised Mama for trying to sterilize Daddy's rotting flesh. Her word—*deceased*—couldn't dismiss the anguish I felt. I hated Daddy for dying and leaving us all alone. And I hated the all-powerful, all-knowing God who could've saved Daddy from the grave but chose not to. Being the daughter of a dead man made me feel dirty on the inside, as if I had done something so wrong, so nasty, so unforgivable that God's only recourse was to take my daddy away.

That intense hatred seared a hole in my heart so big nothing eased the pain. Not that anyone was necessarily trying. Mama certainly never tried to talk me through my confusion. She was too busy trying to salve her own hurts. Linda, Frank, and I never ever talked about Daddy or how much we missed him.

Sometimes classmates at school would ask me about my father. The only comments I remember any of them making were hurtful things. Like the time one of my friends said, "It really bothers me that you don't have a daddy. I don't like being around you because of that."

"I'm sorry," I said, although I really thought she was the sorry one for saying such a horrible thing to me. I learned at a pretty early age that the death of soldiers in Vietnam didn't invoke much concern from others. Truth was, nobody really seemed to care that Frank, Linda, and I were growing up without a father. Except Mama, and it hurt her so badly, she could barely stand to think about it, much less talk about it. So we bore our sorrows in silence, to keep from offending anyone unnecessarily.

Like the multitude of Vietnam veterans who were returning home to empty airports, our family had no one around to embrace us or tell us that they appreciated our sacrifice. Daddy's death made me so angry I just wanted to go out and kick somebody's ass. Anybody's ass. I wanted to spit in God's face and tell Him what a pathetic mess He'd made of things. I didn't realize then that most of the mess was manmade.

WILD DOGWOODS WERE IN bloom when Mama's Aunt Cil died in spring 1968, and it nearly broke Mama's heart. Aunt Cil was her last physical connection to her mama, Granny Ruth, and with those two matriarchs gone, Mama's world just crumbled around her.

Frank, Linda, and I had spent a good bit of time at Aunt Cil's after Daddy died. Mama would drop us off at her farmhouse whenever she had errands to run. Cil (short for Lucille) was a squatty woman, with thick arms, thick legs, and broad shoulders. She had hair as white and fine as powdered sugar. It hung clean to her waist, but she wore it in braids, twisted up into a hair net. She looked like a Native American because she was, partly. Granny Ruth and Aunt Cil's mother, Louisa, was an Englishwoman, but their father was reportedly a Cherokee. Mama says she never met him and can't remember his name, but the grave marker for Louisa at the Tennessee cemetery identifies her as Louisa Matilda Hobbs, wife of Bill Sopshire. Mama's birth certificate spells the name Shropshire.

There were five kids in all—Ruth, Lucille, Pearlie, Ann, and Pet. Pet was the only boy in the bunch; Mama said her uncle was a traveling man who never settled down anywhere. Grandma Louisa lived with Aunt Cil at Christian Bend; Aunt Ann lived at Big Stone Gap; Aunt Pearlie married and moved to Toppenish, Washington; and Granny Ruth settled in Rogersville.

Aunt Cil married a man named Doc Christian. She told me once he wasn't really a doctor. "That's just what everybody called him," she said. Doc already had a son, Lon, from a previous marriage. Lon was the first deaf-mute I ever met. A tall, lanky fella, he was about as old as Cil. Lon wore denim coveralls and tended to the hogs. He filled the water pail from the well every afternoon after dinner and again after supper. Lon seemed to know that his inability to talk made us kids nervous, so he smiled at us a lot and nodded hellos and good-byes.

"People think because he don't speak that Lon's retarded," Cil said one day as we sat on the front porch, rocking and waiting for our dinner of green beans, ham, and biscuits to settle. "He's not retarded. Lon's smart. He just can't talk, that's all."

After that I wasn't afraid of Lon so much. Sometimes Frank and I would climb the rail fence and watch as Lon slopped the hogs. Or we would follow him through the rows of cornstalks out back and watch as he inspected the cobs. Sometimes he would reach up to the apple tree's tallest branches and pluck us the choicest fruit. When Linda and I would tickle each other to tears, Lon would laugh right along with us. Only we couldn't hear his laughter. And he couldn't hear ours.

The other children raised in Christian Bend weren't the least bit afraid of Lon. Patsy Patterson Miller, who grew up in the house down the road from Cil's, remembers the day Lon loaded her up in a wheelbarrow and carried her out of the holler.

"We had a bulldog pup that had crawled up under the house," Patsy recalled. "It was a rainy day. He was whimpering, so I crawled under there to fetch him. I was barefoot and cut my foot on a broken fruit jar."

She was thirteen then and too big to be carried out of the holler by her daddy. Cars couldn't get back in the holler in those days, so Patsy needed to be carted out to the road that leads into Church Hill. Somebody ran down to Aunt Cil's and asked Lon to come help. Patsy said her daddy could communicate with Lon even though he was a mute. "Lon loaded me up in that wooden wheelbarrow of his and carried me out of the holler," she said. "All of us kids thought the world of Lon. Whenever there was any sort of sickness or mess to clean up, folks in the holler sent for Lon."

Aunt Cil was revered for her cooking. "She was a really good cook," Patsy said. "I ate there several times. Lon would pick blackberries for her, and she'd make pies and jellies with 'em."

Patsy loved growing up at Christian Bend, next to Aunt Cil and Lon. "I was a tomboy and we lived way back in the holler," she said. "It was great."

Daddy's death tore up Aunt Cil. She and Frank got into a row one afternoon because he wanted to watch a World War II movie and she forbade it.

"I won't have no war movies in my home!" she declared, ordering Frank to flip the television's station. He protested, but Aunt Cil wouldn't budge. Finally, he turned to a western.

"But Aunt Cil," I said, intervening on Frank's behalf, "they got guns in westerns, too."

"It ain't the same," she said. "I can't tolerate no talk of war since Dave died."

I didn't argue with her. And Frank never did ask again to watch a war movie in Cil's house.

Aunt Cil had a simple house. It had no foundation and was held up off the ground by stiltlike posts. "That's so snakes don't get in the house," Cil explained.

She didn't have any indoor plumbing, so water had to be pumped from a well in the front yard. And for many years there wasn't any electricity. Even when we were kids, the light in the house came from single electric bulbs hanging from the center of each room. I'd have to climb on a stool, hold the lightbulb, and jerk on a chain to turn the light on. Cil cooked everything in her woodstove. She heated the house the same way. Cil kept a porcelain pot under her bed for night. During the day, there was a two-seater outhouse back by the apple grove. Linda and I would never go in there alone, so we always made the other one tag along. Discarded magazines served as wipes. Once, while Linda was doing her business, curiosity got the better of me. "Wonder how far this thing goes down," I said, plunging my head momentarily into the black hole.

I jerked it right back out.

"Whad'ya see?" Linda asked.

I didn't have enough breath to answer her. Pushing the door open, I fell out into the ground, gasping.

"SHUT THAT DOOR!" Linda screamed. "You're letting the flies in!"

Cil performed the same bedtime ritual every night. She'd put on a cotton gown, take out her hair net, and unwrap her braids. Then

she'd take a silver-handled brush and run it through her hair for a
hundred strokes. "If you brush your hair one hundred times each
night, it'll keep healthy," she explained. Linda and I would sit on the
edge of Cil's bed and count the strokes with her . . . seventy-nine,
eighty, eighty-one. Then we'd borrow her brush and do the same to
our hair.

When we finished, Cil would pull out her black Bible with the
words of Jesus printed in red and read us a story. Usually it was a tale
from the Old Testament—the story of a flood, a plague, a king, or a
whale. Cil shied away from the battle stories. Then she'd drop to her
knees by her bed, and Linda and I would follow suit. We'd fold our
hands and listen quietly as Cil asked for God's blessing on us, on Lon,
on Frank, on Mama and Grandpa Harve and all her mountain neighbors. Then Linda would crawl into bed with Cil and I would sleep
on a cot next to her bed.

Cil died in that bed. She died the same way she lived—gracefully
and peacefully. When Mama got word, she loaded us into the 1967
Chevy Malibu that she'd traded her Corvair for and drove through
the night with her friend Dave Gibbons at her side. As we drove over
the bridge that spans Tennessee's Holston River, toward Christian
Bend, Dave turned and chided us kids for cutting up in the back.
"Listen, you kids need to calm down. Can't you see how upset your
mother is?"

I stopped tickling Linda long enough to study Mama's face. Her
forehead was bunched up, her dark eyes troubled, her lips drawn taut.
She was chewing on the inside of her cheek, her habitual worry gristle. She hadn't said much of anything since we left Columbus some
eight or nine hours earlier. She hadn't even told us kids to knock off
our messing around like she usually did. It was as if she was in another place, another time, with other people. And I suppose that's exactly where she was—in a place of remembrance. Thinking about all
the times she and her mama used to board the ferry for the trip across
the Holston River. When Mama was a little girl, there wasn't a

bridge across the shiny silver waters. So she and Granny Ruth would have to hop a ferry, then walk the five or six miles to Cil's.

The road, which is paved now, was a dusty shoelace pathway in those days. It wrapped around the muddy banks of the Holston, and sometimes, especially during spring runoff, water would spill out over the road until there was no sign of it. On those trips, mud would cake Mama's legs like dark stockings. She didn't always like the journey, but Mama loved the time she spent with Aunt Cil. Cil had what country folks called the joy of the Lord. She could always find something to laugh about. Her joy was infectious. With Cil nearby, a person just couldn't have a bad day.

Later as I peered into her casket at the altar of the Freewill Baptist Church at Christian Bend, I thought how lovely Cil looked. I hadn't thought a dead person could be so pretty, but Cil looked beautiful. She wore a pale pink cotton gown. Her white hair was parted down the middle, and two long white braids hung to her waist. The hands that had kneaded flour into biscuits; sliced and mashed apples into sauce, brushed and twisted hair, and embraced family and friends in prayers and love lay folded against her heart. A white Bible was tucked beneath them.

That moment was totally unlike the moment two years earlier when I'd stood on my tiptoes peering into Daddy's casket. Daddy had looked so gawd-awful, not at all like himself, that I couldn't help but cry. But Cil looked exactly like herself, only better. Happier, more at peace than ever before. I was convinced she was in heaven because she looked so angelic lying there. It got me to wondering if the way a person dies determines her disposition in the ever after. If a person dies angry, or violently, maybe he wakes up in a bad mood for all eternity. And if a person dies in his sleep, while in the midst of a really good dream, maybe he wakes up in eternity singing songs about bluebirds and sunny days.

Grandpa Harve came back to Georgia to live with us after Aunt Cil died. Lon moved in with some of Doc's family, and I never saw him again.

THROUGHOUT THE SUMMER of 1968, Floyd begged Mama to marry him, but she kept turning him down. It probably didn't help matters that she had had one marriage end in annulment earlier that year. Mama knew she simply couldn't afford to wind up divorced with children. She wasn't about to take another risk at losing her Social Security benefits and widow's pension on a marriage gone sour.

Floyd tried to convince Mama that he loved her, that they wouldn't end up divorced, that he would always care for us, always. But Floyd was learning, as Daddy had, what a mule-headed woman Shelby Jean could be. "Your mama was a strong woman," Floyd told me later. "The most determined woman I've ever met."

Mama had a multitude of reasons for not wanting to marry Floyd. He was only twenty-four. She knew he'd want kids of his own someday and she wouldn't be able to give them to him. Daddy and Mama had tried to conceive another baby when we lived in Hawaii, but cysts had hardened Mama's ovaries. The doctors told her she'd probably never get pregnant again. Mama explained all that to Floyd, but he said he didn't care. He couldn't imagine loving any kids as much as he loved us or any woman as much as he loved her. "Please, Shelby, please," he begged.

But Mama stood firm. She had learned her lesson. She would never again let herself be vulnerable—emotionally, mentally, or most important, financially. She would not be dependent on a man, even a man who loved her dearly, like Floyd. She would take other lovers, but Mama would never again take another husband.

That summer Mama accepted a job at the Carl Vinson VA Medical Center in Dublin, Georgia. She knew Floyd would be leaving the Army in August. Fearful that he would be leaving her soon thereafter, Mama never gave him that chance. She left him first.

dublin doings

CARL VINSON VA MEDICAL CENTER WAS, AND REMAINS, ONE OF DUBLIN'S LARGEST EMPLOYERS. WE MOVED IN July, undoubtedly the worst time of the year to make a move to central Georgia. Mama sent Grandpa off to Uncle Carl's and then paid a fellow to put our home on wheels and take it east to Dublin. I always thought that Dublin should've been named Halfway. It was halfway between Columbus and Savannah, halfway between Savannah and Atlanta, always halfway to somewhere else. For our family, Dublin was a halfway stop on the road to further turmoil.

The trailer park we moved into was nondescript and situated in a gulleylike clearing near a muddy tributary of the Oconee River. The roadways that led through the park were sparsely graveled, mostly dirt. There were fewer than twenty trailers in the entire park. The only trees were all along the creek bed at the back of the park; these provided the park's only shade.

The air never moved. It just hung in the sky like a damp sheet on wash day. Mary Sue and Melissa made the move with us. Mama worked the day shift, and Mary Sue watched over us.

During the day I'd hang out with Frank and Linda. After a breakfast of cold cereal and cartoons, we'd ride bikes, build forts, or explore the creek bed. But by noon we were back inside, standing in front of the window air conditioner, pushing back sweaty bangs from our foreheads. Afternoons were spent reading or watching more television. It was just too unbearably hot to be outside until dusk. After only a few weeks in that heat, Mary Sue took Melissa and went back to Joe. She couldn't bear Dublin no more.

Hoping to provide us kids some distraction, Mama allowed me to adopt three kittens. I named them Faith, Hope, and Charity and kept them in a cardboard box stuffed up next to the rear wheel of the trailer, the one under Mama's bedroom window. In the mornings I would carry a saucer of milk to them. They were too little to reach over the rim of a bowl. If they got messy with the milk, it was hard to tell, because they all had white markings on their black faces.

One morning I found the cardboard box overturned. I knew the kittens weren't big enough to tip it over. I immediately suspected Frank of some no-good deed.

"What did you do with my kittens?" I yelled into the open doorway of the trailer.

"I didn't touch your ugly kittens!" he yelled back.

"But they're gone!" I cried.

Frank and Linda both rushed outside. Then all three of us began searching underneath the trailer wheels, in clumps of grass, under the cinder block steps. We called out their names, and then listened. But we never heard any meows in return.

Frank hopped on his bike, the one with the banana seat and revved-up handlebars, and began a full-blown search-and-rescue mission. Linda pressed Thumbelina against her hip and declared, "He'll find them, Karen. Everything's going to be okay."

Frank did find the kittens, floating paws-down in the creek. Seemed some neighbor boys, kids whose names we didn't even know, had decided to take Faith, Hope, and Charity for a swim. Picking them up by the scruff of their necks, they'd tossed my babies, one by one, into the muddy creek. Frank rushed back to the house and grabbed me. Together we clamored down the slimy slope of the riverbank and watched in despair as Faith, Hope, and Charity floated downstream. "I'm sorry, Karen," Frank said.

"Stupid boys," I said, wiping away the angry tears streaming down my face. "I hate those stupid boys. I'd like to drown them."

"I know," he replied.

The boys, all about Frank's age, fourteen, stood on a knoll above the river, near an oak tree, laughing at the dead kittens and us. If we had one more kid to help us, I think Frank and I would've taken those boys down to the river and held their heads underwater. For a long, long time.

"Dumbasses," Frank said as we headed back to the trailer.

"Jackasses," I chimed in.

Mama never again allowed me to have another kitten. I don't think she could stand to have anything so defenseless around the house. She didn't get me another pet for a very long time, and when she did it was a German shepherd so fierce and so strong he could easily maneuver his way through the muddy Chattahoochee River and play tag with the waves of the Atlantic Ocean. We named him Bruiser. He'd have seriously maimed anybody who might've tried to throw him in a creek. Mama has always had a great heap of humor mixed in with her sense of justice.

Seeing my kittens murdered in cold water was a horrible enough experience to sour me on Dublin. But the traumas didn't end there. Less than a week later, I broke out in a case of hives that totally disfigured my face. My blue eyes melted away behind puffy scarlet welts. Blotchy, inflamed clumps covered my previously freckled cheeks. Oh, the itch! I would lie in bed furiously rubbing my face back and forth against the ribbed-cotton bedspread. Scratching and scratching.

Mama knew it wasn't a case of poison oak. I didn't have hives anywhere except on my face. She took me to a doctor.

"Gracious, girl!" the doctor said. "You look awful."

It was obvious he wasn't the chairman of the town's Welcome Wagon. I didn't smile or respond in any fashion to his remarks. I just answered his questions with a nod or shake of my head.

"Does this itch?" he said, pressing a forefinger against my swollen cheek.

I vigorously nodded.

"Any other rashes?" he asked.

I motioned "no" with a side-to-side shake.

"Looks like your daughter has had an allergic reaction to poison sumac," he said to Mama as he shined a pen-point light into my eyes.

"I don't know where she would've come across that," Mama replied.

"Oh, she wouldn't have to rub up against it," he said. "Somebody could've just been burning some brush and the smoke could've caused this."

He wrote out a prescription and sent us on our way.

"I've never heard of this kind of thing," Mama said, taking me by the hand and leading me out the door. I hadn't either. But I was worried about more pressing things. If the doctor thought I looked gawd-awful, what were my seventh-grade classmates likely to think? I couldn't start at a new school looking like a circus reject. I hoped the medicine would work.

In early August Mama took one last trip to Columbus to see Floyd. She took me with her, maybe because she felt sorry for me with all my recent travails. Or maybe because she wanted some excuse to flee in case things didn't go well with Floyd.

We stopped by Lake Forest, and Mama let me visit with Leslie and James for the afternoon. James had fallen off the back of a moving car and was suffering a concussion. But despite his injury and my unfortunate disfigurement, he still recognized me. "What are you doing here?" he asked as he raised his head from the sofa pillow.

"Just came up for the weekend," I replied, heartened by his obvious affection for me. James was the first boy besides my cousin Roger that I was remotely attracted to. Both of them pretty much ignored me. "I'm sorry about your accident," I said.

"Me, too," he replied, sinking his head back into the pillow.

Leslie and I spent the afternoon swimming. I told her all about my kittens and how awful Dublin was and how I wished Mama had never moved us away. Leslie told me all about the modeling classes she was taking with her sister at Mable Bailey's. She told me she had a crush on Joe K. and she thought he liked her, too. I told her I was sure he did.

Mama took me out to Floyd's place to spend the night. He had moved into a tiny trailer in a park off Victory Drive. I watched a black-and-white television while Mama and Floyd sat at the table drinking black coffee and chain-smoking. Eventually, they disappeared into the only bedroom in the trailer. I fell asleep praying Mama would move us back to Columbus and marry Floyd.

God granted me one of those prayers. Less than four weeks later, just shortly after school started, Mama moved us back to Columbus. Right back out to Lake Forest. We got a corner lot near the lake this time—prime real estate in a trailer park.

Mama enrolled me at Eddy Junior High and Frank at Columbus High School. Mary Sue, pregnant again, and Melissa moved back in with us. Mama hadn't bothered to tell Floyd she'd made a mistake, or that she'd be coming back to Columbus. By the time we got back, he'd already moved home to Arkansas.

victory drive-in

THE OLD GANG WAS GLAD TO HAVE FRANK AND ME BACK IN THE NEIGHBORHOOD. JAMES LET ME KNOW HOW happy he was by extending a special invitation to me one afternoon.

"Hey, Karen," he said. "You want to go down to the cabin at the lake with me and Joe?" He gave an elbow nudge to Joe K., who was standing beside him smirking.

"What for?" I asked. I kicked at a clump of dirt in the middle of the road that ran between James's luxurious double-wide home and my more modest single-wide.

"For sex," he replied. There were no snickers, no chuckles. Just dead-on honesty.

"What?" I asked.

"There's no one around. It's just a little shed. No one has to know. No one will see us."

I looked over at Joe K., who was one of Frank's closest friends. I didn't think he would let anything bad happen to me.

"Yeah, we've taken lots of girls there," Joe K. said.

"Like who?" I asked. Skepticism was a trait I cultivated early in life.

"Mary Jane," Joe K. said.

"Mary Jane had sex with you?" I asked. Mary Jane was one of my best friends. Certainly if she was doing the big nasty, she would've told me all about it. Mary Jane and I talked about everything.

"Yeah," Joe K. replied.

"What about Leslie?" I asked. I hoped the question would unnerve her brother.

"Her, too," Joe K. answered. James didn't even blink.

The pressure was on now. They both stared at me. If my girlfriends in the park were having sex, then certainly I couldn't turn down their earnest request. "I can't have sex," I replied.

"Why not?" James asked.

"I haven't even had a period yet," I replied. "I'm not old enough to have sex."

"All the better," James quipped.

"Why's that?" I asked.

"If you haven't had a period yet, then you can't get pregnant."

I brushed by them and marched on home. Horny boys, how dumb do I look?

I was shocked that Leslie might have been having sex, but I wasn't that surprised about Mary Jane. Mary Jane's mom, a big-breasted, big-hipped, thick-lipped, boozy blonde, was considered the trailer park slut. My memories of her primarily consist of the times she would order us teens into her car and head out to the Victory Drive-in burger joint, a favorite soldier hangout. Her husband, who wasn't Mary Jane or Joe's father, was fighting for his country in Vietnam. And she was doing her part by entertaining the troops at home.

One night, after we'd made the customary pickup at Victory Drive, she decided to take all us kids and her two new soldier pals to visit a haunted house across the river in Phenix City, Alabama. It was already late, past eleven. The idea of traipsing through a haunted house didn't appeal much to me. I had a tough-enough time dealing with ghosts in broad daylight. Mary Jane didn't want to go either, but what choice did we have? Her mother was a madwoman. She didn't possess a lick of common sense. So I cowered in the corner of the Buick, rolled down the window, welcoming the slap of weighty night air against my cheeks, and prayed that God would protect us from the demons that Mary Jane's mother sought out.

There wasn't any moonlight to illuminate the crumbling concrete path that wound through wrought-iron gates, past an ancient oak, and up to the squeaky front door of the long-forgotten Georgian manor. There, beyond the sloping lawn, hundreds of tombstones protruded from the ground, like elbows and knees only half buried. I shivered and gave Mary Jane a nudge. "Look!" I said as I pointed to the graves.

A shrill laugh startled us both. Mary Jane's mama had a soldier hanging on each side of her. Directly ahead of us, they were all three swaying in a lusty rhythm. The young soldiers were rubbing up against her swollen breasts every chance they got. And she gave them plenty of chances.

Nothing like righteous disgust to overcome one's fears. I grabbed Mary Jane by the hand and marched right past her mama. I wanted to hurry up and get this whole ordeal over with. I about walked right through the front door. "Y'all be careful in there!" Mary Jane's mother shouted out after us.

"Oh, shut up, you ole hag!" I muttered, so she couldn't hear.

Mary Jane giggled.

I wasn't feeling as brave once we were inside the dark caverns of the old home. The wooden floors were covered in dust. The place smelled of dead spiders, live rats, and cat urine. As Mary Jane's mother and her twin escorts bounded up the narrow stairs behind us, Mary Jane and I edged over to the entrance of the living room. We stood there, snuggling up against each other, inspecting formidable furniture draped in cotton sheets and dust balls. We worried about the snakes we feared we might see and the ghosts that we didn't see but could feel were there. Backing out of the house, we stood on the porch and stared out across the neighboring graveyard.

"Do you believe there's really a heaven and a hell?" Mary Jane asked.

"I don't know about heaven, but I believe there's a hell," I replied.

"Me, too," she said. "Me, too."

That night Mary Jane and I shared her bed. I don't know that either of us slept much. Mary Jane's mother and her new pals were carrying on something fierce in the back bedroom. Laughter, the throaty kind that follows a nasty joke, echoed down the hallway. I don't know what Mary Jane was thinking, but I was busy trying to not imagine her mama nekkid. I felt bad for Mary Jane, Joe, and the soldier that wasn't their real father. I wondered if Vietnam was a desolate place and if there was as much confusion over there as there was here at home.

ALL THAT CONFUSION came to a head one day when Aunt Mary Sue and I got into a shouting match. Neither of us remembers what the fight was about. We were in the kitchen, sitting at the dinette table, when I got mad at her and smarted off about something. Mary Sue grabbed the cup of coffee she'd been drinking and doused me with it. I was soaked from neck to thigh. The coffee was warm enough to create flaming red blotches. Angry, I called Mama at work. "Mary Sue threw coffee at me!" I said, bawling.

"What?" Mama asked.

"She threw hot coffee at me!" I sobbed.

Mama drove straight home. I was in the bathroom, cooling the red blotches with a wet rag. From there, events get blurry, as is often the case with violent rages. Mary Sue swears that Mama took the gun from the bedside drawer and cornered her. Mama adamantly denies it. They will go to their graves disagreeing over that gun, but they agree on what happened next.

"Get the hell outta my house!" Mama yelled.

"Shelby, Karen is lying," Mary Sue protested. "That coffee wasn't hot!"

Mama wasn't budging. "I said get your damn things and get out!" Mama yelled again.

"Shelby, just calm down. You can look at Karen and see she ain't hurt. If I'd thrown hot coffee at her, she'd be burned."

Mama was beyond reason. I'd never seen her so mad. What my aunt said was true. The coffee wasn't hot. I didn't have a burn on me. But all Mama saw were the red blotches, and for all she knew, they might blister.

I hadn't intended to put my aunt at such odds with my mother, but I wasn't about to intervene. There's nothing like a mama kicking someone out to prove to a young girl that her mama loves her more than life itself. I was enjoying Mama's overt display of affection for me. I didn't give much thought to my aunt and her situation.

Mary Sue didn't even stop long enough to pack up her things. She just took Melissa and left on foot. Fortunately, she'd just gotten her paycheck. She bought a Greyhound ticket to Tennessee and moved in with Granny and Pap. A couple of years passed before Mama and Mary Sue spoke again.

oh, brother frank!

AFTER MARY SUE MOVED OUT, GRANDPA HARVE MOVED BACK IN. HAVING RELATIVES LIVE WITH US PROVIDED Mama with a sense that someone, no matter how feeble or ill-equipped, was keeping watch-care over us. From where he sat every afternoon, chain-smoking, Grandpa Harve could see that Mama was doing the best she could, considering, but the former lawman could also see that Frank needed more supervision than an Alabama chain gang.

Frank was angry. And he lacked the verbal skills to articulate his frustrations or the emotional fortitude to wrestle the growing madness within him. Frank wasn't crazy. He was just plumb upset. Like me, he was struggling to figure out how to get through life without Daddy. The two of them had been the best of buds. Mama had only had to look at Daddy's shadow to find Frank. He was always tagging alongside Daddy.

Nobody was offering to teach him how to cope with death. So Frank settled for the next best thing—a means to dull the ache. He discovered a fifth of Crown Royal that somebody, maybe Mama, had left in the backseat of the red Falcon and began using it as a pretty effective pain reliever. (Frank had stripped the gears on Mama's Chevy Malibu during an illegal hot-rod excursion down the freeway late one night, and Mama bought the Falcon to replace the trashed Malibu.)

Frank grabbed that bottle and his buddy Joe C. and headed for the
lake. The two of them downed the entire bottle in an afternoon. It
was Frank's first drink. He was fourteen, almost fifteen.

He got sicker than a yard dog with scours. He spent the evening
puking and finally passed out on the living room floor. Mama didn't
have any idea that he'd been drinking. She figured a day at the lake in
Georgia heat was enough to tire anybody out. She left him lying
there.

But she roused him early the next morning. It was vacation time.
He had to help her drive to Tennessee. Mama didn't usually like to
go to Tennessee on her vacations. She'd much rather go to Panama
City, Florida, and bask in the sun. But Uncle Hugh Lee was getting
ready to leave for another tour of military duty, and Mama wanted
the chance to say good-bye.

In 1966, while Daddy was in Vietnam, Hugh Lee wrote him a letter
asking whether he should stay in the Navy or do something else when
his tour was up. Daddy wrote back and told his younger brother to do
something else. Hugh Lee kept Daddy's letter packed away in a stor-
age shed for many years, with his other military gear, at the edge of the
sweeping acre that serves as his backyard. If he wanted, Hugh Lee
could pitch a rock from his backyard and hit the roof of the Elm Street
home where Granny Leona and Pap had once lived. The envelope had
a map of Vietnam on it. On that map, Daddy had marked the spot
where he was.

In the letter, Daddy told Hugh not to reenlist. "Sooner or later,"
he said, "you get tired of being shot at."

"He told me because I had an education I could do anything I
wanted to do," Hugh Lee recalled. "I'm sure Dave's letter was one of
the reasons I didn't reenlist. It wasn't the only reason, but it was one
of the reasons."

So, when his tour was up in 1967, Hugh Lee returned to Tennessee and worked an assortment of jobs. But in 1969, for a variety
of reasons, he joined the Navy again.

Mama had another reason for taking the trip to Tennessee. She was dropping me at Granny's for month.

If I'd been thirteen, Mama could've blamed my sour attitude on puberty, but I was only twelve. Mama's a quiet woman, not prone to outbursts of any sort. She typically doesn't yell. She doesn't cheer. She doesn't say ugly things. And she didn't used to say too many nice things, either. Mostly, she just kept to herself—if I would let her. My temperament is the opposite. My temper fuse is shorter than the used wick of a birthday candle, and the motor on my mouth has more combustion than a gas-fired turbine. I always say the first and last thing on my mind. Mama had run out of energy to put up with me. Granny Leona always enjoyed my company.

In the mornings, Granny and I would visit over bowls of oatmeal soaked with Pet milk. In the afternoons, Pap and I would walk down to Hurd's store for a cold pop and a bag of peanuts. Sometimes I'd pour the peanuts into the neck of the cola bottle, the way Aunt Mary Sue had taught me. In between visits with Granny and Pap, I took walks up the hill to chat with Mrs. Blizzard, a widow who lived near Lyons Park Baptist Church.

A tall, lanky woman, Mrs. Blizzard looked to me like she could reach the kitchen table from her living room couch just by stretching out her arms. I don't know why she tolerated my afternoon visits, but she seemed genuinely delighted whenever I dropped in on her. Sometimes she pulled out the family photo albums and told me about her dead husband and her grown kids.

Her stories were never about them being grown, of course. They were always about when she was a mother of young children.

"I would never let anyone kiss my babies," Mrs. Blizzard would say. "And I never kissed or hugged anybody else's babies. Too many germs are spread that way."

I didn't worry too much about germs then. In fact, one of the reasons I liked visiting Mrs. Blizzard was because I had to walk past Rodney's home. Pretty boy Rodney was sixteen. He lived

smack-dab halfway between Granny's house and Mrs. Blizzard's.
And despite Mrs. Blizzard's warning about the hazards of kissing, I
spent many an afternoon and evening thinking about swapping
slobbers with Rodney. But the most we ever swapped were a couple
of "Heys."

While I lingered around Granny's that summer, snapping peas and
reading and rereading Louisa May Alcott's *Little Women,* trouble was
brewing back in Georgia.

Frank and Joe K. slipped into the projects across the tracks one afternoon, armed with a slingshot and rocks. In their own version of
Army, they tossed their grenades at the enemy until the enemy came
running toward them with real guns a'popping. Nobody got hurt,
but it caused quite a stir on both sides of the tracks for a week or two
when the police paid Mama a casual visit.

The next time the police came calling it was on more official
business. Mama had sent Frank to the store to get her a pack of cigarettes. Frank had turned fifteen in mid-June. He wasn't old enough
to drive, but Mama gave him the keys to her Falcon anyway. Frank
was eager to do any of Mama's errands as long as he had the keys to
her car. Besides, Mama reasoned, she might as well give Frank the
keys, since he was always stealing them anyway.

Frank and Joe K. hopped in the car and headed up Morris Road
to the corner market. They picked up her cigarettes and were on
their way back home when they sped past a motorcycle cop parked
next to Tillinghurst Elementary School.

The officer pulled out after Frank. Knowing full well he was too
young to be driving, Frank figured he was in big trouble. So, he reasoned he only had one option—outrun the cop. Frank knew the
1965 Falcon was equipped with a 289 high-performance engine.
Surely a cop on a bike was no match for such a demon. Frank pushed
the pedal to the floor while Joe played scout.

"Take a right! Take a right!" Joe K. shouted, as Frank came up the
Lake Forest entrance.

Glancing at his speedometer—forty-five miles per hour—Frank kept the pressure on the gas. He turned the car on two wheels.

"That pig's right behind us!" Joe shouted. Frank didn't slow down for the potholes. *"Holy Shit!"* Joe yelled. *"Wipe out!"*

Looking into his rearview mirror, Frank watched as the cop's bike spun out from underneath him. Both bike and driver bit the dust.

"I bet he's gonna be pissed now," Frank said. He didn't stop to offer the fellow a helping hand. He parked the car behind the trailer. Figuring out of sight, out of mind, maybe the cop would forget about him.

He and Joe walked casually into the trailer, handed Mama the paper sack holding her cigarettes, and then headed for Frank's bedroom. They were sitting on his bed, whispering excitedly about their adventure, when the cop rapped loudly on the trailer door.

It was a good thing for Frank that our unsuspecting Mama already had her cigarette lit when she opened that door. She needed something to calm her down. The cop cited Frank for driving without a license and reckless driving. When word got around to the trailer park manager, there was another angry rap at the door. He gave Mama forty-eight hours to put the wheels back on the trailer and get her ass out of his park.

I DIDN'T KNOW a thing about the ruckus Frank was creating in Georgia until it was time for me to leave Granny's. Mama called and said she wasn't going to be able to pick me up. Could somebody please make sure I got on the right dog—Greyhound bus—for the ride home?

Granny scribbled down the new address Mama gave her. Then Uncle Doug took me to town to catch the bus. The bus driver assured my uncle that he would deliver me to the right spot.

It was morning when I left Tennessee and morning when we crossed the Georgia state line the next day. The bus took the milk route, meaning that whenever somebody yanked the cord overhead, we stopped. Sometimes we stopped when they weren't yanking the rope. There was a bellyaching drunk on the bus, and about halfway into the trip, before we'd gotten out of Tennessee, the bus driver pulled over on a grassy spot and chucked him out the doors. There wasn't anything around except a road that seemed to go nowhere in both directions. Then the driver took his seat, looked into the mirror above his head, and said: "The next one of y'all that gives me any trouble is going to get the same treatment."

I hunkered down farther into my seat. "Oh, Lord," I prayed. "Get me home safely."

A crackle of thunder ripped through the heavens. In the distance a finger of lightning flashed, and hard rain pelted the windows. I leaned my head against the pane and exhaled. My breath coated the glass. I watched as the drunken man jerked at the neck of his shirt and yanked it up over his head. I hoped somebody would come along and give him a ride soon.

Some people on the bus had brought a sack lunch with them. I hadn't thought to do that, so I slept through dinner. Fearful and angry, I waited until it got dark enough so I could weep with nobody seeing me. I hated Mama for making me take the bus home. Wasn't she worried about me?

I was relieved when the bus finally rolled into the station in downtown Columbus. It was morning but it still looked like midnight. Dawn was a couple hours off yet. I clamored off the bus with about half a dozen other folks and waited quietly as the driver pulled my suitcase from the undercarriage. Then, lugging it behind me, I made my way into the brightly lit station. I quickly scanned the room for Mama, but she wasn't there.

My chest burned, and I blinked back stinging tears. I didn't know what I was supposed to do. How could Mama leave me down here all alone? For gosh sakes, I was only twelve years old. I wasn't even a mother, and I knew better than to leave a girl like me all alone. It was my first bus trip. It was the middle of dark. And Mama had up and moved to someplace I didn't even know.

I walked over to the pay phone and dialed home. Mama answered, her voice thick with sleep, and told me to take a cab home. She gave me the address of our new trailer lot. I told her I didn't have any money for a taxi. She said she would pay the driver when he dropped me off.

Now I was seething mad. Daddy would've never put me on a bus, much less tell me to catch a cab in downtown Columbus in the dark of morning. I couldn't figure out who was dumber—God or Mama. Why in heaven's name did he trust Mama with us kids? He must've been mental to think she could care for us by herself. Shoot, she hadn't seen me for a month of Sundays, and she wouldn't crawl out of bed to come pick me up. I was ready to get back on the bus and go right back to Granny Leona's.

Instead, I walked to the curb to look for a taxi. I didn't have to wait long before one pulled up. A black cabbie jumped out, tipped his hat, and opened the back door for me. He put my bag in the trunk. When he crawled back in behind the steering wheel, he turned and asked me, "Where to, ma'am?" I passed him the address I'd jotted down on a paper scrap.

"Crystal Valley?" he asked. "Whoo-wee! That's way out Macon Road."

Since I didn't drive, I didn't pay much attention to where things were or how far the road was between them. "I don't know where it's at, sir," I replied. "Mama moved while I was away."

"It's okay, sugar," he said. "I can get you there. Don't worry."

His radio beeped. Somebody else needed a ride, he explained as we pulled up in front of a downtown bar. A man wearing a white dress shirt and dark trousers was waiting. The cabbie rushed around to open the front passenger door for him. I took a deep breath and exhaled a silent "Thank you, God."

A white man. Somebody who could be trusted. I'd been taught from a very early age to avoid black men. I don't actually recall Mama warning me to stay away from blacks. I just always knew that dark-skinned men posed a threat, especially to blond-headed, blue-eyed girls like me. I knew that the same way I knew swimming in the pool with boys or heavy petting could make a girl pregnant.

The rules of social interaction between blacks and whites were part of our daily instructions, like the Ten Commandments. Don't look a black fella in the eyes, lest he think you're easy. Don't lend black girls a comb; they have head lice. Always keep the doors locked when driving through the projects or black neighborhoods. Blacks travel in gangs, and they are violent. Never, ever, be alone with a black man; he'll rape you.

I'd never before had an occasion to be alone with a black man, and I didn't want to now, in the dark before dawn and in the middle of nowhere. It didn't matter to me if the white man was sweating and swearing. The social mores of that time had taught me that I was safer with a drunken white man than a sober black man, any time of the day or night. I didn't have any reason to question that, so I didn't.

As the cabbie drove out past Shoney's Big Boy Restaurant, a couple of churches, and Parkhill Cemetery, I began to wonder if I'd scribbled down the right address. When we passed Macon Road Barbecue, the place Mama took us out to eat occasionally, I really began to fret. There weren't many housing developments past Reese Road. We dropped the drunk off in front of a red-brick colonial in an obscure cul-de-sac.

The cabbie must've sensed my nervousness. "It ain't much farther now, ma'am," he said. Looking into his rearview mirror, I could see the whites of his eyes flashing.

"Okay, sir," I whispered.

My palms were sweating, a nervous habit that plagues me to this day. I watched out the window, but I couldn't see much. There were no streetlights. No moon. No houses with porch lights on. Nothing but the dark shadows cast by pines, oaks, and mimosa trees. And the dark driver in the seat in front of me. He might rape me, cut me with a knife, and leave me bleeding in a dirt ditch out here. Nobody would ever see him. He's as black as midnight.

My next thought was of Mama. I hated her.

"I think the turnoff's right up here," the cabbie said, startling me. I craned my neck to get a look at the corner. There wasn't a convenience store, gas station, or school nearby. A sole streetlight marked our path. A sign, painted blue and white, sat back off the corner, to the right: CRYSTAL VALLEY ESTATES.

Going by name only, a person might think the blacktop at Crystal Valley was sprinkled with rhinestones and the homes were all Georgian manor houses, replete with ornate pillars, stone porches, and sweet-faced women wearing antebellum skirts. Instead it was a sprawling neighborhood with chain-link fences and row after row of trailers with rippled-aluminum skirting.

The cabbie made a right-hand turn. He looked again at the scribbled address and called out the space number of my new home. He drove over several speed bumps, past a lake and lots of single-wide trailers, some with cinder block steps. Finally, at the very back corner of the park, there was our trailer. "That's it!" I said, pointing toward our porch light. The driver pulled the taxi over and jumped out to open my door. Mama must've been waiting up for me, because she was out the door and by my side before the cabbie had time to retrieve my bag from the trunk. Mama thanked him and gave him a fistful of money.

"Long trip?" she asked, turning to look at me. Mama wasn't the embracing sort. Picking up my suitcase, she led me to the trailer's back door. There weren't any steps to the front door yet, and it sat about four feet off the ground because of the slope of the lot.

Inside, the trailer was the same. Same three bedrooms. Same hallway. Same awful couch. But it all felt so strange to me. Like returning to elementary school as a high school senior. You recognize the water fountain you used to struggle to reach on tippy-toes, but now you tower over it. Everything feels familiar, but you don't fit into the spaces anymore. The house smelled of Mama's Salem cigarettes and Chanel No. 5 perfume. I could hear Frank's heavy breathing through the stapled plywood walls. But I felt as if I didn't belong in my own family anymore. It was the most lonesome feeling I'd ever had.

"G'night," Mama said. "Good to have you home."

"Thanks," I mumbled as I slid open my bedroom door. It was attached to a roller that hung from the ceiling, and it often fell right off if I pushed it too hard. Since Linda and Frank were sleeping, I gave it only a light push. It glided open.

I crawled into bed without slipping out of anything but my shoes and fell asleep saying the only prayer I knew: "Our Father, which art in Heaven. Hallowed be Thy name. Thy Kingdom come, Thy will be done . . ."

I hadn't yet learned that it's okay to cry out in prayer, or I might have gone to bed that night hollering: "What's the matter with you, God? If you're so all-powerful, how come you let Daddy die in some foreign country? And if you're so all-loving, how come you don't do better by us kids and Mama?"

What I didn't know then was that Mama was pondering the very same questions. Only she wasn't waiting around for God to get it all figured out. She had a plan.

role reversal

I N THE FALL OF 1969, MAMA ENROLLED IN A NURSING PROGRAM AT COLUMBUS COLLEGE. SHE'D DECIDED THE best way to make a better life for us was to make more money. The only way she could do that was to become a registered nurse.

It was an admirable plan, one that left us kids marveling at our mama once again. Despite all her obvious shortcomings, Mama was the hardest-working person I knew. She never accepted things as status quo. She was forever trying to figure out how to give us kids a better life. Problem was, Mama defined a better life in material terms. This was the result of her impoverished childhood, I reckon. Plus, I guess Mama thought that if she could give us everything our father would have, then we might not miss him so much.

So she began a rigorous schedule, attending college during the days and working part-time, 3 P.M. to 11 P.M., at various nursing homes and hospitals. It was a grueling routine that our entire family endured from the fall of 1969 until the spring of 1971.

Mama had worked the swing shift pretty much since she'd completed the Manpower Program. So there was never much supervision for us kids. Thelma, Floyd, Grandpa Harve, and Aunt Mary Sue had provided some consistency in our lives. Now that we were older, Mama didn't feel we needed as much oversight. Frank was fifteen, Linda, ten, and we were all big enough to be left on our own.

After Frank got us kicked out of Lake Forest Trailer park, Mama sent Grandpa Harve to live with Uncle Carl again. Her plan was to finish her degree and buy a house. Then she'd bring Grandpa back to live with us, forever.

So our entire family began school that fall. Mama at Columbus College, Frank at Columbus High School, me at Arnold Junior High, and Linda at Waddell Elementary. We all went our separate ways in the mornings. And when we kids came home in the afternoons, it was usually to an empty house. Sometimes Mama was there, but if she was, she had a thick medical book propped opened in her lap or on the kitchen table. She was determined to be the best nursing student enrolled at Columbus College.

The college is now known as Columbus State University, and is part of the University of Georgia educational system, but in those days it was often referred to as Cody Road High, a title that offended many of the professionals who staffed the school. So, like most second-ranked schools, they tried harder and pushed their students to their limits. Mama didn't shirk from the challenge one bit, and she repeatedly earned her place on the dean's list. Not bad for a rural Tennessee gal with a ninth-grade education.

One nursing instructor in particular was always giving Mama grief. Not much of a whiner, Mama didn't usually talk much about how difficult school was for her. Although as a kid I didn't understand the magnitude of Mama's accomplishments, I was proud that she was trying to make things right for us.

One particular afternoon, Mama came home frustrated to no end. She said her instructor, Sister Marianella Senft, had chided her in front of the entire class over some procedural thing she thought Mama ought to have mastered already. A shy woman by nature, Mama doesn't like to be singled out for any reason and certainly not for public humiliation. As I listened to her recounting the day's events, I decided right then that somebody had to put the sister in her place, and it might as well be me.

I gathered up a fistful of change and left the trailer. I didn't tell anyone where I was going or what I was going to do. I wasn't too sure myself. But I knew there was a pay phone at the other side of the trailer court. I intended to have a little chat with Sister Marianella.

I found the college's information number in the thick black book dangling from the end of a chain. I plunked a dime in the phone and dialed the number. "Could I please speak to Sister Marianella, ma'am?" I asked the receptionist.

"Just one moment, please," she replied.

There was a long pause before a voice came on the line. I'd half expected the nun to talk in the same deep-throttle voice that Coach Bush employed when instructing the mighty Rams, Arnold Junior High's football team. But Sister Marianella's voice was pleasant, not imposing. That bolstered my resolve a bit. "Ma'am," I said, "you don't know me, but my mama, Shelby Spears, is a student in your class."

"Yes?" she responded, no doubt curious about why some student's daughter was calling her.

"Mama's been having a tough time in your class. She comes home upset all the time. I don't know what you said to her in class today, but she came home almost in tears."

I didn't pause to take a breath or give Sister Marianella a chance to take one either. My voice was growing louder, more intense. "Did you know Mama is taking care of three kids while she goes to school? Did you know that my daddy died in Vietnam? Did you know that when Mama leaves school she goes to work all night? Don't you understand how hard she's trying? She's really trying. You ought not be so mean to her. Can't you see she's doing her best?"

There! Whew! I'd spit that all out.

"How old are you?" the nun asked.

"Twelve," I said.

"Well, young lady, I think it is impertinent of you to make such a call," Sister Marianella said. I wasn't too sure what she meant, but I didn't interrupt her for an explanation. "If your mother wants to be a nurse, she's going to have to earn the right to be one. Perhaps she ought to reconsider, given all you've just told me. I will talk to her about it tomorrow."

Click.

I couldn't believe it! That old bag had hung up on me. She didn't listen to a word I'd said. And she obviously didn't carry an ounce of mercy in her deep pockets. I fumed all the way back home. But I didn't say a word about the phone call to Mama. She was upset enough. No reason to get her more riled up. Besides, I was pretty sure the sister was going to tell Mama all about the phone call.

She did.

It was the first thing Mama wanted to know about when she got home the next day. "Karen?" she called out, walking down the hallway toward my bedroom. "Did you call Sister Marianella yesterday?"

"Yes, ma'am," I replied, pretending to be occupied cleaning up the toiletries on my dresser.

"You had no business calling my instructor," Mama said.

"She's being mean for no reason at all," I said. "I just told her how hard you're trying."

"I know what you said to her," Mama remarked. "She told me all about it. Don't ever do such a thing again."

"Yes, ma'am," I said.

Mama spoke sternly to me, but I knew she wasn't really mad. Otherwise she would've grounded me. I suspected when she repeated the story to her girlfriends that in her own quirky way, Mama was kind of pleased that I'd called the sister. I figured she probably wished she'd been able to tell Sister Marianella a few things herself, if it wouldn't have been such a risk to her future.

I don't think Mama or I realized it at first, but that phone call marked a change in the way we began to relate to each other. Months later, Mama summed up the change this way: "Sometimes I can't tell who is the mother and who is the daughter here."

She was popping off at me at the time. Angry over yet another battle we'd been waging. But she got it right. Our roles had reversed. From the moment I confronted Sister Marianella Senft, I viewed Mama as a needy person, incapable of properly caring for herself, much less us kids. And although she'd never said so, I suspected Mama doubted her own capabilities at the time.

When she wasn't studying or working, Mama was drinking more than ever. Not alone and not usually at home. She often spent the weekend evenings partying with her nursing buddies. I hated Mama's honky-tonking. I was fearful of being left alone at night. Sometimes I made desperate attempts to keep her at home. I'd cry that I had a bad bellyache. Or I'd take the thermometer and scratch it across the bedsheets, trying to raise the mercury level and convince Mama that I was running a bad fever. Sometimes I would tell her that I was scared to be alone and that I wanted her to stay with me. For the most part, Mama ignored me and my fears. She labeled me her "hysterical child" and often laughed off my silly sicknesses.

I didn't make any attempts to hide my disgust with her indulgences. Mama said that before Daddy died she didn't drink at all. Not even one beer. But then again, back then she didn't have any screeching sorrows to quell. As long as she stayed busy, Mama could ignore Daddy's absence. But at night an imposing shadow rested on the pillow next to her. The memories of the man she had loved with her whole heart, mind, body, and soul haunted her. Death is a cold companion to snuggle up next to. No wonder Mama often soaked her slumber in firewater first.

for god's sake don't enlist

THE VERY BEST THING ABOUT ARNOLD JUNIOR HIGH WAS Mrs. ANN ANDERSON. MRS. ANDERSON SPORTED A backcombed hairstyle and sometimes wore white boots that made her look like one of Nancy Sinatra's go-go dancers. But it was her laughter that captured my attention. She was the sort of teacher who kept her frustration burner turned down low and her giggle monitor cranked up high. If a kid acted up in her class, she'd put a dunce hat on him and tell him to take a seat in the wastebasket next to her desk. For that reason alone, very few kids ever acted out in her class.

But it was the stories we read that made me most eager for her English class. Mrs. Anderson introduced me and hundreds of other pubescent television devotees and comic-book readers to good literature. The backbone of our class that year was John Gunther's *Death Be Not Proud,* a father's tribute to his dead son.

The title comes from a sonnet by the classic poet John Donne. Gunther wrote achingly of Johnny, the son he lost in 1947 to a brain tumor. He summed up his son's battle with cancer this way: "A primitive to-the-death struggle of reason against violence, reason against disruption, reason against brute unthinking force—this was what went on in Johnny's head. What he was fighting against was the ruthless assault of chaos."

I read Gunther's words in class under Mrs. Anderson's watchful gaze and fought back my own fury against the "brute unthinking force" that had snatched Daddy from our family and the subsequent "ruthless assault of chaos" we were now enduring. Sometimes, as I read, Mrs. Anderson glanced my way and we locked eyes. I suspected in those moments that she knew how Gunther's book was affecting me. I lived in a home haunted by Death, yet, no one ever spoke its name.

Like John Gunther and his wife, Frances, I wanted to know "Why? Why me? Why him? Why us?"

Frances Gunther summed up her family's loss this way: "Parents all over the earth who lost sons in the war have felt this kind of question, and sought an answer. To me, it means loving life more, being more aware of life, of one's fellow human beings, of the earth."

I didn't know if Daddy's death made me more aware of life, as much as it made my world a much scarier place. I was keenly aware that I could lose Mama, Frank, or Linda. Or my own life, in a lightning-flash moment. Reading about Johnny's brain tumor only heightened my ever-increasing anxieties. My head echoed with the sound of dirt being shoveled onto a steel coffin.

Shoving my way through the school's crowded hallways between classes helped silence the voice of fear growing within me. Arnold Junior High was situated in a cul-de-sac in a middle-class neighborhood. Brick homes with white Corinthian columns and well-tended azalea bushes stretched out in every direction. There were no trailers, no cinder blocks, no rusted-out cars, and no tires with pansies planted in the middle of them. It was a working-class neighborhood, but no people of color lived nearby or attended the neighborhood schools.

There was only a smattering of black people at Arnold Junior High. Mr. James Bell taught math and Mrs. Uretha Gilmer was the librarian. All the other blacks worked in the kitchen or the bathrooms. Segregation didn't seem strange or wrong to me at the time. I didn't think much about it, really. It wasn't something we kids talked about, and it wasn't something Mama was talking about at home. I'd seen the occasional riot on television news. I'd heard Uncle Ray and

Aunt Helen talk about the marches in Selma, but, frankly, since I didn't know any blacks except Thelma, the plight of blacks in general didn't affect me much.

The irony is that I knew what it felt like to be part of a population that others ignored, avoided, or even hated. I'd felt racism's sharp sting as a freckled-faced towhead living in a Filipino village and attending Oahu's Helemano Elementary School. And I felt that singled-out isolation again after Daddy died.

As a child, I was incapable of distinguishing between my father the soldier and the policies and practices targeted by protestors who were sincerely concerned about politicians' misuse of military might. Certainly, the nightly newscasts and the headlines in the daily papers did little to help me make those distinctions. There was nobody sitting beside me explaining that the protestors burning effigies of U.S. soldiers or shouting obscenities about the Vietnam War weren't necessarily angry at *my father.*

Their rage against the soldiers returning from Vietnam terrified me. The more virulent the protestors became, the more shame I felt over my father's death. I feared telling anyone about Daddy's death. I worried that they would label him a murderer and me the killer's daughter. It was the sort of confused shame a sex-abuse victim might feel, as if I was somehow responsible for hurt that had been inflicted upon me. But I didn't talk about my fears or shame with Mama, Frank, or Linda, or with teachers or friends. Frankly, I just didn't even have the verbal skills to articulate my feelings.

For much of my life, I was embarrassed and conflicted over my father's death in Vietnam. I thought he should've known better. All those intelligent people protesting the war certainly seemed to know better. Why didn't Daddy? It was a question I pondered almost daily as I listened to Walter Cronkite's latest war report and heard the growing casualty numbers during dinner each night. Yet, I never worked up the nerve to ask Mama why Daddy didn't just run off to Canada. I knew that the simple answer was Daddy was a professional soldier. Like it or not, going to war was his job. It was a job he took seriously and did honorably.

Daddy, of course, was dead by the time the antiwar, antisoldier, antiestablishment fervor reached its zealous, screeching pitch. For that, I'm thankful. For my hardworking and honest father, coming home to a nation full of ugly folks spitting and spewing vulgarities at him, to people who neither respected nor honored his efforts as a soldier, would've been a death of a different sort, one I'm glad Daddy never had to endure.

Throughout his military career, my father kept a sense of humor about his job. It's evident in a poem he wrote from Camp Gordon. (It's probably a good thing he was a soldier because I don't think Daddy could've earned his living as a writer.) Mama saved the piece of lined notebook paper with the poem scribbled across it in blue ink, the title written in Daddy's best cursive script:

DOING A HITCH IN HELL

Just below the South Carolina border,
Gordon is the spot where I am doomed
to spend my time in the land that God forgot,
down with snakes and buzzards,
down where a man gets blue.
We sweat, freeze and shiver.
It's more than a man can stand.
We are not a bunch of convicts, just defenders of the land.
We soldiers of Signal Corps, earning our pay,
guarding our people of millions, for meals, two-and-half a day.
Living with our memories, wanting to see our gals,
hoping while we are away they won't marry our pals.
The people who know we are living, never give a darn.
Although, we are not forgotten at home, for we belong to Uncle Sam.
The time we spend in the Army, the good times we've never missed.
Boys, we hope the draft don't get you and for God's sake don't enlist.

When I get to Heaven, St. Peter will surely yell,
"He's from Camp Gordon, Lord! He's done his hitch in Hell."

Daddy's keen humor also comes through in a letter he wrote to Mama, postmarked July 22, 1966, two days before his death:

Hi Darling,

Will answer your letter that I got yesterday. Sure was glad to hear from you for we haven't been getting our mail like we should and everyone is pissed off about it. It has been raining here every day now. So we have fun staying wet most of the time, lately. I think they are trying to turn us into ducks. I hope by now that you have slowed down a little for your last two letters sound like you were staying busy 24 hours a day with all the moving and your job too. I always thought staying busy does help a whole lot, but as you say, you can get too much of it, so slow down and catch up with yourself. I know you have been real busy for your letters don't sound like they used to. It sounds like that it is just about as hot there as it is over here. I know that you must have a hard time working inside in that heat. So you are riding to work with your boss? No wonder the others talk about you. (Ha!) You said that rent was high back there. How is the price on food and other things? I am sure glad that you can save a little money. By the time I get back we should have just about enough to buy that trailer. You said that you had $200 in the bank already. Well, I have thought that I would be sending you at least $1,700 next month. So I would say that is a pretty good start on it. . . . Your last two letters have run out of ink. Do you want me to send you some pencils? I know that I told you to save money but I think you can afford a few pencils. (Ha!) I am pulling your leg. Well, Darling, I see that the infantry is going out so I had better get the battery ready to support them. I still think of you every day. I still love and miss you more than ever. Hope to hear from you today.

Love always, your husband
David

slugger mama

MAMA WAS DETERMINED THAT FRANK WASN'T GO-
ING TO GET HER TOSSED FROM ANOTHER TRAILER
court. To begin with, there just weren't that many decent ones in
town, and moving a trailer cost money, something Mama didn't have.
Frank and I didn't hang out much anymore. Probably because I was
the kid sister but partly because he was continuing to run the streets,
and I didn't want to. When he was out drinking, I stayed home
watching over Linda.

Linda and I tried as best we could to help out. We cleaned house
and we cooked meals. We entertained each other and ourselves. On
the rare times when Frank was around, he was bossing or beating us.
Linda and I were both a little bit scared of him. Dealing with Frank
was like playing a game of hot potato. You can't hold it too long or
too close because it'll burn you for sure. His anger was scorching.

I didn't know who his friends were or where he was getting all
the beer he was consuming or how he paid for it, but Mama knew.
Frank was taking money from her purse, along with her car keys.
He'd wait till she was asleep, then steal her keys and anything else he
wanted. Then he and his pals would go for joy rides down Manchester Expressway. They were invariably caught by the police and
marched home. The juvenile judge was getting to know our family
on a real intimate level.

Things came to a full boil early one morning, real early, about 1 A.M. Mama had come home from wherever she'd been. Out clubbing with her girlfriends, or on some date. Linda and I were already in bed, but I wasn't asleep and I don't think Linda was either. "Where's your brother?" Mama asked, standing in the doorway to my room.

"I don't know," I replied. "Out with his friends, I guess."

Mama walked back into the living room. She didn't turn on any lights. She just sat there, on the couch, in the dark. The only light was the red ember of her cigarette. She was smoking one tobacco stick after another, patiently waiting for Frank.

When he finally stumbled through the door at about 2 A.M., she was still there.

SMACK! BAM!

I heard what sounded like a clap of thunder and then Frank, yelling, *"What the hell!"*

He was sprawled out on the floor. Not from being drunk, which he had been when he walked through the trailer door, but from being sucker-punched. Mama had heard him fooling with the front gate. So she'd stood up and planted her feet firmly by the door, angling herself so she could get in a solid right punch. When Frank stepped inside, she clobbered him with a quick jab to the jaw. He'd been drunk enough that he didn't know what hit him.

Mama didn't say a word, and she didn't offer to help him up, either. She just picked up her cigarette and walked off to bed. I turned over and fell fast asleep, grinning at the thought of Frank sprawled out on the living room floor.

MOST OF THE TEENAGERS who lived in Crystal Valley didn't have daddies. The men were off in Vietnam fighting, or they'd run off with some other woman, or maybe they'd been chased off. I didn't have any friends in the trailer park who had both parents around.

Wesley and Angie Skibbey's father had abused their mother, so she divorced him. Vicki Hart's mama had been married and divorced a couple of times. I always thought it strange that while we kids hung together, our mamas didn't. They didn't get together to talk kids, to get the skinny on the single guy up the road, to moan about the increase in the school-lunch fee, or to seek advice about that whine in the car engine. It was as if they had all they could handle just getting up in the morning and getting through another day alone. They seemed to live for Friday and Saturday nights.

The ritual was the same for most of our families. The mothers would come home from work, dog tired. They'd discard their work clothes, put a hair cap on, shower, rummage through four or five outfits before finding something just right. They'd apply lotion, talcum powder, perfume, red lipstick, and a shot of hair spray to hold those updos, then they'd skinny into that perfect outfit. And with a kiss on the cheek or a pat on our heads, they'd be off in a rush.

Often when they returned, they weren't alone.

Whenever I awoke and heard the slip notes of Floyd Cramer's "Last Date," I knew that Mama had brought someone home for more than just a late-night drink. I would stuff the pillow over my head and try to go back to sleep. But sometimes the strains of Cramer's music and Mama's laughter could not be shut out, nor could any other noise. I heard the sounds of lovemaking drifting from Mama's room long before I ever understood what its crescendoes meant.

When Floyd lived with us, it didn't bother me that she was having sex with him. But I'd never actually saw or heard them engaged in lovemaking. By the time I was a seventh-grader I was onto Mama's promiscuous behavior. Once I was so upset by it that I packed my bags and told all my friends I was going to run away to a better home.

Mama got wind of my threat, which is what I was hoping would happen when I told all my friends I was running off. She called me into her bedroom and tried to talk to me. I told her that she embarrassed me. She had come home the weekend before with some man, whose name I don't recall and maybe never knew. I'd heard the two of them stumble down the hallway to her bedroom. Then I'd listened to them carrying on while Floyd Cramer played in the dark. That night was the first time I remember being totally aware of what Mama was up to. The knowledge angered me.

Mama talked me out of running away that day. But she didn't make any empty promises about trying to be a good girl or anything like that. Mama's nocturnal guests were often gone by the next morning. I would only catch glimpses of these nameless, faceless shadow men as they stumbled down the hallway toward her bedroom, but I harbored a seething fury against each and every one of them. I wanted to take the cord of the vacuum cleaner and strangle each one as he lay sleeping next to Mama.

It seemed to me that I knew what she didn't. These men were taking advantage of her, just like that Kirby salesman who'd sold her that worthless armor of steel that cowered nightly in the hallway closet. Mama seemed incapable of protecting her pocketbook or her heart. I figured she'd quit caring about almost everything, except us kids, and I worried obsessively that she might walk away from us one day soon.

hugh lee, did you love me?

MY EIGHTH-GRADE YEAR FLEW BY PRETTY UNEVENT-FULLY, CONSIDERING FRANK WAS BARRELING down a path of perdition. Mama's right-hand blow had sobered him only for a moment. He continued stealing her booze, her loose change, and her car keys, and he continued getting caught.

I'd gotten messed up in a situation or two myself. Mama liked to beat the dickens outta me one afternoon when she discovered I'd been tossed off the bus for refusing to sit with a girl whose personal hygiene was, well, wasn't.

"Find a seat and plant it," the bus driver had ordered, as he eyed me from the mirror above his head.

"There aren't any seats left," I said. I was standing in the narrow aisle, searching for a friendly face and an empty seat. The only empty seat was right next to a tall, skinny girl named Naomi. She wore calico-print dresses and bobby socks with loafers. Her hair was frizzy, like frayed ends of a thick rope. What curls she had were all mashed into complex knots. Naomi wasn't ugly. She was simply unkempt. Her legs were coated with thick, dark hair. Some fundamentalist churches didn't allow girls to shave their legs or underarms, and I figured Naomi must have belonged to one of those. She had so much underarm hair she could've worn matching armpit pigtails. Europeans might find that at-tractive, but folks who live in the heat and humidity of Georgia figure it to be a breeding ground for maggots and other nasty things. Worst part of all, by the end of the day, Naomi's underarm fluff was dripping with moisture, causing her to reek something awful. The pungent stench could singe nose hairs for kids sitting three seats back, so there was no way in hell I was sitting near Naomi and I told that to the bus driver.

"Get off this bus!" he yelled as he yanked on the handle that opened the bus doors.

Flabbergasted, I stood there. "Are you crazy?" I demanded. "You can't kick me off this bus. How am I supposed to get home?"

"By God, I can and I am!" he replied. "I said get off!"

I stood on the curb and watched the bus pull away. I couldn't believe the driver had tossed my butt off. I guess he figured there was nothing uglier than one white-trash gal putting on airs around another one. I tried to call Mama for a ride, but she wasn't home. I didn't know anybody else to call, so I started walking.

The trek home took me nearly two hours. I wasn't even sure I knew the way. I just lit out Manchester Expressway and followed the bus route as best I could, cursing the bus driver between sobs. When I came to the end of the expressway, I wasn't sure which way to turn. I spied an elderly couple getting into a car outside a little country church and approached them. "Excuse me, sir," I said. "Do y'all know which way Macon Road is from here?"

"Where you headed, little lady?" the gray-haired fellow asked.

"Home," I replied. "My bus driver kicked me off the bus, sir. I called my mama but she wasn't home."

"Oh! Mercy me!" the woman exclaimed. "And you've been walking this whole way?"

"Yes, ma'am," I said.

"Well, I'll be," she added. "Get in the car, sugar. We'll take you home."

Mama was at home when I climbed out of the backseat of the Lincoln Continental. I thanked the kindly couple for bringing me home safely.

In those days all the stylish girls wore falls, hairpieces that were held in place by a comb over the top of a girl's bangs. Mama had bought me a beautiful frosted-brunette fall for Christmas. It had a Dutch-boy cut just like the cut the Supremes wore.

When I walked inside the trailer and explained to Mama why I was so late, she ripped that fall straight off the top of my head and began to whack me with it. She went into a flipping rage, screaming and slapping me with that hairpiece. I covered my head with my arms and tried to run from her. She chased after me, screaming about disrespecting elders like my bus driver. Between slaps with the fall, she'd smack me with her hands. I fell onto my bed bawling and kicking back at her, until we both were give out. Mama threw the hair-, piece at me and left the room.

I didn't know whether to laugh or cry, so I did both. It doesn't hurt to get beaten with a wig, but I'd never made Mama so mad before. That scared me.

An hour later, Mama came to my room. "I'm sorry," she said. She was standing in the doorway. "I shouldn't have lost my temper like that."

"It's okay," I said. "I shouldn't have talked back to the bus driver."

"Karen," Mama said, pausing for effect, "if that had been a baseball bat, you'd be dead right now."

"Good thing it was only a wig," I replied with a chuckle.

"Yeah, good thing," Mama said. She wasn't laughing.

"Mama?"

"Yeah?"

"If it had been a baseball bat, you'd have stopped on the first swing, right, ma'am?" I asked.

"I hope so," she said. "But don't test me again."

"Yes, ma'am."

I think the incident convinced both Mama and me that sanity is like a roach with wings—hard to corner and even harder to catch. Just when you think you've got it securely cupped in your hands, it takes flight again. You're momentarily relieved to be free from it, but afraid of what's going to happen now that it's out of your control again.

There is one significant difference, however. Flip on a light, and flying roaches will flee toward a dark corner, whereas sanity makes no distinction between night and day. It scurries about at will. Mama and I were trying our darndest to hang on to it as best we could. I suspect we all were.

THE SUMMER OF 1970, Mama fell in love again. It shocked us all and nearly sent Granny Leona plunging over the ravine.

At first we kids didn't think anything of it when Mama said she was going to fly out to San Francisco and meet Uncle Hugh Lee, who had just completed a tour of duty on a Navy ship parked off the coast of Guam. They were going to take a couple of weeks to drive back across country together. Mama took us kids to Tennessee to stay with Granny Leona before she left.

Mama had been dating another fellow pretty steadily, a redheaded guy named Lewis Jones. Lewis drove a fancy car with leather seats, and he owned his own home, a three-bedroom brick house across the Chattahoochee in Phenix City, Alabama. Lewis drove Mama to the airport, knowing full well that she was going to be traveling across country with her brother-in-law. I don't know if he suspected any hanky-panky or not, but Granny sure did.

Poor Granny. She was fit to be tied over Mama's shameful, immoral, appalling, floozy, bohemian ways. Shelby was taking up with a dead man's brother—both of 'em Granny's boys. I could hear the disapproval in the swish of Granny's wheelchair as it moved across the floor—"For shame, for shame, for shame."

It didn't occur to Mama that there was anything inappropriate about her falling in love with Hugh Lee. It seemed natural to her that if you love a man, you might love his brother, too. "In the Bible, widows marry their dead husbands' brothers all the time," Mama said to me one afternoon as we drove out Macon Road. "That's the way it's supposed to be. You'd think being a Christian woman and all, your granny would like the idea." But Granny made it clear that no son of hers was going to marry her wayward widowed daughter-in-law. She didn't care what kind of foolish things folks did back in Bible times.

All of us young girls were smitten with Hugh Lee. He had this way of studying folks when they spoke. It didn't matter if a person was twelve, twenty-two, or seventy-two, he was eager to scoop up the spills of people's lives. One of the world's best listeners, Hugh Lee would nod in agreement, raise his eyebrows in surprise, or cock his head to one side and turn his ear to hear a person better. His gray eyes locked in. They never strayed to watch passing traffic or the next commercial. Whenever I spoke with Hugh Lee, I always knew I had his full attention.

Hugh Lee was not handsome like Daddy. Nobody in the family was, really. But he has an endearing grin. He turns it up slowly, like it's on some sort of dimmer switch, and in a few moments it's gleaming brightly. He's always been as skinny as a cane pole. We kids loved to sit next to him on the couch and watch his Adam's apple move up and down when he talked. Sometimes he'd let us press our fingers to it. He'd purposely bob it around by taking big gulps from his coffee. We'd giggle; he'd grin and poke at our sides until we giggled even louder. Hugh Lee loved kids better than anything in the world. I think that's one of the reasons Mama loved him. She knew he cared about us kids just as much as Daddy did.

Hugh Lee knew Mama was falling in love with him. That was one of the reasons why he had signed up for that second tour of duty. He was not in love with Mama, but he was youthful enough to be captivated by her sensuality.

The other reason Hugh Lee re-upped was for the sign-up bonus. He wanted to buy Pap and Granny Leona a home, and he did. It wasn't one of the grandiose homes that line the streets of Rogersville, but it was a nice place. It had a sunny spot out back where Pap could grow cukes and 'maters. And it had hardwood floors, so Granny could scooch along just fine in her wheelchair. There were lots of windows for watching the world and the neighbors go by, and a little cottage out back where Hugh stayed. Everybody in the family was proud of Hugh Lee for buying his parents their own home.

Initially, Hugh Lee had intended for Mama to bring us along on the trip. But Mama decided it was better to leave us with Granny. The trip would be too long. Surely, we'd be bored and whining long before they crossed the Colorado River.

Hugh had been the only family member who consistently looked after us. He did the job that Daddy had asked Uncle James to do. I think Daddy would have been proud of Hugh Lee for that. And I don't think he would've minded if Hugh and Mama had ended up married.

Mama never felt guilty about running off across the country with Hugh Lee, but I did. I knew they were violating some moral religious code that ate away at Granny's gut. Granny acted as if somebody was forcing her to swallow a bar of lye soap, chunk by chunk.

Hugh's attraction to his dead brother's wife was purely carnal. He lusted after Mama enough to ignore his own mother's code of propriety, and dismissing all the social mores of that time and place, Hugh and Mama engaged in sexual relations without benefit of marriage.

While Mama and Hugh Lee traversed the country, I tried to distract Granny with stories of the school year. I told her about the wig spanking Mama gave me. I told her about chewing out the nun. I told her about the troubles Frank was causing. Every afternoon, I sat by her bed and rubbed her hands and watched *The Merv Griffin Show* with her.

We chortled loudly one afternoon after watching an interview with Dr. David Reuben, author of the then-shocking book *Everything You Always Wanted to Know About Sex** (**But Were Afraid to Ask*). I was sitting in a chair next to Granny's bed, which was in the living room. Reuben was blabbing away on the television set across the room. Granny shook her head. "I've had eight kids," she said. "I don't care what that doctor says, as far as I can tell, there is only about four ways to have sex."

Just hearing Granny say the word *sex* startled me. I had spent the better part of my visit trying not to think of all the sex Mama and Hugh Lee were likely having. I certainly didn't want to think about any sex Granny and Pap might have had over the years. I could feel a bright red blush color my freckled cheeks.

Granny leaned over my chair, put her face up next to mine, and laughed. I laughed back at her.

I never did read Dr. Reuben's book, but I spent a great deal of idle time during my teen years trying to figure out the four positions Granny was referring to that day. I knew one of the four positions had to be that burrito-wrap straddle that I would later witness my naked mother engaging in.

I made the mistake of walking into Mama's bedroom once when she was in the middle of a lovemaking session. At the time, I didn't know what was going on for sure, but it didn't take me long to figure it out. It was late afternoon and I needed something—I don't remember what. The bedroom doors in the trailer didn't have doorknobs or locks but were attached to a slide track at the top. They were made of hollow wood, so a toddler could push one open. I went barreling down the hallway hollering for Mama, about something, yanked open the door to her bedroom, and found her naked, wrapped like a burrito in a sheet, up on all fours, straddling some fellow.

She reached for her glasses on the bedside table and asked me what I wanted.

Embarrassed and confused, I told her to forget it and hurriedly shut the door.

The flashback of Mama wrapped up in that sheet, reaching for her glasses, spread-legged over some fellow, has haunted me for decades. Perhaps all kids who witness their parents making love are disturbed by it. I suppose it's even more troubling for kids when they see their mamas making love to men who are not their fathers; in this instance, it was my father's brother.

Hugh Lee would never return to Georgia after I barged in on him and Mama that afternoon. He ended their relationship that very day. He refused to come down even when Mama called him late one night, and, in a drunken stupor, threatened to kill herself if he didn't come right that very minute.

"Shelby said she had a shotgun in the closet and that if I didn't come, she was going to kill herself," Hugh Lee recalled years later.

Mama did keep a shotgun in her closet and a handgun in her bed-side table. Many nights she came home reeking of sour beer and sweet tobacco. But I remember one night in particular when she came home shit-faced drunk. She could barely walk down the hall-way. It was the summer she was seeing Hugh Lee. Her stumbling had awakened me, and I heard her crying in the bathroom. I went to check on her and found her sitting on the toilet, dropping a cigarette butt between her legs. "I'm gonna be sick," she said.

Grabbing a waste bucket, I rushed over to her. She puked into the bucket, again and again and again. I ran hot water over a washcloth and washed her face. She was still crying as I took her by the arm and led her to her bed. I took off her heels and nylons and helped her out of her dress and into her silky pajamas. After I pulled the covers up around her, Mama reached up and pushed my hair away from my forehead. "Sometimes I think you are my guardian angel," she said.

Mama was so drunk, I knew she'd never remember what she said the next day. But I never forgot it. Her remark was the closest thing to a loving moment that the two of us had shared since Daddy died.

Was this the very same night she called Hugh and threatened to kill herself? I suspect so.

But Hugh would not be swayed, not even by Mama's pathetic state. "Well, then, Shelby, go ahead and shoot yourself because I am *not* coming back to Georgia," Hugh said.

And he never did.

Guilt drove Hugh Lee away. "I have never been able to forget you walking in on me and Shelby," he said. "Every time I look at you I see the face of that little girl, seeing us like that. What we were doing was wrong. I couldn't let it go on no more."

Years of nagging guilt was wasted. My uncle thought that I knew it was him in bed with Mama that day. But I didn't. I had never been able to recall the man in the flashback. I could only recall Mama in detail. I didn't know until he told me that Hugh Lee had been the man in bed with her that day. My uncle's confession stunned me, but it didn't alter the love and respect I have for him.

Hugh Lee isn't convinced that Mama really loved him. "I think she needed me," he told me. "She needed me to help raise you three kids. I don't know if it was love or need."

But he's sure of one thing. "I didn't love Shelby."

imitating patsy ward

MAMA HAD HER CHARMS, BUT IT WAS HER FIRM BUTT AND COMELY LOOKS THAT SHE RELIED UPON MOST. The men who took advantage of Mama usually did it with her full consent. She knew she could get men to do what she wanted as long as she gave them what they were after.

Guilt and regret are two garments Mama has never wasted any time fussing over. Best to shove those ugly rags to the back of the closet, out of the way. She's always subscribed to the notion that no matter what the situation is, you have to put your best foot forward, especially if you own a pair of good leather shoes. Hold your head up, your shoulders back, and—oh Lawd!—protect the poor woman who faces the world without a good padded bra. Mama wore padded bras like heart armor—the thicker the better.

The bras tossed into the hamper basket held their form so well that Frank's T-shirts boasted breasts. I don't know whether it was those bras or something else that made Mama so confident, she'd string men together like a line of rainbow trout.

She already had a great catch on the line before she ever flew out to San Francisco to meet Hugh Lee. Lewis Jones was the redheaded fellow she'd met on a blind date some six months before. Not a particularly patient fellow by nature, Jones, nonetheless, quietly bade his time until things cooled down between Hugh and Mama. Then, in no time at all, Mama had the hots for him.

Compared with most of the men Mama dated, Lewis was wealthy. An architect, by trade, he owned his own home, a brick house, with a big yard, a couple of bedrooms, and glossy hardwood floors. He had a console television set and a formal dining room with chairs made of polished wood instead of chrome and vinyl. He played tennis and drove fancy cars. He read books and listened to classical music, not Floyd Cramer. He was an avid Auburn Tiger fan during a time when Bear Bryant and Vince Lombardi were demigods of the South. Mama didn't give a hoot about football, but to please her man, she pretended she did. Lewis didn't have a wife, never had, and he didn't have any kids, which was his weakness.

He didn't know how to relate to kids. Oh, he tried. He always greeted us with a generous smile and hello. But beyond that, he didn't really know how to talk to us. We knew what he really wanted to be doing was giving all his attention to Mama. And, in return, getting all of hers.

Lewis tolerated Linda the best because she was quiet and compliant and she kept to herself. An easy child, Linda didn't backtalk, didn't pitch fits, and didn't demand attention. The thing she wanted most was to get through her growing-up years without causing Mama any more heartache. So Linda taught herself how to stay out of the way. I think Lewis wished Frank and I would do the same.

Frank and Lewis disliked each other from the get-go. Frank would hardly make eye contact with Lewis. When Lewis arrived on the scene, Frank knew his days were numbered. It was Lewis who first suggested to Mama that she ought to send Frank away. "A military school will teach that boy some discipline," he said. "He's out of control, Shelby. You've got to do something."

Mama knew Lewis was right, that Frank needed a male figure to straighten him out. Military school would give him plenty of men to model himself after, as well as the structured environment Mama couldn't provide.

When Frank once again landed in juvenile court—this time for stealing Mama's car and wrecking it—the judge threatened to send him to detention school. Mama protested, saying she already had a plan. "I've enrolled him at Lyman Ward Military Academy, sir," Mama said.

"That'll work just as well," the judge said.

The decision to send Frank away convinced me that Mama was, without question, unfit to be a mother, or at least our mother. I viewed it as the ultimate treason a mother could commit. To me, she was choosing her lover over her son.

Up until then, I hadn't harbored the seething resentment toward Lewis that Frank did. I didn't really have any reason to. Lewis tried his best to win over my affections. One Saturday morning he showed up at the trailer door with a gift just for me. A wooden tennis racket, signed by Billie Jean King. I'd never played tennis a day in my life, but Lewis did. He gave me the racket and then asked me if I wanted to go with him to the courts. It was the one and only time that I remember any of Mama's lovers asking me to do anything just one-on-one. Floyd had spent a great deal of time with me, but we never did anything just the two of us, the way a father and daughter might. The way Daddy and I did before he died. I cherished the personal invite from Lewis even more because I recognized how difficult all this was for him. I knew he'd much rather spend his days off with Mama, alone.

Lewis drove me all the way to Phenix City to try out my new racket. The drive, about twenty-five minutes, lasted longer than the actual court time. I am not a natural athlete, I didn't know how to hold the racket, much less hit something with it. Lewis spent more time on my side of the court than on his.

On the ride home, we were both sweaty, frustrated, and thankful for the silence. I didn't take another tennis lesson until I was in college.

Lewis never made any more attempts to cultivate a relationship with me. And I really began to worry that Mama was only keeping me around to care for Linda. I feared she might ship me off soon, too.

I was a horrible caretaker for my sister. Linda and I didn't sit around painting each other's toenails or braiding each other's hair. Instead, we scrapped like a couple of ill-bred barn cats, clawing, pawing, scowling, and ripping out hair. We fought over the dumbest things. I'd order her to dust while I cleaned the kitchen. She'd whine. I'd slap her. She'd grab my forearm and dig in her hardened nails. I'd curse and kick her. She'd kick back. We'd carry on like that for fifteen minutes or better, until one of us tired out or tore away from the other and took off out the door. Usually, it was Linda fleeing. She wouldn't come back until Mama got home. Then she'd recount the scene, replete with crocodile tears streaming down her rosy cheeks. Invariably, I'd get slapped or grounded by Mama. In return, I'd swear to hurt Linda worse the next time we were alone.

Personally, I don't think Linda would've turned out to be the charming soul she is today if not for the bad behavior displayed by Frank and me. She swore as a little girl she would never grow up to be like either one of us. And she never did. Linda was born good-natured and kindhearted. She seemed assured that God's grace greeted her each morning and tucked her in each night. She's never had to arm-wrestle the demons of darkness that haunted Frank and me. God's mercy is wasted on folks like her.

IN JULY 1970, a nursing buddy of Mama's, Mrs. Yearty, asked if she could take Linda and me to Vacation Bible School. Mama didn't mind as long as the lady wanted to drive all the way out Macon Road to pick us up and get us back home. The church, Grace Baptist, was located in downtown Columbus, a good half-hour drive from Crystal Valley. Mama wasn't in school that summer, but she was working.

We had not been in a church since we'd left Tennessee. In the early weeks following Daddy's death, Frank and I were baptized at the First Baptist Church in Rogersville. The same church folks who had filled our refrigerator with platters of crispy fried chicken, heaping bowls of potato salad, and plates of sliced tomatoes when Daddy died later wept as Frank and I were dipped and resurrected from the cleansing waters of the church's baptismal.

"Praise Jesus!" someone said.

"Thank you, Lord!" another shouted.

I cried, too. But not so much because I felt cleansed, or even saved. Fact is, I felt as disconsolate as I had the day I'd walked into Nash-Wilson Funeral Home and seen the dead man, cold and blue, lying in the casket and heard the strains of that forsaken song: "Just as I am, without one plea, but that Thy blood was shed for me."

I got baptized that day for two reasons—neither of which were very good. First, because Frank was doing it. During my early life, I patterned my steps after his. The second reason was because I was afraid not to. Baptism was my pass to heaven. I couldn't get in without it. And since Daddy's last orders had sent him marching there, I certainly didn't want to be locked out, standing on the other side of the gates and screaming out his name for all eternity. I had to make sure that I could get in should I tragically ended up dead, too.

Throughout my childhood, death struck me like a bad fever. Whenever I thought about it, pearls of perspiration rolled from the crevices of my neck, my crotch, and my palms. My stomach cramped. My eyes glazed vacant as my mind lumbered toward a black forest, where, I figured, dead souls gathered and waited in silent agony for Jesus to return and guide them toward the light of heaven. The fever gave me fits, causing my mind to pitch back and forth, as if in the throes of some horrific dysentery. I thought about the here and now and the hereafter. I thought I would literally go nuts. "Stop it! Stop it!" I would cry.

But those cries would only echo between my ears. No one else knew how terrified I was, so no one was ever capable of calming me. Besides, I knew from the get-go, death would never yield to

anyone. Sooner or later, even the most powerful people alive suc-
cumb to its violent strangle. There's no escape. No way out.

Not even the salvation I'd found in Jesus Christ that summer offered me much assurance.

I'd participated in Vacation Bible School during summer trips to
Granny's. And I'd attended church in those amber years before
Daddy died and Mama got so mad at God she quit speaking to Him.
As a teenager I didn't relish the idea of going to church. I was, after
all, an incoming high school freshman. Mama had bought me a new
bedspread (bright orange) and a rug (royal blue) to honor my position among the Columbus High School Blue Devils. (I suspected
Lewis might have had something to do with her purchases, since
Columbus High bore the exact same school colors as Auburn University.) But I agreed to go to the Vacation Bible School because I
was a people-pleaser; and since Mama's friend had been generous
enough to invite me, I didn't want to disappoint her.

To my good fortune, Grace Baptist Church had a slew of teenagers,
some even older than me. They were friendly and embracing. One
girl in particular seemed genuinely glad to make my acquaintance.

Patsy Ward was an itty-bitty thing. But she had the golden looks
of the beauty queen she would one day become. She had a mass of
honey-hued hair, which she wore in a Marlo Thomas–style flip. Her
white-hot smile could melt frozen butter. But it was her voice that
made people plunge headlong into worship or idolatry, depending
on whether they focused on Jesus or on the lovely Patsy. Even today,
a quarter century after her untimely death, the memory of Patsy
singing "When I Survey the Wondrous Cross" or "Something About
That Name" causes me to weep in sheer admiration. Patsy loved Jesus with a wholehearted purity that was as uncommon then as it is
today.

Many people are glad if they can produce a flicker of Christ's reflection during their daily lives. Not Patsy. She wanted to be a spotlight for Jesus. She had a way of drawing people away from the lure

of evil's darkness to Calvary's hill, where a luminous transformation awaited them.

I was no exception. From the moment I met her, I wanted to emulate Patsy. I was thirteen and she was about to turn sixteen. Patsy loved birthdays, especially her own. She would announce to anyone within earshot: "Only seven shopping days left. Better hurry up and buy me a present!" Young men and old codgers vied for Patsy's affections. And because she was a generous soul, who loved to be loved and to love, she never denied anyone a hug, a smile, or a wink. She charmed us all.

Patsy did not, however, lead a charmed life. Like me, she was missing a parent. Her mother died when Patsy was too little to fix her own ponytail. Patsy had a younger brother, Mike, who came to church with her sometimes, and an older, very handsome brother, Danny, who didn't, and a sister, whose name I can't recall. Patsy, Mike, and Danny lived with their father and his parents in a house in an older neighborhood, near historic downtown Columbus. I think the home was formerly a mill house built for the textile workers who once made up the fiber of the town's business district. The house had two separate kitchens and living areas.

Patsy's younger sister didn't grow up with her older siblings because she was a baby when their mother was killed in a car crash. She was sent to live with another family member. It wasn't until 1979, when Patsy tragically died from a brain aneurysm a week after the birth of her only child, a boy named Stephen, that some thought that perhaps Patsy's mother had really died from the same troubling defect, which could have caused the car crash.

Patsy's father did not share her love for Jesus. I don't ever remember him attending church to hear his talented daughter sing. The church elders took Patsy in as their own daughter. In the hundreds of times I was at Patsy's home, I never saw her father much. Sometimes, we would daydream that her father and my mother would find Jesus, find each other, and fall in love, and we would all live happily ever after. It wasn't my first attempt at fiction, but it was likely one of my poorest efforts.

I continued attending Grace Baptist Church long after Vacation Bible School ended. The youth pastor, a kindly gentleman, and his wife invited me to participate in car washes, bake sales, and other fund-raising activities. The youth were planning a big summer-blowout trip to Atlanta's hottest theme park—Six Flags over Georgia—and invited me along.

I had never been to an amusement park of any sort. I'd never ridden a roller coaster or a Ferris wheel, never plucked my way through a puff of cotton candy or licked the skin of a candied apple. Going to Six Flags seemed as foreign to me as a trip to Mozambique. I'd wash a hundred muddy tires for the chance.

We made the trip in mid-August, the week before the start of my freshman year at Columbus High. Patsy, her cousin Darlene Jackson, and I joined a slew of other teens on the church vans shortly after daybreak. We didn't return until almost midnight.

I discovered two things that day—the sheer thrill of a log ride through shallow water and what it means to be immersed in the cleansing blood of the Lamb. The latter I learned when the youth pastor dropped me off at home.

I paused momentarily before jumping out of the van and rushing into the trailer house. "Pastor," I said. "Can I ask you something?"

"Sure," he replied. "What is it?"

"What makes Patsy so different?"

"What do you mean, Karen?" he asked.

"I don't know," I replied. "It seems that Patsy has a light about her. Something from the inside that sets her apart. I mean, I don't know, she's just different, that's all. She seems happy. Not perfect, but sure of herself or something."

I knew Patsy was as human as any girl when she sat in the back of the van on that ride home necking and snuggling with a blond, bronzed stud in the youth group. At first I was shocked, but then

I thought it was funny the way the two would pop upright and not even touch shoulders whenever the youth pastor glanced in the rearview mirror. I could tell Patsy was pleased that he never once caught them. Stolen kisses in the back of a church van were about as risqué as Patsy allowed herself to be—at least, as far as I ever knew.

"Patsy doesn't have anything you can't have yourself," the pastor replied. He pulled a tiny black Bible out of his shirt pocket. Then, turning to John 3:16, he began reading: "For God so loved the world that He gave His only begotten Son that whosoever believeth in Him shall have eternal life."

I had no idea what he was saying. He must've noticed the confusion in my eyes.

"Karen, there isn't a person alive who doesn't need God," he said. "God created us to need him. He wants to have a relationship with us, but our sin gets in the way of that."

I knew all about sin. It was an honored guest in our household. I recalled the lecture I'd gotten about sin from a drugstore owner after I'd been caught stealing a box of eye shadow. Linda watched in horror as the store manager whisked me to a back room and jerked the makeup out of my hands. "She was trying to get out the door without paying for this," the woman informed the store owner.

A skinny man with puffy cheeks, the owner bent over, shook his finger in my face, and said sternly, "Don't you know that it's because of thieves like you that Jesus had to die on the cross? You ought to be ashamed of yourself! I ought to call your mama."

Frightful tears rolled down my cheeks. Linda was crying, too. She hadn't done a thing wrong, but the man's outrage scared her. She wasn't yet ten, but she already figured Frank and me to be the family idiots.

The fellow didn't call Mama. Instead, he shooed me out of his store with a warning and a threat: "Go home and seek God's forgiveness so you won't burn in hell. And don't you ever come back to my store again, young lady!"

Linda never told Mama about the incident. I went on to steal again. I didn't quit stealing stuff until after Mama confronted me. The most expensive item I stole was a fourteen-karat gold bracelet off a manikin at Kiralfy's Department Store.

Mama had admired a row of gold bracelets in the store's showcase while buying a dress one afternoon. While she was making her purchase, I slipped over to a manikin and picked a bracelet off its wrist. I had nothing to fear. The dummy couldn't push me away, and the sales clerk was too busy to notice.

But by that evening the guilt and shame I felt were heavier than ten blocks of gold. The chain links of the bracelet felt like shackles. So I did the proper thing and gave my shackles away—to Linda.

"Where did you get that bracelet you gave your sister?" Mama asked later. She was standing in the doorway of my bedroom, taking a slow drag from her cigarette as she waited for me to answer.

"I bought it at the drugstore," I replied.

"Where did you get the money for that?" she asked. Mama returned my answer with a cool stare that let me know she didn't believe a word I was telling her.

"From baby-sitting," I said. I had no qualms about expounding the lie.

"It's a really nice bracelet," Mama said. "It doesn't look like a drugstore bracelet. It looks like the ones we saw downtown today."

"Yes, ma'am," I said. "I wanted to give Linda something nice for her birthday. I've been saving up for a long time."

Mama didn't say another word. She blew a ring of smoke into my room and walked off. She took the bracelet from Linda and kept it herself. She wore it sometimes. I always knew that she knew I was lying. She knew I had swiped that bracelet from Kiralfy's. What she couldn't figure out is how I'd been able to do it without her or the sales clerk seeing me. That was the last of my five-finger discount days. Not because I was afraid of getting caught but because I didn't like the way I felt afterward.

I considered myself a pretty good kid once we'd left Lake Forest. I'd quit running the streets with Frank. I hadn't kissed a single boy during my entire eighth-grade year. I knew Frank was still going to make-out parties around the neighborhood, but I refused to go along. I didn't drink, didn't smoke, didn't cuss. And I didn't let boys with stubby fingers touch my breasts anymore. I was trying oh so very hard, to be a good girl. Like Linda, I, too, wanted to be a help, not a burden, to Mama. I was proud when Mama made the dean's list at Columbus College, a feat she accomplished several times. I told all my friends about how smart my mama was. Sometimes I would help her study for her spelling tests. I marveled over the medical terminology that seemed to take up forty-eight letters of the alphabet.

But despite all my good behavior, I knew I lacked something. That something was what Patsy Ward possessed. I wanted it. My breathing grew shallow as the youth pastor flipped through his little pocket Bible, showing me the words of Jesus highlighted in red. Then he turned and placed the book into my hands. "Here, take this," he said. "I've marked some things for you to read. What you need, Karen, is God. He loves you and wants the best for you. But he won't force his way into your life. You have to ask him in."

"I can't take your Bible," I said. I tried to hand the book back.

"No, you keep it tonight," he replied. "You can give it back to me later."

"Thanks," I said. "I had a great time today. It was really fun."

"Thanks for going!" Pastor called out his window as I rushed into the house.

Frank was curled up in front of the television, watching a black-and-white late-night show. Mama was sitting at the dinette table, smoking a cigarette and drinking a cup of coffee. Linda was in bed. "How was your trip?" Mama asked, looking up from the book she was studying.

"Really fun, ma'am," I said. "The log ride was my favorite. I got soaking wet. We gotta go, Mama. You'd love it."

"Yeah, maybe one day when I'm out of school," she said. She turned back to her book.

I rushed to my bedroom, flipped on the light. I had to blink a couple times to adjust my eyesight. That tangerine-colored bedspread caused blind spots. I plopped down across the bed and began flipping through the Bible. I hunted for the red words—the ones Jesus spoke.

I read John 3:16. Then Romans 3:23: "For all have sinned and come short of the glory of God." I wept as the words washed over me. Those bright red words scoured my heart's tarnish better than a team of Merry Maids.

I slipped off the bed, onto my knees. *Rat-tat-tat. Rat-tat-tat.* My heart pounded harder than a woodpecker on a chimney chute. Blood coursed through my body until my cheeks were hotter than an oven coil. Gasping, convulsing sobs racked my body, leaving me as exhausted as an epileptic after a bad seizure.

"God," I cried. "I don't even know if you're there or not. I don't even know how to pray. But if you can hear me, I need you. Everything is so messed up. Frank's leaving. Mama's never around. I miss Daddy so much. Why did he have to die, God? How come you didn't save him?"

I kept on going. "Everything has been so messed up since Daddy left. I know I've done some bad things, God. I'm so sorry. I hope you'll forgive me. Will you, God? Will you forgive me?"

I took a deep breath and held it for a long moment. Waiting expectantly. But God didn't bust through the trailer roof with a dozen angels flanking his side. So I kept talking.

"These words say that you're standing at the door of my heart knocking, ready to enter." I could hear the pounding of my heart but I couldn't tell if it was God or not. "I want you to come in. I want you to be Lord of my life."

My body heaved with relief, the kind that comes at the end of the first day of a really long hike when the heavy pack can finally be slipped off and the trekkers can kick back. Immediately the faucet of tears shut off. I blew my nose on the edge of the bedspread. I looked around the room, but I didn't see any incandescent figures hovering. That was a relief in itself.

I'd had a visitation once in the first year after Daddy died. The spirit who came into my room that night was not my father's. It was not a woman or a man. No wings or halos adorned this presence. I remember the luminous figure perched on the edge of my bed. I wasn't afraid, but I was a bit startled, just as I might be if I woke up and found Linda sitting on my bed studying me.

"Karen, don't be afraid," the voice said. It was neither a male nor female voice. Just a voice of calm assurance.

"I'm not," I replied.

"Your daddy is okay," the voice said. "He wants you to know that. He wants you to quit worrying so much."

"I'm trying," I said. "But I miss him. I want him to come home."

"He can't do that," the voice answered. "But he misses you, too. He loves you. Never forget how much he loves you, Karen."

"Okay," I said. I tried hard to stop crying the way I had the night when Daddy came to my room before leaving for Vietnam. But, like before, I wasn't able to.

I quit believing in fairy-tale endings the day the man in the jeep showed up. I knew Daddy was in no position to make empty promises to me anymore. I believe the visitation was simply my father's way of letting me know he was sorry for breaking his promise and for breaking my heart.

Death took Daddy away, but his love for his family remains unrestrained. A short round didn't kill it off, and a casket didn't seal it away. It was the love of my earthly father that first convinced me there was such a thing as eternity and a heavenly Father who cares for me.

fending off
the boogeyman

I WAS SITTING IN THE LIBRARY IN THE BASEMENT OF COLUMBUS HIGH THAT FIRST WEEK OF SCHOOL IN AUgust 1970 when a group of very big upperclassmen pulled out wooden chairs and sat down beside me. "Whaddya' reading?" one fellow asked.

"Victoria Holt," I replied.

Another boy reached over and took the book out of my hands. I kept my head down.

"You a freshman?" the third fellow asked.

"Yes," I replied. I looked up at them.

"What's your name?" the biggest of the three boys asked.

"Karen Spears," I said.

"You have a brother who goes here?" he asked. "Is your brother Frankie?"

"Yes, sir," I replied. Frank's name is John Franklin. Lots of folks called him Frankie.

Then the three boys looked at one another, grinned, and stood up. They pushed in their chairs, and without saying another word they walked away from the table and never bothered me again. They didn't even give me time to tell them that my brother was no longer at Columbus High but at a military school some seventy miles away in Alabama.

My brother laughs whenever I recount that story. But what he never understood is how much I depended on him for my security. When he went away, my fears soon overshadowed me. I grew convinced that someone was going to do me or Linda or Mama some great harm, and I had no idea how to protect any of us.

For safety's sake, I devised an escape route from the trailer. With Mama often gone at night, I slept on the floor of my room, with my head sticking out into the hallway. The front door was to my left and the back door to my right. I figured if anybody came through the front, I'd be able to see them, grab Linda, and run out the back door. And vice versa if they came through the back door.

Needless to say, I got very little sleep. Every time the wind blew a pine branch up against the trailer, I jumped up and stared out the windows into darkness with my heart pounding, my stomach cramping. If I heard Mama coming in, I hopped up into my bed so she wouldn't know what a fraidy cat I was.

I hated the nights when she went barhopping with her girlfriend Betty. Or over to Lewis's to spend the night. I continued to feign sickness, hoping she'd postpone her plans and stay home for the night. That never worked, since Mama was a nurse. She would tell me to take two aspirin and go to bed. What she didn't understand was that I was feverish with fear. I couldn't sleep. I couldn't eat. I couldn't think clearly and I cried constantly.

I had quit going to church, since I had no way of getting there. Mama wasn't about to run me to town three times a week for Sunday school, evening service, and Wednesday-night prayer meeting. The only book of the Bible I'd studied so far was Revelation. The sight of locusts made me tremble. God's promises in Revelation did not offer me any assurances—they terrorized me: "I gave her space to repent of her fornication; and she repented not. Behold I will cast her into a bed, and them that commit adultery with her into great tribulation, except they repent of their deeds. And I will kill her children with death; and all the churches shall know that I am he which searcheth the reins and hearts; and I will give unto everyone of you according to your works." Rev. 2:21–23.

I was sure Mama's sinful ways were displeasing to God, so I was constantly worried that He was going to take her from me. My own salvation did not comfort me because my image of God was terribly distorted. I knew nothing of mercy and grace. I felt completely abandoned by my father, my mother, and now my brother. My world grew so dark that not even daybreak offered me a sense of relief.

I didn't want Mama out of my sight. On the nights when she was home, I pleaded with her to let me sleep next to her. But because she didn't understand my gnawing fears, Mama told me I was acting childish. "You're too old to be sleeping with me," she said. She banished me from her room. "Go to bed in your own room!"

Often I lay on my bed until I was sure Mama was asleep, and then I snuck back into her room and curled up on the rug by her bed. The floor was hard and usually too cold because of the window air conditioner. But I slept better there than anywhere else during that first year after Frank went away.

When my sleeping pattern didn't improve, Mama decided something was horribly wrong. So she took me to see a counselor at Martin Army Hospital. She told him how I slept on the floor in my room or beside her bed. She told him there was really no reason for me to be acting out like this. She suggested maybe I was just trying to get attention. I'd always been her most hysterical child.

Then the kindly man sent Mama out of the room.

"Karen, what do you think is wrong?" he asked me.

"I don't know," I said. "I just get scared when Mama's away."

"What are you most afraid of?"

"That she'll die, too," I replied.

He paused for a moment, and a heavy silence fell between us. I studied the stacks of papers piled across his oak desk and looked out the window at the twisted oaks. He studied me. Then he asked, "What should your mama do to help you?"

"She ought to take me to church," I said.

"Why's that?" he asked.

"I like going to church," I said. "But I can't drive. I don't have any way of getting there."

We visited some more, and then he called Mama back into the room. "Your daughter wants to go to church," he said. "Perhaps you ought to consider getting involved in one."

Mama thanked the man and left. We drove home in silence and never returned to that counselor. Mama didn't take his advice. She wasn't speaking to God, and she didn't care if I cracked like a hard-boiled egg; there was no way in hell she was taking me to church. As far as she was concerned, I was just overreacting.

But to be sure, she did take me to see another counselor. A woman therapist in downtown Columbus who specialized in troubled teens like me. But I was on to her scheme.

On occasion, Mama and Aunt Mary Sue visited palm readers. They'd pay twenty dollars or whatever the going rate was for a glimpse of their futures. What they wanted to hear was that very soon a well-to-do, handsome pirate would come steal them away to some exotic island. When, instead, the readings cautioned Mama or Mary Sue about a short lifeline or a troubling intersection ahead, they would dismiss the gypsy's reading as pure foolishness. That particular palm reader would be stricken from their list of wise advisors. Then, after a sufficient time lapse, they would seek out another fortune-teller, hoping for a better outcome. I knew Mama was applying the same approach to therapy that she did to palm reading. The trick was to find someone who would tell you what you wanted to hear.

The counselor, a juvenile specialist, didn't tell Mama to take me to church like the man at Fort Benning did, but she didn't dismiss my fears as easily as Mama had hoped. After our second visit, as we drove home down Macon Road, Mama and I got into a shouting match about who was at fault for what. When we pulled up to the red light near Shoney's Big Boy, Mama turned to me and said, "Shit fire, save matches, Karen! I can't do anything right by you. I'm not wasting any more time or money going to see more therapists! As far as I can tell they just make aggravating matters worse."

"Fine with me!" I yelled back. After all, no teen in her right mind wants to be identified as mental and hauled into therapy. I was furious with Mama. She was troubled enough by my insomnia to try and get me help, but only as long as it didn't require any effort or change on her behalf. That was just further evidence to me that Mama was unfit.

In an almost prophetic twist of literary irony, the first book to enrapture me as a youngster was Madeleine L'Engle's classic novel *A Wrinkle in Time*. I had read and reread it while attending Helemano Elementary School in Oahu, long before Daddy died. The mystery is about a brother and sister's quest to find their father, a scientist who is missing due to a time-warp experiment gone awry. Her father's absence makes the temperamental Meg explosive and emotionally unstable: "But it was still not possible to think about her father without the danger of tears."

Only Meg's brother, Charles, whom the townspeople generally consider to be slow-witted, seems to understand her. The brother and sister duo travel through time and space and spiritual boundaries in order to restore their family. They are aided in their search by Mrs. Whoo, Mrs. Which, and Mrs. Whatsit.

"If you want to help your father you must learn patience," Mrs. Whoo warns Meg. "To stake one's life for the truth. That is what we must do."

By the story's end, Meg's greatest weaknesses prove to be the source of her inner strength. What are her greatest faults? Anger, impatience, stubbornness. Yes, it was her faults that she turns to to save herself.

Unlike the fictional Meg, I did not recognize that weaknesses, either Mama's or mine, could be useful. For the next year or better, I struggled to iron out wrinkles in my own blurred reality. I traveled along dark borders and traipsed through warped places that Mama couldn't see or comprehend. I had absolutely no coping skills to handle the fright that seized me each night or the guilt and anger that I harbored toward Mama by day. I never understood why she couldn't just hold me and tell me everything would be okay. What difference did it make if I was eight or eighteen? I was scared. I missed Daddy, and Frank, and I was haunted by the thought of losing Mama.

The guilt I felt over my sprawling fears was as heavy as an iron maul. I lugged it around all day long. I'd tell myself how stupid it was to be so afraid. I'd resolve each day at noon never to let darkness frighten me again. But every night at suppertime, as the sun set and the sky's light dimmed, a big swell of dread filled my belly until it ached fiercely. I'd try to fight off the anxiety with prayer, but that was never as comforting as having a grown-up nearby. I suspect Mama could see the fear clouding my eyes, but she turned away from it.

Years later Mama told me: "The more hysterical I saw you becoming, the more I tried to push you away. And that just made you more hysterical. I should have just let you get into the bed with me. I should have just comforted you. But I didn't know that then."

DADDY'S LAST INSTRUCTION to me was to stop crying because it upset Mama. I tried as best I could to do as Daddy had asked. But what he didn't know then is that Vietnam would upset a lot of people. I learned at an early age to handle the burning things of life with mitts of silence. So for many years I didn't talk about losing Daddy, about death, or Vietnam. I especially didn't talk about such things with Mama. Yet, neither one of us could escape Vietnam's far-reaching shadow. It was featured prominently in the nightly newscasts and in the daily papers. Political debates reached a feverish pitch once Fort Benning was selected as the site of the court-martial of Lieutenant William "Rusty" Calley, Jr., for his role in the My Lai massacre.

Whenever Mama watched the newscasts or read the newspaper reports about the Calley trial, she'd gnaw on that worry gristle inside her cheek, over and over again. It was as if she had a mouthful of words she was chewing on but couldn't quite spit out. I could tell she was troubled by what she was hearing and reading, but she wasn't one to divulge her worries.

November 1970 was a month chock-full of news. A lot of it was election stuff. Jimmy Carter, a plainspoken peanut farmer who promised to be a "working governor," handily earned Georgia's top spot. It was the biggest Democratic victory Georgians had ever seen.

But not everybody in the city or state was rejoicing. Family members of the sixty-seven Georgia servicemen listed as missing in action or prisoners of war gathered in Atlanta and drafted a letter to the Viet Cong delegation at the Paris Peace Talks. They also urged their fellow Georgians to join in a "Write Hanoi" campaign, asking the Communists to release names of those being held captive, and they pleaded for the release of any prisoners who were sick or wounded. At Columbus High School several of my classmates wore engraved bracelets bearing the names of those men. I didn't need a bracelet to remind me that our family was held hostage by what had already happened in Southeast Asia.

Some of the jury-selection proceedings in the Calley trial occurred on my fourteenth birthday—November 12—the day after Veterans Day.

Calley, then twenty-seven, was charged with murdering 102 Vietnamese civilians in the village of My Lai on March 16, 1968, in Quang Ngai Province of South Vietnam. Several other soldiers were also facing murder charges because the troops, under Calley's command, reportedly killed as many as five hundred unarmed civilians during that same rout.

The highly publicized trial was never discussed in my classes at Columbus High. Most of the kids there were the children of civilians, yet many had fathers or grandfathers who'd once served in the military. Columbus has always been very patriotic and deeply loyal to the military community at Fort Benning. Churches and civic organizations make it a point to "adopt" young servicemen and to give them a family away from home. Sometimes literally. But soldiers are warned not to marry local girls. A fellow fishing off the banks of the Chattahoochee once told me, "They taught us at Fort Benning, 'Don't marry a Columbus girl unless you intend to stay here because Columbus girls don't leave home for long.' "

Lieutenant Calley, a Florida native, was one of the many soldiers who married a local girl and made Columbus his home. He married Mrs. Tilly Vick's daughter. The Vicks were a prominent Columbus family. Well loved and highly regarded, they own the popular V. V. Vick Jewelers at Cross Country Plaza. Calley still runs the family business.

Teachers weren't given any edict about avoiding discussion of the trial; it was just part of the constrained society in which we all lived. It was considered uncouth to discuss unpleasant topics. The trial that made daily headlines nationwide was largely ignored at dinner tables and in civics classes. But occasionally I would overhear discussions among the students as we waited between classes for the bell to ring:

"Do you really think he killed all those people?"

"Yeah, I do. He's a murderer. A trained killer, like all those other soldiers over there."

Frank said the teachers at Lyman Ward Military Academy weren't making Calley's trial a point of current events there, either. He said the general feeling among the teaching staff was that Calley was being made a scapegoat. "This was a military community," Frank explained. "Everyone in the military community knows a lieutenant doesn't have that much rank. The only teachers I heard talk about Calley felt that he was just doing what he was ordered to do."

That wasn't the case among Frank's peers, though. The talk in the locker rooms and dorms painted Calley as a bloodthirsty maniac. Frank listened in silence as his classmates debated the issues among themselves. He never once chimed in. And he certainly made it a point to not divulge that his own father was a casualty of Vietnam. "There was no point in saying anything," Frank noted. "The attitude of the day was that all American soldiers were just like Calley. I was made to feel ashamed over Dad's participation in Vietnam."

The worst part of it all was that there was no place for kids like Frank and me to escape from the daily deluge of stories about the trial. We had no one we could talk to about it, not even each other. And so it was, month after month after month. Calley's trial was one of the longest-running military trials in history. A verdict by a six-officer jury was returned on March 29, 1971. Calley was convicted of premeditated murder of twenty-two civilians, including women and infants. He also was convicted of assault with intent to murder a child, believed to be about two years old. Throughout the trial, Calley maintained that he was acting upon the orders of Captain Ernest Medina, his superior, to kill everyone in My Lai. The jury didn't buy it. Calley was sentenced to life in prison. On November 9, 1974, a few days before my eighteenth birthday, he was released on bond after a federal judge overturned his conviction. I was a freshman in college. He had served three and half years, most of that under house arrest at Fort Benning.

oh! happy day!

WE SPENT MUCH OF THE FALL OF 1970 RUNNING BACK AND FORTH TO LYMAN WARD MILITARY ACADEMY in Alabama, where we cheered Frank as he played lineman on the school's football team. He came home for the holidays, but the family gatherings had turned into unpleasant affairs after Frank and Lewis got into a spat over Thanksgiving.

Lewis and Mama had prepared a festive dinner while we kids sat in his living room watching his big console television. We knew better than to cause a disturbance at Lewis's house, so we did our best to act like little grown-ups. We were practicing what Mama called "our best behavior." A lace tablecloth was spread across the shiny wooden table. Thin sheets of plastic covered the satin upholstery of the dinette chairs. Creamy tapered candles in brilliant silver candelabras and gleaming plates with delicate rims as thin as paper decorated the table. Frank and Mama were seated on one side, with Linda and me on the other. Lewis sat at the end, like a king on a throne. I was picking my way through a saucer of ambrosia when Lewis looked over at Frank trying to eat a slice of turkey with his left hand and a fork.

"Frankie, pick up that knife and cut that meat," Lewis ordered.

My brother lifted his right arm. It was wrapped in a cast from above the elbow down to his palm. He'd broken it playing street football with his buddies at Crystal Valley. "How do you expect me to do that?" Frank replied. "Can't you see my arm is broke?"

Lewis didn't tolerate backtalk. "Damn it!" he replied. "I said, pick up that knife!"

Frank shot him a look that clearly said "Go to hell, buddy." Then he put down his fork and didn't take another bite. I looked at Linda. She kept her head down and kept eating. I looked at Mama and could tell she was annoyed at Lewis for speaking so harshly to Frank, but she didn't say a word. It was a miserable holiday.

Frank didn't come home much after that. Maybe because the staff at Lyman Ward was never as demeaning to him as Lewis was.

Besides, at Lyman Ward Frankie had found a way to alleviate some of his teenage angst—Colombian gold. The military academy had a generous population of boys whose fathers had sent them to the historic school with hopes of turning them into solid citizens and tough soldiers. But folded between the pairs of white socks neatly ordered in their dresser drawers were Baggies of potent pot. Frank grew especially fond of his cadet pals and their pot. By the time he returned home that spring, my brother and I had grown distant. I barely recognized him as the boy I'd once adored.

I'd changed, too. Patsy helped me escape from the shadow of terror that had besieged me. She and I attended different schools—she was at Jordan High—so there wasn't opportunity for us to see each other every day. But she would call me nearly every other week, just to see how I was doing. And she made a couple of trips to Lyman Ward with the family to watch Frank play football. Mama didn't readily embrace my friends, but Patsy was a rare exception. Mama liked having Patsy around and often invited her to join us for Frank's games.

During a slow weekend in March, Patsy invited me to spend the night with her. She drove out to Crystal Valley and picked me up before dinner. Her grandmother fixed us a meal of pork chops, mashed potatoes, and green beans. Her brother Danny asked her to iron one of his shirts, which she did without complaint. Then I sat on the foot of one of the twin beds in her room while Patsy pinned her hair up into large pink curlers. We talked about church. Patsy told me she wasn't attending Grace Baptist anymore. She was at Rose Hill Baptist, a bigger church out on Hamilton Road.

Without going into a lot of details, I told Patsy that I'd been having some problems. I didn't tell her about sleeping on the floor in Mama's room, but I did tell her I'd been having a hard time sleeping and that no amount of prayer seemed to help. I didn't say it aloud, but what I really believed was that God just didn't favor me as much as he did Patsy. As I told her about the growing anger I felt toward Mama and the guilt I felt over not being a good Christian girl, I began to cry.

Rather than coming over to comfort me, as she normally would have, Patsy got up and left the room. She said she had to fetch something and would be back in a moment. I learned later that she'd been so worried about me that she'd left the room to call someone for advice on how best to help. When she returned, Patsy told me a story.

"Ever try to make a fire?" she asked. "A fire with one log doesn't burn nearly as well as a fire with several logs. You're like the log burning by itself, Karen. You need to be with others to keep the fire going."

I had no idea why Patsy was telling me some campfire story. I quit crying and fell to sleep. The next week Patsy called and asked me to attend a prayer meeting at Rose Hill Baptist Church. It was a Monday night, an odd time for a prayer meeting. But Patsy told me it was for teens only. She said to meet her at the youth building out behind the church, about a twenty-five-minute drive from our house. Mama dropped me off but only because Patsy promised to drive me home.

Patsy hadn't told me what to wear. I showed up in an eggplant-colored skirt and jacket. All the other teens turned out in cutoffs and T-shirts. Patsy wore jeans and a halter top. I couldn't have been more conspicuous if I'd been an armor-clad knight at a nudist camp.

Wide steps of concrete led to the front door of the youth building, a brick house modified into a meeting place. Prayer meeting was held in the living room and dining area. Orange shag rug covered the hardwood floors. Folding chairs were circled around the rooms and around a musty old couch. There was a kitchen at the back of the house with an empty refrigerator and a white wall phone that was continually in use.

"Hi, I'm Steve Smith," one of the older boys said. He held a Bible in one hand and offered me his right one.

"Hey, I'm Karen," I said as I shook his hand.

"This your first visit?"

Nothing like a purple suit to blow a girl's cover. "Yes," I said. "Patsy invited me."

"She should be here soon," he said. Then Steve began introducing me to the other kids, many of them siblings—Jimmy and Jerry Burke; Andy Kelley; Steve's sister, Sharon; Sherri Davis; David Toney; Jimmy Owens; Debbie and DeeJo Baker; Debbie Harrison; Karen and Ken Mendenhall; Lynn and Buddy Wilkes. Steve explained to me that his father, "Smitty," was the pastor at Rose Hill.

When Patsy finally arrived, she introduced me to the youth pastor and his wife, Charlie and Gail Wells. I don't remember much else about that evening other than the praying. Kids sprawled across the shag carpet, the couch, and the folding chairs. They took turns making prayer requests for upcoming tests, friends, and troubled family members. I sat stiffly in a folding chair in a corner between Steve and Patsy.

When somebody reached up and turned out the lights, I was startled. I'd never been at a meeting where anybody prayed in the dark or out loud. I hoped they didn't expect me to pray. Although I'd asked Jesus into my life the previous summer, I wasn't accustomed to the ways of the devoted. When I needed to talk with God, I did it one-on-one, when nobody else was listening. I clutched the Bible on my lap and listened as kids around the room prayed for their mamas and their daddies, their teachers and their friends.

But when Steve began to pray, I lost my composure. "Lord Jesus," he said. "I don't know Karen or what her life might be like, but you do. You know everything there is to know about her. And you care about her. I ask that you meet her where she's at. Thank you for bringing her to us tonight."

I'd never had anybody pray over me like that. I was weeping. Steve didn't know how hard the previous years had been for me. He didn't know anything about my family's history. He didn't know about Daddy bleeding to death in South Vietnam or of Mama's subsequent drinking and running around. Or of Frank getting us kicked out of the trailer park or his fondness for pot. He didn't know about the boys in the trailer park who had enticed me to have sex with them before I was old enough to menstruate. And he didn't know about the anger and guilt and fears I had toward Mama or the terrors that were seizing me at night.

But his simple prayer of concern touched me. As I wept, Patsy put her arm around me, and then she prayed for me, too. Patsy didn't know about all my sorrows, but she knew about some.

The group prayed for an hour or more. Long enough for me to wipe away the streaks of black mascara staining my cheeks and to regain my composure. Charlie Wells, the youth pastor, closed the meeting.

I crawled into bed later that night and thanked God for giving me a friend like Patsy. Then I slept soundly for the first time since Frank went away. Something about those prayers lifted the despair that had been hanging over me like mosquito netting.

With Patsy serving as my chauffer, I began attending Rose Hill Baptist. The church gave me a place to feel safe and to root my faith, and it gave me something else as well—a group of sorely needed friends who would come to love me no matter how badly I disappointed them or how quirky I acted. Those friends I made in those tender teen years remain among my most cherished pals.

Most of these new friends came from two-parent families. They lived in subdivisions with fancy names like Brookstone or Windsor Park. But when we gathered at Rose Hill's youth house, none of that seemed to matter much.

Rose Hill Baptist Church is located not too far from downtown. There's a well-known seafood joint nearby, a barbecue house down the way, and a complex of low-income apartments around the corner, usually referred to as the Peabody projects or just plain ole Peabody. Nearby are a few once-stately historic homes, many of which have been converted to medical offices or some other functional purpose. The neighborhood is definitely low-income and mostly black. It's that way now, and it was that way in the 1970s. But at one time, during the 1960s, the church drew people from all over Columbus and even across the Chattahoochee, from Alabama. There were fourteen hundred people on the attendance roll, and it wasn't uncommon for as many as eight hundred to attend Sunday school. That's why they built a new sanctuary.

Rose Hill was an imposing place of worship. Instead of using the pine so common to Georgia, they crafted the facility from expensive walnut. Gilded lights dangle from the ceiling that, from the inside, looks to be three stories high. The sanctuary can easily hold eight hundred people, although fewer than a hundred attend today. A magnificent organ, with more than fifteen hundred pipes, is situated directly behind the pulpit, in the choir loft. Striking white columns face Hamilton Road. Over the years, those columns have provided a good spot for the deacons who smoked to lean and loiter.

It didn't make sense to build such a formal sanctuary in an older, poorer neighborhood, where many of the residents were lower-income and black. The church membership was dependent upon drawing from other communities because whites and blacks didn't worship together. By the time Pastor Smith arrived, attendance had plunged to three or four hundred people. It was on a slow but steady decline. The church that was home to so many for so long struggles to keep its doors open today.

If it had been solely up to him, Smitty would have welcomed the neighbors with open arms. Prior to taking the job at Rose Hill, Smitty was pastoring a church in Quitman, a rural town in South

Georgia, where he'd been for thirteen years. Smitty and his wife, Betty, came to Columbus with their two kids, Steve and Sharon, in the summer of 1970, just prior to Steve's senior year of high school. He pastored Rose Hill for seventeen years. When he arrived, the church already had a good number of problems. Other than declining attendance, there was the issue of that ostentatious sanctuary located only blocks from the low-income projects. The youth program was lacking. As the father of two teens, Smitty was committed to building a strong youth program. He supported Charlie Wells and his wife, Gail, in their endeavors, even when it put him at odds with some of the church's staunchest supporters.

Today Smitty laughs at all the things that seemed so important during the 1970s that seem downright ridiculous now. For instance, segregation was not an idea saved solely for blacks and whites in the churches of that era—men and women were segregated, too. We could pray together for hours on Monday nights, but on Sunday mornings, the teen boys were taught in one classroom and the teen girls were taught in another. "Under the old Sunday-school system, it was considered a very dangerous thing to teach mixed sexes," Smitty said. "Even the married people were separated for Sunday school."

And there was always a group of folks who thought it wrong for churches to sponsor car washes or bake sales or hot dog feeds. It's a matter of bringing moneychangers into the Lord's house. That group of naysayers became very vocal when Charlie Wells held such events to help us raise money for the choir trips we took every summer. We called our choir Prophecy, and we took our first trip during the summer of 1971, through Southern Georgia and into Florida.

"When we came to Rose Hill, there was a handful of youth already there," Smitty said. "But when Charlie came, that youth group really took off. The kids really loved old Charlie, and he really reached out and touched a lot of people. Rose Hill's youth choir was probably the best in the area at the time."

There's no question that with Smitty and Charlie at the helm, Rose Hill was taking some bold steps. And everyone agrees that perhaps the pluckiest thing Charlie Wells ever did was to enlist us teens to begin a tutorial program for kids at Peabody, the neighboring housing project for some of Columbus's most disadvantaged families.

"I was already in college when Charlie started that program," Steve Smith said. "But I've remembered it because I thought it was such an excellent idea. Nobody else was doing much for Peabody at the time. It was extremely innovative, very cutting-edge."

I remember it vividly because it put me in touch with kids who were without a doubt far more disadvantaged than I was. And given my trailer park existence at the time, I often felt like I had a pretty sorry life. I soon learned otherwise. It was also the first real encounter I'd had with blacks, other than Thelma.

We would go once a week to the church, after school, and work one-on-one with elementary school kids. We weren't well trained, but the kids came in droves. They gobbled up Kool-Aid and cookies and then opened their books and began to read to us. Or they listened as we read books to them. We didn't whisk out church pamphlets or thump Bibles. We simply read library books together and sometimes shared a smile or a hug. I don't recall the name of the girl that I worked with every week, but I remember her lightning smile. And I loved the colorful plastic clips that she wore in her braids. She would sit on the edge of her chair as we read together. Stories were manna for both of us.

Sadly, it was the constant bruising Charlie Wells took for this and other programs that drove him away.

"There were people unhappy about it," Smitty said. "The kids were black, and they just didn't like that. They would say, 'I don't want those—and they would use the *n*-word—kids running through the church halls.' That kind of thing. We tried to overcome it, but you never really eliminate that sort of thing."

Smitty always felt churches shouldn't be so class-conscious. Mama would've been welcomed into the Rose Hill community by any number of people, but she refused to attend. Regardless, most of the people at Rose Hill embraced me, even though I could offer them nothing in return. No money. No talents. Nothing but sure trouble brewing.

IT WAS DURING those afternoon tutorial sessions and the Monday-night gatherings that I struck up friendships with Karen Mendenhall and Lynn Wilkes. Karen was two years behind me, while Lynn was a year older and a grade ahead of me. Both went to Columbus High. Lynn and I couldn't have been more different in personality, and Karen and I couldn't have been more alike.

Lynn's parents both worked for the school district. Her mother was a business teacher at Baker High School. Her father headed up transportation for the schools, one of the most demanding jobs in the district once integration was implemented. Lynn was like Mama in that she didn't display her emotions. All the Wilkes kids were responsible, but as the eldest girl to three brothers, Lynn set the standard. She earned straight A's throughout high school, and she was the only girl in her physics class.

Lynn had naturally wavy hair that she wore cut short, during an era when most girls wanted long hair like Cher. She didn't worry herself over the latest style of make-up or clothes. She was meticulously organized and a born nurturer who attracted strays of all sorts—dogs, cats, girls like me.

We did most of our hanging out together at church or school functions. On occasion, Lynn's mother would invite me to stay for dinner. Lynn's father was an imposing man, large in both stature and personality.

I was on my best behavior around him. Eating at Lynn's home was like watching a ballet of chaos. There was lots of frenzied motion as plates of biscuits, platters of chicken, and bowls of mashed potatoes were passed back and forth among the family of six. Lynn's mother was always hopping up to get one more item.

Once, as we were all about to enjoy a piece of blackberry pie, Lynn's daddy got up from the table and started pulling out all the drawers in the kitchen and riffling through them. "What are you doing, Guy?" Lynn's mama asked.

"I'm trying to find the hammer," he replied.

"Why do you need the hammer?" she asked, baffled.

"So I can eat this pie," he answered. His laugh bounced around the room like a basketball. Lynn and her brothers doubled over their plates in fits of laughter. Mrs. Wilkes rolled her eyes at me and at her husband.

Karen Mendenhall and I occasionally, meaning whenever we had extra change, ate lunch at Dinglewood Pharmacy. Lieutenant Stevens, the main cook at the lunch counter, prepared his renowned Scrambled Dawgs from extra pink hot dogs layered under a heap of onions, dill pickles, chili, and oyster crackers. During the summer or early fall on sunny Saturdays, we'd walk from Karen's home on Birchfield Drive to Dinglewood; along the way we shared the latest in Mary Jane jokes: "Mary Jane was walking down the street one day and she saw a fly sitting on top a pile of turds. Mary Jane she just laughed and laughed and laughed, because she knew that fly couldn't do all that." Most often, however, we talked about our mothers and what they'd done to drive us crazy that week.

Karen's mother, Donna, was an Italian Catholic from Boston. Her father, Hunter, was a hillbilly Baptist from Alabama. Karen had three brothers and an older sister. I once asked Hunter where he was from in Alabama. "Plumnealy," he answered.

"Where's that?" I asked.

"Plumb out in the sticks, nealy out of the country," he replied with a chuckle.

A World War II veteran, Hunter was on the USS *West Virginia* when Pearl Harbor was bombed. He claimed it was hunger that kept him alive that day. He'd been on laundry duty all night. When morning came he headed to his bunk for some shut-eye, but just as he started to doze off, the call for breakfast came. Hunter decided to get up and have a bowl of cornflakes. He was at the top of the ladder on his way to the mess hall when the first bomb hit the ship. Had he been in his bunk, he would've likely been killed.

Hunter loved all his children, but he and Karen had a special bond. She possessed her father's easygoing, good-natured manner. She didn't have the blond hair or blue eyes commonly associated with Southern coeds, but she was unquestionably beautiful. Her Italian heritage had gifted her with strong features: full lips, hazel eyes, a definitive nose, olive skin, and thick russet hair that fell way past her shoulders. Because her hair was naturally wavy, Karen would often sleep with it pulled atop her head in a ponytail and wrapped around an orange juice can. She covered the can with a pair of silk panties to keep it in place. And if that didn't take the wave out, the next morning she would spread her locks out across the ironing board and, with the iron set on low, press her hair straight.

Donna Mendenhall didn't know what to make of me at first. She was a disciplinarian who didn't tolerate much foolishness from her brood. I was about as foolish a girl as she could abide. She was worried, and rightly so, about what kind of influence I would have on her daughter. Karen was a good student, unfailingly polite and respectful. I, on the other hand, was a constant challenge.

When Mr. Smith, my chemistry teacher, explained that all matter is made from atoms, I scoffed aloud at him. "You mean to tell me my eyeballs are made of the same thing as the walls of this room?" I asked.

"Your eyeballs and the walls are both made of atoms," he replied.

"How can that be?" I pressed, absolutely befuddled by the concept.

"It just is," he said.

"Well, I don't believe it," I replied.

"It's true whether you believe it or not," Mr. Smith remarked, his round cheeks now inflamed at my impertinence. "I've heard about you from Mr. Barfield."

Mr. Barfield was my algebra teacher. I'd gone head-to-head with him over the idea that $A + B = 0$. I didn't understand why all of a sudden math was about mixing up numerals with the alphabet. "What's that supposed to mean?" I asked, stung by the idea that two male teachers, both single, would be discussing me at all.

"I know you have an issue with men," Mr. Smith answered. The entire class was silently watching the two of us, eager to see who would back off first.

His remark angered me. It was obvious that the conclusions reached by Mr. Smith and Mr. Barfield were based upon my not having a father around the house. "That's not the problem," I replied heatedly. "It's just that I simply don't believe in atoms!"

"What do you mean, you don't believe in atoms?" Mr. Smith said, challenging me.

"Some people choose not to believe in God even though he's there," I answered. "I choose not to believe in atoms!"

In a fit of sheer frustration, Mr. Smith chucked the eraser he was holding in his right hand directly at my head and stormed out of the room.

I ducked swiftly and the eraser struck the wall. SPLAT! A cloud of white dust erupted as atoms mingled with atoms.

Part III · 1971—1975

the years of
plenty want

moving on up

ON JUNE 8, 1971, OFFICIALS AT COLUMBUS COLLEGE BESTOWED ASSOCIATE'S DEGREES IN NURSING TO thirty-seven people. Mama was one of the honored. Her graduation from Columbus College was cause for celebration. She was the first person in her family and my father's to obtain a college degree. Lewis told Linda and me to order Mama a store-bought cake, with lard icing. It had pink flowers and the inscription CONGRATULATIONS SHELBY, R.N.

Mama received a new nursing cap with her diploma. It had a black velvet ribbon across the edge of the brim. I loved to rub my fingers across the velvet on that stiff, starched cap. After the graduation ceremony, Lewis took us all out to dinner. Then he and Mama went dancing while we stayed home and ate all the roses off the store-bought cake.

The following weekend Mama took us on a family vacation with one of her nursing buddies. It would be the first of several annual trips we would make to Panama City, Florida, often referred to as the Redneck Riviera.

Mama had always loved the beach. While on Oahu, she had lived in bathing suits. If she wanted to dress up, she'd put on a pair of shorts, a sleeveless top tied around her waist, and a pair of flip-flops. Sometimes she'd take the pink rollers out of her hair or tie a scarf around them. Other times she'd just run a brush through her lush brunette curls and call it good enough. Daddy would fish from the rocky cliffs of the North Beach, while Mama slathered baby oil on her thighs and watched us chase after the foamy waves.

In Panama City, Mama rented a room for $18.99 a night in one of those stucco-pink motels with a name like the Surf-n-Sun so common along the town's strip. There were so many and they all looked nearly identical, Mama would often forget which one was ours. Especially if she'd been lying out in the sun all day. Mama could afford only one room, with two double beds, so she and Linda shared a bed, I slept with her nursing buddy, and Frank slept on the floor. The sheets and towels always had traces of sand in them, as did the green carpet covering the floor.

Some of the beaches were marked "private," which meant they belonged to the people with money. We'd walk to the areas marked "public access" early in the morning and lay out big towels to mark our spot before the crowd arrived. We'd take turns during the day running back and forth, bringing one another sodas and bologna sandwiches, getting Mama another pack of cigarettes or the suntan lotion that somebody, not me, had left in the room.

The sand at Panama City is white and fine, not like the gritty, coral sands of Oahu's North Beach. It looks and feels as if somebody, maybe God, dumped over one of heaven's sugar bags. And the water has that turquoise tint of Depression-era glass. Postcards of the beach label it "the Emerald Coast."

During one of my trips between the beach and the motel, I passed a vendor's table stacked with airbrushed T-shirts. Plucking through a pile, I picked out one of the colorful, cheap ones—$3.99—and forked over four one-dollar bills. Then I rushed on back to the motel room, grabbed a couple of Cokes, and headed back down to the beach, wearing my new shirt. I hadn't even bothered to read the inscription: FREE SEX. GOT A MINUTE? written above the face of a bulbous-nosed character that looked ever so much like Mr. Magoo.

A group of college boys, perched on a couple of chrome fenders, wolf-whistled as I strode past. One of them yelled out at me: "A minute? Honey, I got a whole half hour!" Then the group of them howled as I walked on by, red-faced and confused.

When Mama saw my new shirt, she laughed and pointed out the inscription. She told me that I'd better take it off, unless, of course, I was begging to be assaulted. I never wore the shirt again.

That night Mama took us out to a fish house called Allen's for supper. We ate two baskets of hush puppies—cornmeal mixture, deep-fried—and emptied the tall glasses of sweet tea before the heaping plates of fried catfish and French fries arrived. Allen's sat on the bay, so we could stare at the boats and the fishermen out the big picture windows that surrounded the dining room. We'd never eaten at such a fancy place before.

When we got back to the motel, Mama and her buddy went out, and we sprawled across the bed and the floor and watched television. Frank and I were as red and hot as peppers. Our freckled features didn't tolerate Florida sun as well as Linda's bronze skin did. We wet down rags with cold water and held them over our faces and thighs. We didn't know about the soothing qualities of aloe vera in those days. We were all asleep when Mama and her buddy came stumbling in. It was the sound of one of them vomiting that woke me up. "Food poisoning," Mama said.

Alcohol poisoning was probably closer to the truth.

On Sunday we shook the sand from our towels, shorts, and heels and drove back to Columbus. Our two-day family vacation had come to an end. We didn't know it then, but all sorts of new adventures awaited us, down the road a bit.

FRANK STARTED ATTENDING Rose Hill with me that summer. He and Patsy had become good pals. And even when he wouldn't go to church, he was always willing to take me. This was great, since I still couldn't drive and we lived so far out.

I had two distinct personas that summer: the one I displayed at church and the one that surfaced at home. At church, I was the cutup, the quick wit. I could not sit through a sermon or a prayer meeting or a training-union class without popping off with some remark that would cause others around me to burst into fits of giggles. Grabbing a hymn book, I'd open it up and randomly pick a title, something like "There's a Fountain Flowing" or "Amazing Grace," and poke the person sitting next to me, usually Karen Mendenhall or Beth Mc-Combs, and add on the following line: "Between the sheets." "Look, Beth, *Just as I am between the sheets!*" I'd say, choking back a laugh.

On down the pew the joke would travel, until soon coughs filled the sanctuary as everybody tried to suppress laughter. Charlie Wells would glare at us from the pulpit as he led worship. The kids at Rose Hill usually filled up the first three or four rows of the church. We couldn't escape Charlie's glares, but he couldn't do much about our irreverence, either. After all, Charlie was probably the one who taught us that little ditty.

At Rose Hill I never used swearwords, and I acted like the virgin I was. Curious by nature, I wasn't afraid to question folks much older and wiser than me. The adults at Rose Hill encouraged this in me.

Mama, on the other hand, had long grown weary of what she referred to as my inquisitions. Often she'd ignore the questions I asked about Granny Ruth or her own childhood, or why she and Granny Leona didn't get along. She pretended to be too busy or lost in thought to answer me. Sometimes she reprimanded me for asking so many questions. "What do you wanna know that for? Are you planning on writing a book?" The sharpness in her tone usually shut me up, at least for an hour or so.

At home I was often petulant and mean-spirited. I was filled with self-righteousness over the indignities I felt I suffered because of Mama's errant behavior. I wanted a mother who wore a string of pearls, linen suits, and pillbox hats. Who went to church, read her Bible, belonged to the Women's Missionary Union, and preferred sweet tea to beer. Come to think of it, I guess I thought all mothers ought to be like Pastor Smitty's wife, Betty.

While I prayed faithfully for Mama every day, my prayers were limited in nature. My first prayer was that Mama would quit smoking. My second was that God would send Mama a handsome rich man to take care of her, and me, for the rest of our lives. Lewis had given Mama a sparkly engagement ring, and they said they would marry someday. But I wanted God to send Mama somebody else to marry. Frank, for sure, didn't want her to marry Lewis. Neither of us ever told her how we felt, but she had a pretty good idea anyway.

When I wasn't at church or school, I was often hanging out at the home of Angie and Wesley Skibbey. Like so many of us Crystal Valley kids, Angie and Wes didn't have a dad. Pauline, their mother, was a native of Italy who'd married a soldier boy from the Carolinas and followed him to the U.S. She left him because he'd used her as a punching bag once too often.

Pauline was a beautiful woman, with olive skin and close-cropped brunette hair, and a seductive but subtle cut to her waist and breasts. Angie didn't look a thing like her mama. She had hair the color of wheat at harvest, and Dolly Parton–sized boobs. She never could wear the button-front shirts that were so popular in those days. Pauline didn't smoke, but Angie did. I can't ever remember her not smoking. She held her cigarette in that same elegant but exaggerated fashion of screen star Bette Davis, as if the thing she held between two fingers was a glittering wand, not a cancer stick. Her nails were long, shaped into ovals. Angie liked to watch soap operas all day long and hold séances at night. She bored me. But I felt differently about her younger brother, Wes.

Even as a seventh-grader, Wes towered over me. He hadn't quite reached six feet, but he wasn't far from it. He was almost too skinny. His hair was blond like his sister's, and he wore it long, as was the fashion. He was always flipping his bangs off to one side because they kept falling down to his nose. His eyes were blue. Not silver-blue but bright blue, like the sky above Waikiki Beach. And when he smiled, it always looked as if he was holding something back. He had a lop-sided grin that gave him a perpetual sly-dog look. He wasn't the kind of guy who stopped a gal in her tracks, but he could slow her down.

For the most part, I kept my infatuation with Wes a secret. I pretended he was a bother, a nuisance, like all younger siblings. We called each other stupid names and wrote ridiculous notes in each other's yearbooks. Like this one, scripted by Wes in one of mine: "To a big bag of trouble. I hope you straighten out."

Sometimes I invited Wes and Angie to go to Rose Hill with me, and sometimes they did, but neither of them ever felt like they belonged there the way I did. The whole time I lived at Crystal Valley, Wes and I never did anything more than hold hands, when we thought nobody else was watching. But as fatherless children, I always felt we shared a common destiny, something I didn't have with the boys at Rose Hill.

My friendship with Angie and Wes began to diminish during the fall of 1971 because of two events—forced busing and an impending move.

SOMETIME SHORTLY BEFORE Frank headed back to Alabama for his senior year, Mama suggested I consider going to a boarding school in Virginia. I'm not sure if it was Mama's idea or Lewis's, but I wasn't going anywhere, and I told Mama so.

It didn't matter what a person's income bracket was, a lot of white folks who could ill afford to do so began sending their kids to private schools when busing was implemented. It was the only way to make sure their kids didn't get bused clear across town to Carver or Spencer, the town's two predominately black high schools.

As far as I was concerned, the only school I wanted to attend was Columbus High. I had gone to three different junior highs and four different elementary schools; I was bound and determined I would go to one high school, come hell or high water. And it didn't matter one bit to me how many blacks I had to maneuver my way around in the hallways; I had started high school as a Blue Devil, and I wanted to remain a Blue Devil until I collected my diploma. I was fed up with transferring schools and trying to find somebody to eat lunch with. I certainly didn't want to go to some hoity-toity boarding school in Virginia. I figured I had more in common with black kids from the projects than with a bunch of rich white girls. I knew I might end up at Carver or Spencer, but I was more worried about Hardaway High, a relatively new school in town that might as well have been a boarding school because it was full of white kids from middle- to upper-class neighborhoods.

The bus that picked up kids at the Crystal Valley trailer court stopped at three high schools—Hardaway, Jordan (pronounced "Jerden"), and Columbus. When the Fifth Circuit Court issued an order to the district to integrate, the Muscogee County School Board approved an assignment plan striving for a 70–30 white-to-black ratio in each school, with a faculty ratio of 75–25. Sometime before Labor Day weekend, I got a letter confirming me as a Blue Devil for at least one more year. But my sophomore year started off with a tension that hadn't been there my freshman year.

For the most part, Columbus is a town of well-mannered people, so the protests against forced busing had a modicum of civility to them. To be sure, there was a lot of ugliness involved, but nobody burned down neighborhoods or shot the sheriff. Prior to the first day of school, hundreds of white parents gathered at the school district office and burned an effigy of William Shaw, the superintendent of schools. A petition was circulated calling for his resignation. Many threatened to pull their kids out of public schools. Hundreds did.

What I remember best were the school fights, many of them in the student parking lot out behind the school. I was fourteen and too young to drive, so I wasn't worried about getting hurt. I was standing outside the music class, leaning on a railing in the courtyard, when a boy ran up to a group of us and said, "There's a big fight going on. They got knives and switchblades. Somebody got cut already." I heard later that that somebody was Frank's old pal Joe K., from the other trailer park.

I got into a few scuffles myself and had a couple of near misses. One occurred while I was walking to my locker, which was in the school basement. I headed there with Fran Hart after lunch. Fran was a little thing, probably not quite five feet tall, and about eighty-five pounds. But I was already five feet six, and I've never been slight of frame. We approached a set of stairs where a group of four black girls sat. One girl called out to me. "Where did you get that skirt?" she asked.

I was wearing a blue skirt with a patchwork pattern, a common style in those days. I didn't answer because white girls like me were told to never speak to blacks, under any circumstances. Fran and I stepped around them as we headed down the stairs.

"I think that is about the ugliest skirt I've ever seen!" another girl called out. Then they laughed.

Now, that made me mad. Whipping my head over my shoulder, I called out, "I don't rightly care what you think!"

Fran was mortified. "You shouldn't have done that, Karen," she said.

We kept going. The hallways were empty. The bell hadn't rung yet, and most kids were still in class or eating lunch. Fran waited as I turned the combination lock on my locker and reached for my history book. All of sudden, we were surrounded on either side.

"Hey, girl, what did you say to me back there?" The girl asking the question towered over me. Her buddies were glowering at the two of us. I think Fran quit breathing. But I wasn't about to back off.

"I said I didn't care much what you think about my skirt," I answered, trying to feign a coolness I didn't feel.

She moved her head in closer to mine. "Well, you ought to care," she hissed. Her girlfriends snickered.

I wasn't that good at math, but it only took me a moment to do the counting and to figure out that I was about to get my butt kicked. I wasn't worried too much about myself; I'd been in some dogfights before when I lived at Lake Forest. But I was pretty sure

Fran had never been in one and would never talk to me again for involving her.

But in one of those saved-by-the-bell moments that honestly do happen, it rang, and the hallway was flooded with kids. The four girls turned and walked away, their glares still fixed on me in warning.

"That was so dumb of you," Fran said. She spoke in a whisper full of exasperation and relief, the kind of tone a mother might use in a hospital emergency room. "They could've killed you. Don't you know you never talk back to blacks?"

About a month later I heard that same remark when a black girl came up to me in the school bathroom after I backhanded a black boy in homeroom class because he wouldn't quit playing with my hair. "Whoowee, girl!" she said. "Don't you know better than to slap a black man? Nobody slaps a black man and lives to tell about it— especially not a white girl!"

The ruckus had started shortly after I'd taken my seat. The pudgy-faced boy sitting behind me fingered the ends of my hair every single day. It annoyed me like all get-out, and I'd told him so on several occasions. I started out asking him to "kindly leave my hair alone, *please.*" But he kept doing it. To avoid a confrontation, I'd lean forward as far as I could, out of his reach. Or pull my hair down around my shoulder as I hunched over a book. He would laugh and continue messing with me and my hair.

After a couple of weeks of this, I grew downright pissed. So one day when he reached up and began playing with my hair, I turned around and backhanded him across the face. "Leave my hair alone!" I screeched.

Momentarily stunned, the boy jumped to his feet. He grabbed me up out of my chair and slapped me with powerful force across my left cheek. Before I could reach up to my face, hot and flushed, he grabbed my right arm and twisted it up behind my back, between my shoulder blades. The whole time he was screaming at me. "Stupid bitch!" he said. "I'll teach you to hit me."

He was pushing me down the aisle.

Miss Patch, a new teacher, was on her feet, her face as flushed as mine.

"Stop it! Stop it!" she yelled. "Let go of her now!"

The boy ignored her cries. *"I'm going to throw this dumb bitch out the window!"* he yelled back as he shoved me toward the open windows that faced the school's courtyard. We were on the second floor. The courtyard was mostly concrete. I was struggling to break free, but I wasn't about to hit, slap, or kick the kid again. I looked at Miss Patch, my eyes pleading with her to do something.

She pulled out a silver laser device. With one flash of that laser pen she could activate an emergency call to the front office. The burly security staff, typically retired or off-duty firemen and police officers, would be at the door within minutes. The class of onlookers who had only moments before been yelling "Fight! Fight! Throw her! Throw her!" grew silent. Nobody had ever been in a situation that required activation of the laser pen. All eyes were upon Miss Patch. Would she really do it?

"LET GO OF HER RIGHT NOW!" Miss Patch yelled, pointing the pen toward the call box bolted to the far wall. She had yet to activate the laser.

The boy dropped my arm, but he didn't quit quietly. "Don't you ever touch me again!" he said. "I'll kill you."

I didn't say a word.

Miss Patch pulled us both out into the hallway.

"I'm referring you both to the principal," she said. She was visibly shaken. Her hands were trembling.

Fighting for any reason was cause for expulsion. I knew if I got expelled, Mama would send me to a boarding school for sure. But first, I figured, she'd take a shotgun to the school and put the fear of God into the boy who dared slap her daughter. I begged the principal not to call Mama. I told him she was itching to send me off to a private school, and this incident was all she would need to seal my fate. The boy didn't say a word. He didn't care if he got expelled. He didn't care if the principal called his mama. I was pretty sure he didn't care if all the white girls at Columbus High got sent off to boarding school. It wasn't going to affect his life none.

The principal rubbed his hands through a thick fluff of his silver hair and lectured the two of us on the need for "everybody to be nice and get along." He made us swear we'd leave each other alone from now on. And he ordered us to sit on opposite sides of the classroom. Then he dismissed us to our next class and told us he'd "study the matter some more" before calling our parents. Mama never did get a call, but I figured what she didn't know couldn't hurt me, so I never told her about the incident.

Mama might not like her kids going to school with blacks, but I don't ever remember her using the ugly slang, the *n*-word, that some of our kinfolk used. However, there was no question that she felt, then, that blacks and whites shouldn't run in the same circles or attend the same bars, churches, or schools. But she didn't put up a fuss about it either. And she would never join a segregationist group creating the ruckus at the district office. Mama was never the kind of woman to jump on a bandwagon for any cause. She was way too independent for such nonsense. Besides, she was too busy for marches or boycotts. She had much more practical matters to tend to—like finding her family a new home.

EVER SINCE AUNT CIL had died, Grandpa Harve had been shuffled around from pillar to post. First, Uncle Carl and Aunt Blanche took him home to Clinton, Tennessee. Carl's home wasn't big, but it was bigger than our trailer. And it was probably as comfortable as anything any of the Mayes family owned at the time. But Grandpa hadn't been there very long before Carl and Blanche decided he'd be better off in Oregon with Uncle Roy and Aunt Katherine. Mama wasn't involved in the decision-making process and wasn't even told about the move until after it was done.

She wasn't happy about it, but at the time there wasn't much she could do other than make plans to bring Grandpa back to live with us. As soon as Mama started bringing home a regular paycheck from her Medical Center job, she started talking to a Realtor about finding a house she could afford.

In the meantime, she gave Lewis back that big ole diamond ring he'd bought her and called off their engagement. Mama decided she couldn't marry him after all. Not because she didn't love him, but because she feared he didn't love us kids enough. And Mama simply could not bear to be hitched to a man who didn't adore us kids the way Daddy had. She broke the news to us casually over supper one night.

She'd brought home a bag of Krystal hamburgers. The steamed burgers were smothered in mustard and pickles and could fit in the palm of a kid's hand. Since they only cost a quarter each, Mama could buy a sack of twenty for five bucks. Still, a meal from Krystal was usually reserved for special celebratory events. As she stood at the kitchen counter, taking the burgers from the bag, Mama told us that she'd given Lewis his ring back.

"How come?" I asked.

"Just because," Mama said. I knew better than to press her for any more explanation than that. The "Just because" answer meant all discussion was finished as far as Mama was concerned. I don't recall any of us kids being upset about Mama and Lewis breaking up.

A change was taking place in our lives. Once she finished school and started working full-time, Mama quit her honky-tonking. She was working the 11 P.M. to 7 A.M. shift. She'd start getting ready for work at about 9:30 P.M. She'd leave at about ten-thirty and get home in time to see Linda and me off to school in the mornings. When we got home in the afternoons, Mama was up, the trailer was cleaned, the laundry was all folded, and dinner was being contemplated. Except for the obvious absence of men in our household, life seemed almost routine, like it had been before Daddy died.

In fall 1972, Mama up and sold our trailer and bought a house. It was a three-bedroom brick home, just a block off Manchester Expressway, on Johnson Drive. It wasn't anything fancy, less than fifteen hundred square feet, but it was situated on a corner lot, which meant we not only had a front and backyard, but we had a side yard as well. And the house had a concrete foundation, instead of cinder blocks to hold it up. There were lots of windows and glossy hardwood floors in the living room and bedrooms, and a bathroom with a tub and shower. The trailer had cost $5,700. Mama sold it for $2,000 five and a half years later. She used that money to put a down payment on the house and financed $14,000. That was a great sum of money for a woman making less than three dollars an hour.

It didn't take us long to box up everything we owned. A bunch of the kids from Rose Hill got their parents' cars and trucks and helped us move. Mama appreciated that. All day long she kept humming that Roger Miller tune—"King of the Road"—"Trailer for sale or rent."

Linda and I got to decorate our room the way we wanted. We picked out a pair of hot-pink curtains with ruffles on the valances and the hem. Our bedroom faced west, so when the sun set, its dappled light came right through our window. The afternoon sun drifting through those cotton curtains gave the room a rosy glow that seemed magical to us.

Mama's room was next to ours, facing east. And even though he wasn't living at home, Frank got a little corner room that was big enough for a twin bed and not much else. Every door had a glass doorknob, and there was even a dining room separate from the kitchen. The kitchen seemed especially spacious. I couldn't just turn and reach the refrigerator from the stove or sink. I actually had to walk across the linoleum floor to get eggs from the fridge. But the best thing about the kitchen was the picture window above the sink. It looked directly into the bedroom window of the very cute teenage boy who lived in the house next-door.

Rudy used to take off his shirt whenever he saw Linda or me

standing at the sink washing dishes. He'd pick a vinyl record and put it on the turntable and sit there flipping through a magazine and pretend like he didn't know we were staring at him. Other times he'd talk to us through the window screens. One night, when a fellow who had given me a ride home from church attempted to kiss me good night on the back stoop just outside the kitchen door, Rudy flipped on his bedroom light and scared the dickens out of the poor guy. That fellow never did try to kiss me again.

Lust wasn't the only fire to heat up that kitchen. Once while Mama was working, I was at the stove, fixing me and Linda some BLTs for dinner. I'd been cooking for years, so frying up a skillet of bacon was sort of a mindless chore for me. But on that afternoon, I turned up the front eye too high. I stood with my back to the stove, talking to Linda about something, when flames a half-foot high shot up from the pan. *"Karen! Look out!"* Linda screamed.

I grabbed the skillet's handle and moved the pan to the stove's middle. Then, forgetting everything I'd been taught in home ec about not throwing water on hot grease, I yelled at Linda to get me a glass of water. I poured it in the pan.

"Oh! Shit!" I screamed. Too late. Bacon torch.

"Gimme a towel," I said. Linda threw a dish rag my way. Smoke was filling the kitchen and streaming out the side door. *"Get outta my way!"* I shouted as I picked up the frying pan and ran with it to the sink. *"I need some flour!"* I yelled. Finally, the home ec lesson on cooking fires had kicked in.

Linda handed me the flour canister. I scooped up a handful, tossed it into the pan, and turned on the water at the same time. The fire in the pan died out, but the kitchen curtains above the sink were aflame. Linda ran out the side door and yelled at Rudy to call the fire department. I reached for the sprayer and drenched the blazing curtains. The flames were out when a fire engine pulled up in our drive. Rudy never had time to call them. Someone else in the neighborhood, seeing the smoke pouring out of our house, had already called the fire department. Several firemen rushed through the side door, scaring the bejesus out of Linda and me.

"You girls okay?" one of the men asked as he stood in the middle of the kitchen assessing the damage. Smoke, black like a thundercloud, settled on the ceiling.

"Yes, sssir," I stammered. I was certain Mama was going to go apeshit. I'd just managed to torch her new kitchen. The firemen insisted I call her before they left the premises. One of the men got on the phone with Mama and assured her we were okay, but that the kitchen had extensive smoke damage. Mama left work and came straight home. She didn't yell at me, but the next week she bought a four-hundred-dollar fire-alarm system from some man who she then ended up dating. Mama made Linda and me listen as the fellow gave us all a terrifying presentation on death by fire.

There seemed to be no escape from the idea that one of us was fated to burn up, either in this life or the next one. It wasn't long after that incident that I introduced my sister to Christ. Linda was in the bathtub, shaving her legs. I went in and sat on the toilet lid to visit with her. When you live in a household full of women, the bathroom often serves as a conference room. It wasn't uncommon for all three of us girls to be crowded in there at once, but Mama was at work that night. Black-and-white images of nude Grecian women graced the matching wallpaper, shower curtain, and window coverings. Mama had gone all out decorating that bathroom.

I had been praying for Linda's salvation for a long time. My heart thudded and my palms grew clammy as I worked up the courage to talk to her about God's saving grace. "Do you know what a Christian is?" I began.

"Sure," Linda said. "Somebody who believes in God."

"Yep," I replied. "But not only in God, but in his Son, Jesus Christ."

"I believe in Jesus," she replied.

"I know you do," I said. "But have you ever invited him into your life? To be Lord of your life?" Linda looked at me quizzically. "The Bible says in James that even the demons believe in God," I explained. "It's not enough to believe. You have to ask Jesus to forgive you of your sins and to be Lord of your life."

"How do you do that?" she asked.

"Well, you just pray. I could pray with you if you like."

"No," Linda said. She'd responded so quickly and sharply, I thought I'd offended her. I rose to leave.

"It doesn't have to be anything fancy, Linda." I said. "You just say that you know Jesus died for your sins, that you're sorry for them, and then you ask him to come into your heart and be Lord of your life."

"Okay," she said.

I left the room without shutting the door behind me.

About ten minutes later, Linda called out to me. "Karen," she said.

I came and stood in the doorway. Linda's dark hair was soaped up and piled high atop her head. I couldn't tell if she had been crying or if the soap had reddened her eyes. "I did it," she said.

"Did what?" I asked stupidly.

"I asked Jesus into my heart," she said.

I squealed. Tears streamed down my face. At least one other member of my family was saved from hell's eternal flames. And now, finally, there was somebody else in the house that could help pray for Frank and Mama.

Once the smoke-damaged kitchen, covered by insurance, was restored, there was nothing about that house that needed changing. We all loved it. It felt permanent, like a home should. We'd been living in a trailer since June 1966. Mama had spent years going to school, first to get her GED, then her LPN, and finally her RN certification. It hadn't been easy, but she didn't have time for complaining. She just did what she thought needed to be done. Mama couldn't fix the fact that Daddy had died, but she was bound and determined that his death wasn't going to keep us from having the kind of life he would've given us. She had wanted a home of her own since she'd returned stateside. She'd been saving for a down payment from the moment she got back to Rogersville.

Now that we had our own place, Mama wanted to bring Grandpa Harve back to live with us. When his health started to decline, Mama's brothers had placed Grandpa in a skilled nursing facility. Now that Mama had a nursing degree, she figured she could care for him better than anyone. But before she could make arrangements to bring her daddy home, he died. He had taken ill with pneumonia. Mama didn't know until the brothers called to tell her their daddy was dead. Uncle Roy and Aunt Katherine sent Grandpa back to be buried in Rogersville.

We made the trip to Tennessee during November 1971. There wasn't any snow on the ground, but the sky was the color of concrete and the ground was frozen and nearly as hard. Only a handful of people showed up at the burial. Mostly family members and a few of the townsfolk, whom Grandpa used to greet on the street, back when he was walking patrol as a Rogersville policeman. Uncle Woody, who worked part-time as a preacher doing pulpit supply, gave the eulogy. Mama didn't say anything. She shed her tears only when her brothers weren't around.

Mama thought crying was a weakness. She was always trying to be strong whenever Uncle Carl or Uncle Woody was nearby. Only Uncle Charlie, who was the closest to her in age, was allowed to see beyond Mama's tough-gal demeanor. She couldn't fool him. Charlie knew Mama better than any of her brothers. But he wasn't at the funeral because he couldn't afford to make the trip from Oregon. He was self-employed as a roofer, and any time off meant a loss of income.

Mama was thirty-four when Grandpa Harve died. She was now an orphan, a widow, and the mother of three fatherless children. Grandpa Harve didn't live long enough to tell his daughter how proud he was that she'd gotten her nursing degree. He never told her that she was sure brave to tackle her education while trying to care for three kids by her lonesome. I don't even know if he ever told

Mama that he loved her, but she knew he did and he knew she loved him. That was enough for the both of them, and to hell with what anybody else thought. Mama never said it, but I always knew that losing her daddy hurt her. Other than her son, the two men she'd loved most in life were both dead. And shortly after Grandpa died, Frank ended up in the hospital.

spiraling down

FRANK ARRIVED BY AMBULANCE AT THE MEDICAL CENTER IN COLUMBUS, THE SAME HOSPITAL WHERE MAMA worked the night shift. By the time we arrived, he had an oxygen tube up his nose and an IV pumping fluids into his vein. Doctors weren't sure what happened to him. Frank had collapsed after class. A classmate had found him, barely breathing. They administered CPR and called for an ambulance. So far the tests were inconclusive.

Mama had been unusually quiet on the way to the hospital. The trip from our new home to the hospital took fifteen minutes, long enough for her to smoke two cigarettes. She didn't have to warn Linda and me to behave; hospitals put the fear of death into us anyway. We didn't say a word to her, to each other, or to Frank. I stood at least a foot away from the bed and watched his chest rise up and down, ever so slowly.

Mama walked up to the bed and touched his arm. Frank's eyes fluttered, then opened. "Hey, son," Mama said.

"Hi," Frank replied. He looked quizzically at the IV.

"You probably don't remember collapsing, do you?" Mama asked.

"No, ma'am," he replied.

"You'll be fine," she said.

I looked over at Linda. She looked at me. We both wondered the same thing—how did Mama know Frank would be okay? Mama conferred with a doctor for a while, then she told Linda and me to wait outside for her.

There was a row of chairs in a television room at the end of the hallway, but Linda and I stood, silently, watching as glassy-eyed people wearing hospital gowns and fluffy slippers stared at the TV or at us.

Mama smoked three cigarettes on the drive home. The only thing she said was "You ought to pray for your brother."

When I got home I called Pastor Charlie and my friends Karen Mendenhall, Patsy Ward, and Lynn Wilkes. I told them Frank was in the hospital and the doctors were running tests. We didn't know what was wrong. Mama wasn't saying much, but I could tell she was worried sick. Mama has a nervous stomach. Whenever she gets upset, she gets sick to her stomach. She'd been in the bathroom since we got back home.

"You want me to come over?" Lynn asked.

"Nah," I said. "We'll be okay. Just pray for Frank."

"All right," she said. "But call me if you need anything."

Frank spent four days in the hospital. If the doctors knew what was wrong with him, they never told Mama. They just sent him home with a handful of prescription drugs, mostly antidepressants. It was actually drugs that had landed him in the hospital to begin with. The morning he collapsed, Frank had taken about twenty barbiturates.

A month or so later he was in the hospital again, this time for taking a handful of uppers. Frank had never smoked pot until he was a cadet at Lyman Ward. It was there that a buddy from Birmingham introduced him to pot and other recreational drugs. The classmate, a doctor's son, had unlimited access to all sorts of red, white, and blue goodies. And being a generous soul, he shared them freely with my brother. Frank left Lyman Ward with a ferocious craving for something he couldn't quite figure out.

As a nurse. She had to wonder if Frank's problems were drug-related, but if she suspected it, she didn't let on to any of us. What she told us was that Frank's asthma was acting up. She never once mentioned the possibility of drug abuse, and it never occurred to me. I was pretty sheltered from the drug culture. Shoot, beer was considered taboo by most of my friends. Our Southern Baptist Sunday-school teachers had given us the drill about the evils of alcohol. I believed Mama when she claimed Frank's problems were asthma-induced.

We were all worried that Frank wasn't going to make it to his graduation in May 1972, but he did.

Patsy went with us. Mama had invited her to come along; Patsy had been praying for Frank and Mama for a long time. All of us girls dressed up, like we were going to church on Easter Sunday, except instead of wearing pink floral outfits, we all had on various hues of navy and red. The ceremony was held on the lawn directly in front of the school. We sat on bleachers and folding chairs as somber-faced cadets marched before us, wearing spit-shined shoes, white gloves, and hats that hid their eyes, and carrying rifles. A military band played, and we stood every time the Stars and Stripes passed. There was nothing lighthearted about the event. The cadets flipped rifles and flags with the precision possessed by military drill teams. And when they sat down or stood up, it was in perfect harmony, as one body, not as individuals. At Lyman Ward, individualism was regarded as self-indulgence. Nobody ever wanted to be singled out—they all wanted to fit in, to be part of the whole. On the surface, Frank appeared to fit in very well. He was a model cadet.

To celebrate Frank's graduation, Mama took us all out to a catfish house for dinner. The waiter, a young college kid from nearby Auburn University, asked Patsy how she wanted her fish cooked.

"What do you mean?" she asked. Typically, Southerners prepare fish one way—deep-fried. But this was a nicer restaurant, one that broiled fish. The waiter explained to Pasty that she had a choice.

"So what if I tell you I want it raw?" she asked.

"You can have the fish prepared any way you wish, Miss," the fellow replied. If he was flustered by her question, he didn't show it.

"I'm only teasing," Patsy said, flashing a smile. She ordered her fish fried like everybody else. But not one to be outdone by Patsy's flirtatious manner, the waiter served her a platter of raw catfish. Patsy's jaw dropped as she considered for a moment that she really might have to eat the cold flesh. (This was long before the sushi craze swept the country.) The rest of us burst into a fit of laughter. Even Mama was tickled by the smart-aleck stunt.

Later, Mama took us on our second family vacation since Daddy died. We spent a week in Orlando at Florida's newest attraction, Walt Disney World. This time Mama didn't take along any of her nursing buddies. The only thing she drank that week was iced tea.

Frank's future plans were unclear. Lewis had made some calls to some high-ranking officials, and they helped get Frank an appointment to the Naval Academy, but he blew that off and enrolled at Columbus College for the fall term.

Mama was disgusted with his decision. Frank had earned a near-perfect score on the Scholastic Aptitude Test. He had a natural mathematic bent and had done well in physics and calculus. More than one teacher told Mama her son was almost a genius. His decision to stay in Columbus and attend a community college stupefied all of us. But as was her nature, Mama didn't say much about it. She just quietly pondered the matter.

In September 1972, a businessman knocked on our door and offered Mama sixteen thousand dollars for our home—two thousand in cash, and he'd pay off the loan balance. The man went to all the neighbors and bought their homes, too. Eventually, all those homes were bulldozed away and they put up a parking lot and a new business, Victory Auto Parts.

Mama found another house, a couple of blocks away, on Fifty-second Street, just down from Allen Elementary School and around the corner from Arnold Junior High (now Arnold Magnet Academy), where I'd finished out my middle-school years. A couple from Rose Hill Baptist Church owned it. They sold it to Mama for nineteen thousand dollars. We moved in before my sixteenth birthday that November.

The new house had a backyard that seemed as long and wide as a soccer field. For my birthday Mama bought me a used car, a Simca sedan. The only difference between the Simca and a Tyco was the Simca came with an engine in the trunk, whereas toddler feet powered the Tyco. The car was so compact Frank taught me how to drive it in the backyard. Even in third gear, I could still manage to maneuver that baby between the tall pines. About a month after I got my driver's license, Frank borrowed my car without my permission and blew up the engine. I never saw it again.

The three-bedroom brick house Mama bought wasn't much bigger than the house she sold. In fact, the kitchen was only about half as big as the other one. But it had one advantage the other house didn't—central air-conditioning. The first night in the house, I slept on the floor of my room with a sheet spread out over the floor vent. No more running back and forth to a window air conditioner with a sheet over my head, trying to cool down. Now I could sleep all night long without breaking a sweat. I didn't have to snuggle between the bed and the wall to keep cool. The entire house was a comfortable temperature. The freon air made the sheets feel like silk against my skin, instead of like warm compresses.

Frank's bedroom had been a den. He painted the entire room, including the ceiling, black. Then he tacked up posters of rock groups like Black Sabbath and the Rolling Stones. His room was situated in the middle of the house, and to get from my bedroom to the kitchen, I had to walk either through the living and dining room or through his bedroom. Most of the time I avoided his room. It always had a funny smell to it. At first I thought it was from his dirty socks. I didn't know about his stash of pot.

I found a Baggie full one morning while rifling through his pockets for lunch money. Frank was already at school. I snuck into his room and began scavenging for change. I found a pair of his jeans on the floor. I picked them up and reached into a pocket, and pulled out a cellophane bag of what appeared to be oregano. I had no idea what it was, but I figured whatever it was I'd better put it back. When Frank returned home later that day, I asked him about it. "Hey," I said. "How come you keep a bag of herbs in your pants?"

"What are you talking about, stupid?" he replied. Stupid had long been his pet name for me.

"I was looking for lunch money this morning. I found a bag of stuff in your pocket. What is that? It smells bad."

"*Stay out of my room!*" he yelled. "And don't say anything to Mama, or I'll kill you."

"*Don't yell at me!*" I screamed back. "And don't worry, I didn't tell Mama anything."

I had no idea why he was so upset. Mama wouldn't care if he carried a five-pound bag of turnip greens in his pocket. Linda and I agreed that Lyman Ward had turned our brother into a raving idiot. I told her about the bag I found, but she didn't have any idea what it was, either.

That Christmas Frank bought Mama new lamps for the coffee table in the living room. We still had the same uncomfortable couch of carved koa wood. The lamps were expensive, about forty dollars each, but he bought them at the furniture store where he worked. Still, eighty dollars was a lot of money for a kid making about two dollars an hour. Mama asked him where he got the money to buy her such nice gifts. He told her not to worry about it; she was worth every penny he'd had to save for them. I think he meant that, but he was lying about everything else.

Frank was dealing dope. LSD and marijuana, mostly. Mama learned of Frank's drug problems from Dave Gibbons, a family friend. Dave was single. His wife had up and left him and their three sons. He and Mama shared their parenting struggles. Dave told Mama about Frank's drug problems in the nick of time. The Georgia Bureau of Investigation and local law enforcement officials had been keeping close watch on Columbus's drug traffic for months. In early 1973, they'd arrested over a hundred people. About a third of those people were business associates of Frank's. He was either selling drugs to them or buying drugs from them. The GBI didn't have enough evidence to arrest Frank yet, but Mama knew that if he continued his wayward ways, they'd catch him soon.

Mama cried. It was the first time I'd seen her weep since Daddy died. I was furious at Frank for upsetting her so much. She didn't know what to do. Although she was a nurse, she didn't know much about drug addiction. She was scared she was going to lose her only son. So she figured out a way to save him.

Mama never discussed any of this with Linda and me. We didn't know Frank was dealing drugs. We didn't even know what that meant. I just told my friends at Rose Hill that Frank was in a lot of trouble. Mama was upset. And they both needed Jesus. The Monday-night prayer group kept Frank's name at the top of their list. To his credit, Charlie Wells tried to come alongside Frank. He would call him, invite him to join in all our activities at church. But honestly, to my knowledge nobody at Rose Hill had ever dealt with drug addictions before, so they had no idea how to help.

One night Frank stumbled into the house about 1:00 A.M. I found him in the bathroom bent over the toilet, throwing up, hollering, and holding his head with both hands.

"What's the matter?" I asked. I'd never seen him so sick.

"I don't know!" he cried. "My head hurts so bad. *Oh God!*"

Frightened, I returned to my room and woke up Linda. Mama was at work. "Frank's sick," I said. "He said his head hurts really bad."

"You'd better call Mama," she said.

We rarely called Mama at work. We knew she was tending to really ill people and didn't have time to chitchat. "I don't know," I said. "Maybe he's just been out drinking or something. I don't know what to do."

Frank continued to yelp. He was pleading with God to make his head stop hurting.

"I think you better call Mama," Linda said again.

I picked up the receiver of our white princess-style phone and dialed the number to the Medical Center.

"Nursing supervisor, please," I said to the operator.

Mama answered.

"Something's the matter with Frank, ma'am," I said.

"What do you mean?" Mama asked. I could hear worry in her voice.

"I don't know, exactly," I replied. "He got home about a half hour ago. He's been in the bathroom throwing up. He keeps screaming that his head hurts really bad."

"Well, hang up and call an ambulance," Mama said. "Right now."

A crew of emergency personnel arrived at our door within fifteen minutes. I let them in and led them to the bathroom. They began to work over Frank, while Linda and I hovered about in the hallway. They took his blood pressure. Checked his eyeballs. Strapped him to a stretcher and went out into the black night with sirens silent but lights flashing. I called Mama back. "He's on his way to the emergency room," I said.

"Okay."

When I woke the next morning, Mama was in the bathroom, sitting on the toilet, smoking a cigarette. Her nervous stomach was upset again.

"The doctors think your brother has an aneurysm," she said.

"What's that?" I asked. I stood at the sink brushing my teeth.

"A blood-vessel problem. It could burst. They have him in ICU. They're watching him."

"What happens if it bursts?" I asked. I spat into the sink.

Mama dropped the cigarette butt between her legs into the toilet. "I don't know," she said. She was lying. Mama didn't want to tell me Frank could die. "Gawd, my stomach hurts this morning."

"You want me to stay home?" I asked.

"No, go on to school," she replied. "He can't have visitors. I'm going to try and get some sleep and then go back up there later."

"Okay."

Linda and I both prayed for Frank that day. We weren't sure that he didn't cause this aneurysm thing himself. We just didn't know what to think.

Frank spent nearly a week in ICU. Then the doctors sent him home. He slept for another couple of days in his darkened room, but he didn't put on any of his Black Sabbath records.

Mama had him pack his bags as soon as he felt well enough to eat. "You've got a few choices," she said. "Either go to Oregon and live with Uncle Charlie, or join the Army. If you don't do one of those two things, I'm calling the police and turning you in for dealing drugs to the neighborhood kids."

Mama had been doing some spying on her own. Before Frank got the headache from hell, she'd seen him hanging with kids from Arnold Junior High. She figured rightly that he was hustling drugs.

I didn't know much about Mama's brother Charlie, other than he didn't have any sons of his own, so I figured he'd be pretty strict. Like Lewis Jones, probably. I might have chosen the Army or jail if I'd been Frank, but he chose Oregon.

In late March 1973 Mama put Frank on a plane headed to Portland. He'd been home less than a year. He had a drug addiction and an unstable blood vessel that could burst and kill him at any minute. Even Mama was beginning to think life couldn't get any crazier for us. But sure enough, it did. And this time I was the one stirring the pot.

virginity's burden

ALMOST FROM THE VERY FIRST MOMENTS THAT FRANK STEPPED FOOT IN OREGON, MAMA BEGAN TO TALK about moving west. She had all sorts of reasons for wanting to go—more job opportunities, better pay, she'd be closer to her brothers Charlie and Roy. "I hear it's beautiful there," Mama said. "They've got real mountains, and the ocean's only an hour from Portland."

But I wasn't buying it. "I'm not going anywhere," I said. "I've been to umpteen elementary schools, three different junior highs. I don't care what you do, but I'm not going anywhere. I'm staying here until I graduate from Columbus High."

Mama and I must've had this same argument a hundred times between the spring of my junior year and the summer leading into my senior year. She wanted out of Columbus. It had too many hard memories for her. But Columbus was home for me. It held good memories. I had a church family that treated me like I was their own daughter. I had good friends whose parents watched over me. I wasn't a great student, but I had people like Marjorie Sewell, my English teacher, who treated me as if I was as capable and intelligent as anyone else. Reading had always been one of my favorite pastimes, so I took an immediate liking to Mrs. Sewell. She taught English lit with the same passion that Miss Virginia Harwood brought to my world history lessons. In their classrooms, Edgar Allan Poe and King

Henry VIII loomed as larger and more important characters than President Nixon and John Dean.

Like church, school had become a refuge for me, a place where I could forget about the chaos of my life and focus on something or somebody else.

Once a week Lynn, Karen, and I attended the school's morning prayer group. The meetings were usually led by Sammy Ellis, a classmate and a preacher's kid. I met Sammy one spring afternoon when I was a freshman. We were both going home early. He had a dentist appointment, and I wasn't feeling well. We were waiting on the school steps for our parents to pick us up. Sammy began the conversation with a lighthearted "Hi, I'm Sammy." But it seems to me his very next words were "Do you know Jesus?"

It took him less than five minutes to find out my entire spiritual background. Because he was so engaging and pretty cute, I wasn't offended by the interrogation. I thought he was sweet to be concerned about me.

Sammy and I became good friends over the next couple of years. We didn't have the sort of relationship that comes so easily to boys and girls today. Good girls weren't supposed to call boys at home. And it would never have occurred to me to confide any of my personal life to Sammy or any other boy. I didn't even confide much about my personal life to Lynn or Karen, my two closest friends. They usually knew when Mama and I were fighting, but they rarely knew what we were fighting about. I wasn't even sure myself sometimes.

Looking back, I realize what a confusing time it was for Mama and me. We didn't seem to have any common ground from which to form a relationship. It was during this time that Mama hurled burning words at me, accusing me of wishing she had died instead of Daddy. She never understood how truly terrified I was of losing her.

For the most part, Mama had quit partying. She went out with her girlfriends occasionally, but that wasn't a regular part of her routine anymore. Sometimes she took pills to help her sleep or get through the day. She wasn't using drugs recreationally, the way my brother had, but she was self-medicating her pain as best she could.

Her moods seemed to be more pronounced to me than in the past. She was quick to anger and often impatient. Mama isn't a cross person by nature; she usually isn't high-strung. But she was during this period of her life. Everything I did seemed to agitate her, and I pretty much felt the same way about her.

My world caved in one night when Charlie and Gail Wells announced that they were moving to Memphis. Charlie had grown weary of his battles at Rose Hill. They were expecting their first child. They would be gone before summer's end.

Hot tears rolled like a flash flood and heavy sobs racked my body. Karen and I were on the phone, trying to figure out what church would be like without Charlie and Gail. Neither of us could stop crying. I hung up when I saw the headlights of Mama's car in the driveway. I was lying across my bed, still crying, when she and her friend Betty walked in. "What's the matter with you?" Mama snapped as she flipped on the overhead light in my room.

Sucking back yet another sob, I said, "Charlie and Gail are leaving Rose Hill."

"*Oh God!*" Mama replied. "The way you're carrying on I thought somebody had died."

"Mercy, Karen," Betty chimed in, "there's no need for all this crying."

"You don't understand!" I cried out.

"You're right, I don't," Mama said matter-of-factly. "People move on, Karen. Get used to it."

I cried harder that night than I had since Daddy died. In many ways, Charlie represented a father figure to me. I think he understood that role and took it seriously. He was never too busy to take a phone call from me and never too weary to listen to the struggles I was having, even though he had forty other kids with other problems to deal with. He never said a discouraging word to me regarding my family.

He once told me that he didn't know how to help Frank because he'd never known anybody with such a severe drug problem. But instead of despairing over it, Charlie just bowed his head and prayed for me, for Frank, for Mama and Linda, one more time.

Sometimes Charlie's humor was biting. Like the time he told me I had on so much green eye shadow it looked like mold was growing around my eyes. Or when he asked me for the pattern number for a new dress a friend had made me. The dress was smocked at the bodice. "That's a perfect maternity dress," he said.

I'd been self-conscious about my size since my art teacher, Mr. Dozier, informed me I was built more like a defensive lineman than a girl. But Charlie was such a funny guy, it was easy to dismiss his remarks as just more of his silly humor.

I didn't realize it then, but Charlie and Gail's leaving marked an irrevocable shift in my own life. It was like a small earthquake that caused fissures deep below the earth's surface. All I could see was the brokenness of my life. Nothing made any sense to me any longer.

I had never really resolved my anger at God, my anger at Daddy and Mama, or even my anger toward Frank. Charlie and Gail's leaving made me feel utterly abandoned. Despite all my efforts to be a good kid, to make others happy, the investment wasn't paying off. No matter how hard I tried, people still found reasons to leave me. By the time August rolled around, I was in a fit of despair.

I'd quit going to church so much. Several of my good friends from church were headed off to college. Lynn Wilkes went to Berry College near Rome, Georgia. Steve Smith and Sherri Davis were across the river at Auburn. The Burke boys, Jimmy and Jerry, were attending Columbus College, as was Andy Kelley. Patsy Ward was working a full-time job.

I started spending more and more time hanging out at my old haunt—the Crystal Valley trailer park—with Wes Skibbey. Wes's sister, Angie, was a student at Hardaway, where my good friend Beth McCombs also went. Wes was confined to parochial school at Pacelli

High, because that was Pauline Skibbey's solution to dealing with her son's waywardness.

Wes and I had nothing in common, except for absent fathers and hardworking mothers. Even more troubling, Wes was a pothead. He usually had a joint or beer in one hand and a cigarette in the other. I didn't smoke pot, ever. Not once. And because of those foul experiences with both Uncle Joe and Mama, I hated the stench of alcohol. I hadn't smoked a cigarette since trying my first and only one in seventh grade.

Yet I was still physically and emotionally drawn to Wes. He was a handsome boy. He'd cut his eyes at a person rather than turn his head and look straight at you, and his smile crept up slowly whenever he thought something was funny. Since he smoked so much pot, Wes thought everything was funny.

Although he attended parochial school, Wes didn't go to church and had no use for God. Most of my friends couldn't figure out what a nice girl like me was doing with a fellow like him. I didn't ever talk about him with Karen or Lynn. I knew that they would never approve.

Discontent is what led me back to my trailer park buddies. I was miserable after Frank and Charlie Wells moved on. I was often lonely and depressed. Trading one obsession for another, Mama became a workaholic. She left Linda and me to ourselves much of the time. For six weeks that year, she was off in Saint Petersburg, Florida, taking a class on cardiac care at the Rogers Heart Foundation. Her friend Betty checked on us while Mama was away, but otherwise, there was no one providing any supervision or care for us. I grew increasingly bitter toward Mama.

In August, after a particularly heated screaming match, I threw myself across my bed and railed against God and the situation he had put me in: "I have tried so hard to do everything right, but nothing I do seems to matter!" I cried. "Frank is gone. Charlie is gone. All my school friends are leaving me. I'm just sick of trying to be a good girl. I'm not even sure you pay attention to me anyway, God. I wish Daddy had never died. And I want you to go away and leave me alone. *Just leave me alone and let me live my life the way I want!"*

There. I'd dared to say what I really felt. My sobs subsided and I went quiet and listened. I was half expecting lightning to crackle or thunder to roar. Nothing happened. At least not outwardly. But inside I felt a sense of calm. Resignation, perhaps? Empowerment? I got up and washed my face, determined that from that moment on I would live my life to please me. Not Mama. Not Frank. Not Charlie Wells. Not all my friends. I was going to do whatever it was that made me happy.

The first thing I did was to get in my baby blue Dodge and head out to the trailer court to see Wes again. Mama had bought the push-button Dodge to replace the Simca Frank destroyed. It's hard to strip the gears of a push-button car. By November our relationship turned a corner—from friends to lovers. I'd never had a steady boyfriend before, a source of much consternation for me. Mama had more boyfriends than I did. Even Linda at age thirteen did. I desperately sought the affirmation of a male in my life. In the past, I'd turned to my brother or Delmer Floyd, Charlie Wells or Pastor Smitty, for assurance. But as my own sexuality surfaced, their reassurances were no longer good enough. I wanted a romance. Of course what Wes wanted was sex. I was naïve enough to think I was the first girl he cared about, and he was savvy enough to let me think that.

Wes and I never really dated. In other words, it wasn't a matter of going places together. Most often he would come to my house while Mama was at work, or I would meet him at his place. By then his mother had moved across the river to a small trailer court outside Phenix City. But more often than not, Wes could be found at Crystal Valley hanging out with his pothead buddies.

Wes made his first serious attempt to relieve me of virginity's burden in a darkened cul-de-sac of a subdivision that was being constructed near Crystal Valley. Up until then, our serious petting had amounted to extended periods of French kissing, a couple of hickeys, and his constant effort to fondle my breasts. For me, these sessions were always more like wrestling matches than anything else. I was always trying to stay one move ahead of Wes. By this time, I was almost seventeen and had been playing make-out games since I was eleven. I thought I was experienced enough to keep Wes interested and my virginity intact.

I was wrong.

We were sprawled across the front seat of my Dodge, and it was pitch-black out. Since it was a new development, there were no streetlights up yet. Tall pine trees provided a blanket of thick shadows. The condensation on the car windows added another screen to the outside.

Or so I thought.

Suddenly, a football-stadium-sized spotlight flashed through the windshield near the driver's door. Wes's white butt lit up the night like a harvest moon. He grabbed for his pants, which where somewhere between his knees and his ankles. My jeans weren't yet below my knees, but they were below my hips. I yanked them back up.

Two police officers—one a rookie, one a gray-haired veteran—stood knocking at the driver's door. The older fellow moved his flashlight over to peer into Wes's face. By that time Wes had managed to get his pants pulled up, although his belt remained unbuckled and his pants were still unzipped. He rolled down the window and greeted the officers.

"Can I see your license, please?" the old cop ordered. Wes's wallet was on the dashboard. He reached for it and handed over his license.

"And yours, young lady?" the cop said, pointing the light into my face.

"I don't have my license with me," I lied.

The rookie cop was smirking. But I wasn't the least bit amused. That light was jarring. I was afraid they were going to arrest us. How was I going to explain *all this* to Mama?

"What's your name?" the wizened cop asked.

"Leslie Johnson," I said, combining two things from my past—a friend's name and the street I used to live on.

Wes whipped his head around and stared at me like I was plumb crazy. I could tell he was upset with me for lying to the cops. I didn't care. I was more afraid of Mama than I was a squadron of Columbus police officers. My nickname for Mama was "Dragon Lady" because, as I told my girlfriends: "Mama can spit fire."

The older cop handed Wes's license back to him. Then, keeping to his oath to honor and serve the public and to lecture all scantily clad people under twenty-one, he gave Wes and me a scolding not unlike the one I had gotten from the drugstore owner when I stole that box of eye shadow. He finished his tongue lashing by ordering Wes to take me straight home.

I was crying by the time I walked into the house. Only Linda was there. "What's the matter?" she asked.

"Nothing," I mumbled, avoiding her gaze.

"Well then, why are you crying?" she pressed.

"Wes and I had a fight."

Linda rolled her eyes, let out a big sigh, and returned to the math book propped open in her lap. She didn't like Wes, and she especially didn't like me hanging out with him. Linda was going to church more than me now. Patsy had taken Linda under her wing shortly after I started bringing Linda to church with me. Just being in my sister's presence made me feel guilty. I was too ashamed of myself to be much of a sister to Linda, but nothing, not even guilt, deterred me from a path of self-destruction.

Sometime later that week, while I was still a virgin, I prayed another prayer. "I'm going to get pregnant," I said.

It wasn't a prayer as much as it was a statement of my intentions. My reasoning was convoluted. I figured if I got pregnant, Wes would marry me, and then I would finally have two people who would love me unconditionally—Wes and my baby. Our own little family.

I didn't think about the fact that Wes was only a junior in high school and likely a poor candidate for fatherhood, given his taste for marijuana and beer. I refused to dwell on the fact that he wasn't a Christian and that we had absolutely nothing in common, other than our fatherless childhoods. I tried unsuccessfully to ignore the mounting guilt I felt about my own sorry choices. The guiltier I felt, the angrier I got; the angrier I got, the more determined I was to do things my way. And God, being who He is, let me.

My girlfriend Beth had no idea how heated up things were between Wes and me. But she was always willing to hang with me, to go with me whenever and wherever I went. I picked Beth up at Hardaway High School almost every afternoon in the Dodge we called Old Blue. Sometimes we would hang out at her house, but that afternoon I wanted to go out to Crystal Valley and see if we could find Wes and his buddy Tom. Tom was a scrawny, dark-headed kid. Beth tagged him as "Bag of Bones." She didn't feel any attraction to him, but he felt plenty for her. Beth was generously endowed with a figure as voluptuous as any of those Grecian goddesses depicted on that shower curtain hanging in our bathroom.

I headed east on Manchester Expressway, avoiding the afternoon bus traffic on Macon Road. We were well past the grassy knoll where Kadie, a monstrous-sized cow sculpture, kept watch over Kinnett Dairies and the acreage where the Peachtree Mall would later be constructed, when Beth spotted Wes's Volkswagen Beetle headed west. Tom was with him.

"Hey! There they go!" Beth shouted as the boys whizzed on by us in the opposite direction.

"Hold on!" I yelled back, and applied my foot to the brakes. Then, making sure no one was behind me in either lane, I gave the steering wheel a sharp turn to the left. The car left the expressway at way too fast a speed and jolted to a hard stop. Beth and I were tossed forward, then backward. "You okay?" I asked.

"Yeah," she said, laughing.

Old Blue was resting on her nose. I'd run her aground in the grassy median. Beth and I got out of the car to inspect the damage. We were both laughing, more from nervousness than anything funny. The car had so many dents in it already, it was hard to tell if this would leave a noticeable abrasion or not. Traffic whipped by us on both sides.

I got into the car and tried to back it out. But the front wheels had dug into the ground, and the rear wheels weren't touching Mother Earth.

"What are we going to do?" Beth asked.

"I don't know," I said. "Let's trying pushing it."

I put the car in neutral. Beth took one corner and I took the other. We might as well have tried moving Kadie the Kinnett cow, whose hooves were encased in cement. Old Blue didn't budge.

A car pulled off the expressway. "Y'all girls all right?" a silver-haired woman wearing bauble jewelry called out to us.

"Yes, ma'am!" Beth called back. "We're fine. Thanks, anyway."

"Well, if you're sure," she said, without getting out of her car. "I'm going to call the police for you." She rolled her window up and drove off.

"The police!" Beth said, panicked.

Every cop in town knew Beth's mama, Rufe McCombs, the Legal Aid attorney. We both knew that if her mama found out about this little escapade, she'd skin us alive.

Another car pulled over. A muscular man wearing a short-sleeve shirt and dress pants approached us. "Y'all okay?" he asked.

"Yes, sir," I replied.

"What happened?" he asked.

"I swerved to miss a dog that ran out in front of me," I lied.

"A dog?" He looked at me suspiciously.

"Yes, sir," Beth interjected.

"Where's the dog?" the fellow asked.

"Done run off, sir," I replied. "It wasn't hurt though."

Beth could barely contain her giggles.

Another car pulled off the roadway. In those days, people thought nothing of stopping to help stranded motorists.

A fellow even bigger and buffer than the first one approached us. The two men conferred as Beth and I tried to figure out how we were going to get out of this mess. The men decided they would push Old Blue out for us. In less than ten minutes, they had backed her up and righted her nose. Old Blue didn't appear to be any worse for the wear.

"Oh, thank y'all so much," I gushed, glad for the help.

"Yes, sirs," Beth said. "Thank you so much. We sure appreciate it. Some lady had stopped and said she was going to call the pigs for us, but we could've been here hours waiting."

The first of the fellows turned and stared at us. "No problem," he said. "I'm a pig. This just happens to be my day off."

In the 1970s, *pig* was the degrading slang term used for cops. Beth was mortified that she'd just called this police officer a pig to his face. Her jaw dropped, and her brown eyes grew dark with anxiety. If he'd known that she was Rufe McCombs's daughter talking so disrespectfully to him, it would have been all over the downtown precinct by midnight.

Beth and I drove back to my house. Wes and Tom had been there, Linda said. They'd waited around for us about fifteen minutes, then left. I took Beth home. I knew Wes would likely be back later.

He was.

And nearly every night thereafter, right up until the moment I had to see a doctor about a pregnancy exam. After that, Wes wasn't around much.

I didn't get pregnant on November 12, my seventeenth birthday, even though Wes and I did the big nasty for the first time ever. It happened after a couple of more intimate encounters.

All the telltale signs were there. Puking, puking, and more puking. My morning sickness extended through most of my waking hours.

Mama would get home from her graveyard shift sometime after I left for school, and a few mornings I was so sick, I couldn't get out the door before she got home. She never quizzed me about why I was throwing up. But after a few weeks of constant nausea, I left school early, went home, and woke up my slumbering mama.

She reached for her glasses as I sat on the edge of her bed. "What's wrong?" she asked.

"I've been sick a lot lately," I said.

"What kind of sick?" Mama asked.

"I've been throwing up a lot."

"Are you pregnant?"

"I don't know, ma'am," I said. "But I might be."

I knew Mama wouldn't yell at me. She never had been one to raise her voice much. It was her quiet disapproval that I dreaded more than anything. Frank had given her grief for years. Now here I was, the daughter she once called her guardian angel, sullied by the sperm of a boy she barely knew.

Mama tapped a cigarette from a pack and lit it. With her elbows resting on her knees, she took a long drag.

"I'm sorry, Mama," I said. Tears of sorrow tumbled down my cheeks. I was overcome by the shame of a child who has disappointed a parent.

"What are you going to do?" she said.

"I don't know," I answered.

"You need to see a doctor," she said. "I'll get you an appointment."

"Yes, ma'am," I replied.

She did not reach out to embrace me. While I really wanted her to hug me at that moment, I appreciated that Mama didn't offer me trite reassurances, such as "Don't worry, everything will turn out okay." She knew better than that. And so did I.

january 1974

MAMA MADE THE DOCTOR'S APPOINTMENT, BUT SHE DIDN'T GO WITH ME. I WENT ALONE, BUT WES found out where I was and showed up while I was waiting in the reception room.

"What are you doin' here?" I asked.

"I wanted to see how the test goes," he said.

"Go home," I said. "Leave me alone."

"Nah, you don't need to be alone," he replied, giving me one of those slow grins.

I don't remember much about the exam, other than that the soft-spoken doctor confirmed that yes, I was pregnant.

Wes and I drove out to Flat Rock Park in his car and talked. "What are you going to do?" he asked.

"I dunno," I said.

"Well, you can't keep the baby," he said.

"Why not?" I asked.

"How are you going to take care of it?" he asked. This was Wes's subtle way of telling me not to count on him for any help. "Maybe you ought to have an abortion," he said.

"What?" I asked, stunned by his suggestion.

We rode around the park in silence for a long time afterward. We passed the picnic area where I had first learned of the locusts and the coming holocaust predicted in the Book of Revelation. A couple of those Grace Baptist Bible-study sessions had been held here at Flat Rock. Those studies had frightened me so badly I couldn't sleep for months afterward. Back then I was too afraid of God to ever defy Him. Now look at me.

We passed the swimming hole where our Rose Hill Baptist youth group had often gathered on hot summer days. We had bruised our thighs and elbows slipping over those slimy black rocks, and gone home sunburnt and dog tired but with laughter still ringing in our ears. What were my friends going to think of me now? I didn't think I would ever be able to look Pastor Smitty and Betty in the eyes again. Or Patsy Ward. Maybe, I thought, I will just never, ever go back to church.

Wes lit a cigarette.

I told him I didn't want him coming around the house anymore. That I didn't want to see him at all. I didn't cry or yell. I just said it matter-of-factly. He didn't argue with me. He just took me home and dropped me off.

Lynn Wilkes was the first friend I told. She was home from college for the weekend. I drove out to her house and found her in her bedroom, books propped open, reading, as usual. Lynn graduated from Columbus High with highest honors. I knew she'd probably do the same at Berry College.

Lynn was pre-engaged to Jimmy Burke by that time—the 1970s version of getting pinned. The promise ring Jimmy gave her meant they would eventually marry when they had both finished school and gotten their careers on track. Lynn was majoring in home economics, and Jimmy was attending Columbus College and thinking of heading to seminary one day.

Lynn and I had never discussed sex, under any situation. She knew nothing about the kind of home I had grown up in, and she certainly knew nothing of my sexual exploits. She barely knew who Wesley was. But I went to Lynn for one reason only—she was the most spiritual woman I knew; besides, she loved me unconditionally. I knew that even if Lynn was disappointed in me, she would never say so. I could trust her to be a friend to me, no matter what.

We were sitting on the twin bed in her tidy room when I just blurted it out. "I'm pregnant, Lynn."

I'm sure it was the last thing she ever expected me to say. But she responded as if I had just told her that a rainstorm was headed our way. She studied me for a moment and then, very calmly, said, "I don't even know what to say."

"Me neither," I replied.

I told the whole story. About how alone I had been feeling without Frank or Charlie Wells around. How it seemed nothing I ever did turned out right. How I prayed and asked God to just get out of my life and leave me alone. And how easily God had complied with that rebellious prayer.

We both mulled over my situation. Lynn encouraged me to go to Pastor Smitty and ask for his help. I promised her I would. She told me she wished she could offer me better advice. I told her not to worry; I just needed someone to listen to me. I couldn't bring myself to tell Patsy what a mess I'd gotten myself into. I don't think I ever did tell her. But I did make that appointment with Pastor Smitty as I had promised Lynn I would.

Meanwhile, Mama had come home one afternoon and announced two things—first, she thought I should have an abortion; second, she wanted me to go on birth control pills immediately afterward.

Abortions were uncommon in 1974, particularly in Georgia. I didn't even know exactly what an abortion was, or how it was performed. I just knew you went to sleep pregnant and woke up unpregnant.

I told Mama that under no circumstances would I have an abortion. Furthermore, I didn't need any birth control pills because I'd given Wes the boot. I didn't intend to see him anymore, ever.

Mama scoffed at me. "Yeah, right," she said, turning on her heels and walking out of the room.

Linda and I never ever discussed my pregnancy. She was ashamed of me, and I knew it. What more was there to talk about? She spent more time with Patsy and at church. I spent more time alone.

Once when Wes did show up at the house, I hid in the den closet. Linda told him I wasn't there. He didn't believe her, so he came into the house and said he'd wait for me to show up. I spent nearly forty-five minutes in that closet waiting for him to leave. Linda didn't have any idea how to get rid of him, but she kept telling him every ten minutes that I was with a friend and wouldn't be home for a very long time. Eventually he left, and she rescued me from the darkness.

It was while I was stuffed in between the coats and old baseball bats that I determined Mama was probably right, I should have an abortion. Wes wasn't fit to be a parent, and I couldn't raise a child without a daddy around. That was too hard. Besides, I was too embarrassed to go through the rest of my senior year pregnant. All of a sudden I had a burning desire to go to college—something I'd never even really thought about before.

Problem was, by the time I'd decided this was likely the best course of action to take, Mama had changed her mind.

Seems she and Frank had been discussing the situation during their weekly phone calls. Frank urged Mama not to give me permission to have an abortion. It's murder, he declared. He told Mama she should raise the baby, or I should give it up for adoption.

Frank had been in Oregon less than a month when he met up with some fellows from Multnomah School of the Bible. They invited him to church on Easter Sunday of 1973, and he went. Soon, he was going to Bible study as well. Frank's battle with drugs was far from over, but finally he was turning to God for help. And he was trying to become a person who would make Mama and Daddy proud. But I was too caught up in my own rebellion to be thankful for the changes that were taking place in Frank's life. I was furious with my brother when I found out he was opposed to the abortion.

"There is no way I am going to let you raise a baby of mine!"

I screamed at Mama when she told me she didn't think I ought to have an abortion after all.

"You're just too ashamed to go through your senior year pregnant," Mama said.

"Maybe so!" I replied. "But you were never around when I was growing up, why would I give you a baby to raise?"

"It's wrong!" Mama said, reiterating that she didn't want me to have an abortion.

"Says who?" I implored. "My brother? Is that who is telling you all this? Mr. Sanctimonious himself? He goes to Oregon and finds Jesus and now he thinks he has a right to tell me how to run my life?"

"I could refuse to sign the paperwork, you know," Mama said. She turned and walked out of the room. Mama hated arguing of any sort.

Frank called me on a Sunday afternoon. It was the first time we'd spoken in months. His voice was gentle but firm. "Karen, don't do this," he urged. "I've been studying up on this in my Bible group. Abortion is murder. Have the baby, give it up for adoption. Let Mama raise it, but don't do this, please."

I was touched by his concern but angered by his interference. "Isn't it funny that you are now giving me advice when for so many years you did nothing but cause grief for all of us around here?" I asked. My words were intended to burn him. It worked.

"I know, I know," he said. "But don't mess up your life just because I screwed up everything in mine."

Frank tried to explain to me why abortions were wrong and why I ought to reconsider. He quoted numerous Scripture verses on the value of life. I heard him, but I didn't listen. He had long since lost the right to be my advisor. It had been years since I'd admired him or valued his opinions. It would be another decade before I would do so again.

I knew Mama could stop me from having an abortion by refusing to sign for it. But I also knew she wouldn't do that. She always subscribed to the theory that once a person makes up her mind, there is little anyone can do to dissuade her. Mama hadn't really had a handle on parenting any of us for quite some time. Our relationship, in particular, had always been a tumultuous one. Our personalities frequently clashed. I was emotive and backtalked her all the time. Mama didn't much care for emotions. They complicated life. And she rarely, if ever, expressed her emotions in words.

She once pitched a can of beans at my head in a fit of anger. It was her way of telling me to shut up. I ducked and the can crashed clean through the wall behind me. That scared us both so bad neither of us said a word for a minute or two. Then we both burst out laughing. I think that was the closest I've come to being decapitated, thus far. As far as I know, those beans are still in the walls of that house on Fifty-second Street. Mama just plastered over the hole without ever retrieving the can.

I didn't really value Frank's or Mama's opinion one way or another about the pregnancy. Still, I did have enough sense to realize that I had to patch things up with God as quickly as possible. I was obviously a failure at handling things by myself. I grabbed my Bible after school one afternoon and drove over to Rose Hill Baptist for a meeting with Pastor Smitty.

His office was located on the second floor of the building, down the hall and around the corner from the primary and nursery classrooms. His door was open, but I knocked on it anyway. Smitty had a pen in hand and was studying a book.

"Karen, come in, come in," he said. He rose from his chair and gave me a big grin. Smitty was a handsome man when he smiled, which he did almost all the time. A bomber pilot during World War II, he possessed that natural athletic look. His brown hair was graying but still as thick as it was when he was twenty. He had broad shoulders and a trim waist. Had he lived, I imagine my own father might look like Smitty, only Daddy would surely have had less hair. It was already beginning to recede when he was killed. "Have a seat,"

Smitty said, waving to the leather armchair facing his desk. Books filled the shelves behind him.

"Thank you, Pastor," I said. My hands were sweating and my face was flushed. I gripped the Bible in my left hand and offered him my right one. Smitty shook it. I had never been in his office before, for any reason. It was more daunting to me than the principal's office. Smitty, after all, was a man of God.

Other than Charlie Wells, I'd never really talked to grown men about things of a personal nature. And that didn't count, because Charlie was more of a pal than an authority figure. But Smitty was definitely in a powerful position, appointed by Almighty God Himself. My heart was beating so hard I could hear it in my ears. "I'm glad you called," he began.

"Well, I don't know, but I imagine you might have heard some rumors, sir," I said.

"As pastor, I'm always hearing things, Karen," he said reassuringly. "But I don't pay much attention to rumors. Why don't you tell me what's on your heart?"

That invitation was all I needed. For the next half hour I told Smitty everything. About my feelings of frustration, anger, and abandonment. I told him about my awful prayer, telling God where to get off. And then about how I'd barreled headstrong into this relationship with Wesley Skibbey, fully intent on getting pregnant so I could finally have the affection and love I sought. And about how, too late, I came to realize what poor choices I had made and, ohmygosh, what was I going to do now? I didn't think Mama capable of raising a baby. Besides, I knew what it was like to grow up without a father, and I didn't want any child of mine to grow up like that.

I told him about Frank's phone call and his admonishment to not have an abortion because it was murder in God's eyes. And about how angry it made me that my brother dared to make such a phone call after all his foolishness over the years.

I told Smitty all this in an urgent and intense manner, the way a bystander tells a cop about the horrific wreck he's just witnessed. My confession was punctuated by sobs of shame. Smitty reached over his desk and handed me a box of tissues. He leaned back in his chair, his hands crossed in thoughtful reflection. I knew he was searching and praying for the right words to bring me both comfort and wisdom. I was praying for the same thing. He let me cry in silence for a while before speaking.

"Karen, it's a terrible situation for you to be in," he said. His tone was soft. Smitty never spoke with a tone of condemnation. Even when he preached, he wasn't preachy. He was a teacher at heart, imparting life's lessons as best he knew them. "What does your mama think?"

"She was the first one to suggest I have an abortion, sir," I replied. "But then, I think it was after she talked with Frank, she changed her mind. She's decided she wants to keep the baby and raise it herself. But I could never let her do that."

"You could always adopt the baby out," Smitty said.

"Yes, sir, I thought of that. But I've decided I really want to go to college. And I have five more months to go until graduation. I'd have to go away somewhere."

Nobody went to school pregnant at Columbus High in 1974. At least not visibly so. There were no school programs for pregnant teens. Girls who got pregnant always disappeared for six months or better.

Smitty considered the situation before advising me further.

Uncomfortable with the silence hanging between us, I blurted out, "I just don't know what's the right thing to do."

"Well, Karen," Smitty said thoughtfully, "in situations like these, I'm not sure there is a right thing to do. You've made a terrible mistake. When we invite sin into our lives, we are left with the consequences of our choices. The question before you is what's the best thing you can do now that the wrong choice has been made. You have a list of consequences to choose from. I can't tell you which one to pick. That's a decision that you will have to make. But I know whatever you decide, your church family is here for you. We care a great deal for you. We want to help in any way we can."

I didn't question for one moment Pastor Smitty's concern for me. I knew he cared immensely about all people.

MAMA WROTE A NOTE for a preexcused absence that I had to take around to all my teachers at Columbus High. She could've written a note that said I was going out of town for a few days because somebody in the family had died unexpectedly. She could've told them I was going to be visiting college campuses. But Mama's note said I was going into the hospital to have a D&C. A couple of my teachers looked at me quizzically after reading it.

"Everything okay?" Mr. Dietrich, my music teacher, asked. He often held Bible and prayer-group sessions in his classroom before school. He'd been my teacher for all four years at Columbus High. I missed several of his classes during December because he was my first class of the day and about that time I was usually holding sessions with the porcelain throne.

"Yes, sir," I said. "Everything's fine. I'm just having some female trouble, that's all."

He signed his name to the note and told me not to worry about missing class.

Marjorie Sewell was the next teacher to express concern. She read the note and studied it for a moment or two before looking at me. "You're going into the hospital?" she asked.

"Yes, ma'am," I replied. I was praying that she wouldn't ask me why. I didn't think I could lie to her.

She pressed her hand over the note, ironing it out. Three or four other kids crowded around us. She signed her name.

"Karen," she said.

"Yes, ma'am?"

"I hope everything turns out. If you need anything . . ." Her voice trailed off but her eyes were locked on mine.

"I'm fine, ma'am. Really, I'm fine." I could feel blood rush to my neck and cheeks as I grabbed the note, folded it up, and stuffed it into a book. Kids poured into the room as the late bell rang. I sat down and avoided all further eye contact with my teacher. I was afraid she knew the truth, and that shamed me.

I was admitted to the maternity ward of Columbus Medical Center on January 29, 1974. My roommate was a black woman who was older than Mama. She already had a litter of kids and didn't want no more, she told me. Mama had stayed only long enough to sign the paperwork and make sure I was situated. She said she'd stop by during her shift that night and check on me.

I unpacked the overnight bag she'd given me for Christmas. Then I sat down on the edge of the bed and continued reading Richard Llewellyn's classic, *How Green Was My Valley*. I needed to finish reading it so I could write a book report. It seemed fitting to be reading a book about how gossip destroyed a minister's career.

Pastor Smitty had asked me how I was going to deal with all the gossip that would surely circulate among the youth group at Rose Hill.

"I'm not going to worry about it," I said. "The friends who really love me will come and talk to me about it. The others? Well, they're going to talk about somebody—might as well be me."

I wasn't quite so cheeky when the orderly showed up in the doorway and took me by wheelchair to get a lung X ray. The technician was Debbie Baker, a good friend of Patsy's.

Debbie handed me a hospital gown and told me she needed to take a chest X ray. I never asked why and she didn't say. We acted as if we barely knew each other as she hid behind a glass pane flipping a switch and I was exposed in a gown as thin as cheap toilet paper, knowing that somewhere on my medical file was the word *abortion*. I felt like somebody had stamped a big red *A* across my chest. Debbie flashed me her best smile and thanked me. The orderly waited for me to get dressed before wheeling me back to my room.

Sometime that afternoon the doctor stopped by. Somebody had

told Mama that Dr. Dennis Whitfield was the only doctor in Columbus who performed abortions. *Roe v. Wade* had legalized abortion
only a year before. There weren't big protest groups marching
around holding up placards of bloody fetuses, but there weren't that
many physicians practicing suction abortions either, especially not in
the South, where life is considered a holy sacrament.

But I'd heard that Dr. Whitfield was not a native son. He was
from Montana or Wyoming or some other place out West where hip-
pies lived in communes and had group sex. Dr. Whitfield sure didn't
look like any other doctor I'd ever known. He had reddish blond hair
that hung around the nape of his neck. He walked in that same mo-
seying fashion that stoners used, rather than the clip style of the military doctors at Martin Army. He spoke to me as if I was an adult,
much the same way Pastor Smitty did.

I followed him to an exam room at the end of the hallway and
propped myself up on the end of the exam table while he pulled up
a chair and grabbed a clipboard. "Karen, I want to explain some
things," he said. "Today, I'm going to insert a substance made from
seaweed that will help dilate your cervix." Then, taking the clipboard,
he drew a picture of a tiny hole and then a bigger one. "It shouldn't
hurt or cause you any discomfort. We'll leave that in overnight. You
can't have anything to eat tonight. That's because we're going to give
you anesthesia in the morning, and we don't want you to have an
upset stomach. I will use a tool like this." Dr. Whitfield showed me
a shiny long instrument that looked like an enlarged version of
the thing the dentist used to clean my teeth. "With it I will scrape
out the inside of your uterus. Then we'll use a machine that's sort
of like the hose on a vacuum cleaner to remove any other fetal
tissue. It won't take long. And you won't remember a thing. Any
questions?"

I shook my head no. I didn't have the heart to tell him I understood very little of what he said. The mechanisms of my womanhood

were as foreign to me as Latin verbs. I'd heard them all before, but I just didn't know what they meant. The part that really troubled me was that seaweed substance in my privates. That was just plain nasty.

Wes and his buddy Tom were sitting on my bed when I got back to the room. I could tell they'd been smoking pot. They smelled like field hands who'd come in from the noonday sun, and they were giggling like a couple of preschoolers who'd just discovered Barbie's pointy breasts. I was annoyed as hell. "Get off that bed," I said.

"Hey, whoa!" Wes said. "We stop by to pay our respects, and you're bitching at us." He and Tom jumped up off the bed.

"I don't really want you here," I replied.

"Okay, okay, that's cool," he said, smiling. "I'm just trying to do my fatherly duty." He and Tom laughed. I didn't.

The old woman in the bed next to mine snorted, apparently put out by their behavior, too.

"Listen, go away and don't come up here no more," I said. "Especially don't come up here when you're loaded."

Wes and Tom laughed. Bad boys nailed again. They seemed to relish the thought.

"Hey, we're going," Wes said. "But remember I tried."

"Yeah, sure," I said. "Where would I be without you?"

"Probably someplace else," he said.

"That's for darn sure," I quipped.

I was so mad at Wes I could spit nails. About a week before I went into the hospital, I'd found out that he had told his mother I was going in the hospital for a root canal. She'd asked me about it one day when I called up to his place. "Wesley tells me you've got to go to the hospital for a couple of days," Mrs. Skibbey said.

"He told you that?" I asked. I was surprised he'd mentioned anything at all about it to his mama.

"Yes. He said you're going in for a root canal. But that's not why, is it, Karen?"

"No, ma'am."

"I didn't think so. People don't usually go in the hospital for dental care. What's the matter, honey?"

I didn't know how to answer her. I was furious at Wes for lying to his mama, but I didn't want to be the one to tell her I was pregnant and her son was the sperm donor. So I didn't say anything. "Karen, are you pregnant?" she asked.

"Yes, ma'am."

"I thought so. Are you having an abortion?"

"Yes, ma'am."

"It's the right thing to do," she said. "I had one too, you know."

I couldn't believe what I was hearing. Pauline Skibbey had an abortion?

"When I was a young girl, living in Italy. They weren't legal then. But I found a doctor who did it. This is better. You'll be okay."

Why did everybody keep telling me that? I wasn't at all sure my life would ever be okay again.

"Mrs. Skibbey, please don't tell Wesley I told you," I replied.

"Don't worry. I'm not going to say anything about our visit. You deserve better than my son, Karen. Forget about him. He needs to grow up."

"Yes, ma'am," I said.

When I hung up I realized that in all the years we'd known each other that was the longest conversation Mrs. Skibbey and I had ever had.

Several more visitors dropped in on me, including the new youth pastor at Rose Hill. His visit just made me feel more ashamed. He didn't know what to say and neither did I. Thankfully, he stayed only a few minutes.

Beth McCombs came and brought me some magazines and a Snickers bar. I'd told her about the abortion shortly after I'd discussed it with Lynn. I was shocked when Karen Mendenhall and her mother, Donna, paid me a visit. Karen thought I was in the hospital to have my tonsils removed. She and her mother hadn't a clue why I was really there.

I hadn't told Karen anything about the abortion because her friendship was too valuable to me. I figured if her mama knew the mess I'd gotten myself into, she'd forbid Karen from ever hanging out with me again. Donna Mendenhall was a stern mother. She had a conniption fit when she learned that several of us kids in the youth group had been caught toilet-papering Pastor Smitty's yard. Smitty and Betty didn't seem to care; in fact, they had invited us all in for a cola, after we'd cleaned out the trees, of course. But Donna gave Karen and me such a lecture you would've thought we'd stolen a car or held up a 7-Eleven store.

Karen told me she found out about the abortion later, from Beth. She also told me that her mother was angry to arrive at the hospital and discover that I'd been stuck on the maternity ward. Donna, who'd quickly figured out why I was really in the hospital, worried about the emotional impact that would have on me.

She didn't come bearing flowers or candies, but Donna brought me a treasure that night that has lasted me a lifetime—the gift of grace. Her concern for me was only slightly veiled behind her dark eyes. She didn't mention the word *abortion*. And she didn't scold me for my folly the way she had the night I'd helped trash Pastor Smitty's yard. Instead, she reached out her tiny hand and patted mine. "We love you, Karen," she said.

And I knew that she did. I was never afraid of Donna Mendenhall after that visit. I knew that while her expectations for her daughter— for all us kids—were high, ultimately she wanted only what was best for us. Her wanting that for me made me want it for myself.

Linda didn't come by the hospital. I hadn't expected her to, really. We never talked about the abortion. Not then and not now. I was a big disappointment to my sister. Linda was the lone child that Mama and Daddy really could be proud of. Although the youngest when Daddy died, Linda has handled the loss better than the rest of us.

I suspect that's because she learned from her siblings' mistakes. But maybe it's because she was born with a stronger heart. One that didn't tear so easily. I've always envied her that.

Mama did check on me during the night, but we didn't have much to say to each other. I knew she was wishing I would change my mind. I felt guilty for putting her in a situation where she had to give me her permission to do something she didn't want me to do. But I was still convinced that letting her raise my child was a bad idea. Pastor Smitty was right. There were no easy answers, just a list of wrong choices from which to pick. I'd made my choice, and Mama was forced to agree to it. Seemed like the only thing we had in common anymore was our mutual resentment of each other.

I woke up early Wednesday morning. Surgery was scheduled sometime before noon. I was not allowed to eat or drink anything. I was terribly thirsty. Mama stopped by after her shift ended. I was lying in bed, reading. There was a lot of activity in the hallways as nurses carted hungry, squalling newborns to their mothers. Any other time I'd have been tempted to sneak off and get glimpses of the babies, but not on this day. "How'd you sleep?" Mama asked.

"Fine," I replied.

Mama looked tired. I could barely see her brown eyes behind their heavy lids.

"I'm really thirsty," I said.

"I'm sure you are," Mama said. "But don't drink anything, otherwise that anesthesia will make you sick. Has the doctor been in yet?"

"No, ma'am, not this morning," I said. "I saw him yesterday."

"You sure you want to do this?" Mama asked. "You don't have to, you know."

"Yes, ma'am," I said without pause. "I'm sure." I didn't feel nearly as convinced as I tried to sound, but I wasn't about to let on to Mama that I was having doubts. Whenever I felt like maybe, just maybe I ought to keep the baby, I envisioned the bickering that would surely take place if Mama was raising *my* baby. And if that wasn't enough to persuade me, I thought about what an absolute cad Wesley Skibbey had turned out to be. The last thing I wanted to do was to be tied to him for the rest of my life.

My answer disturbed Mama. She looked away and began shuffling through the side pockets of her uniform for her cigarettes. When she found the cigarettes and the lighter, she took her leave. "I'm going to go on home and try and get some sleep, Karen," she said. "I'll be back later this afternoon. Don't worry. They'll take good care of you."

Mama did not lean over and kiss me on the forehead, and she did not hug me. She simply turned and left.

"See ya later, alligator," I said. Without trying really, Mama had taught me how to take shelter behind my insecurities and just push on through the hard things in life without too much thought. In doing so, she taught me how to shut down emotionally, how to be just like her.

After she left, I went back to reading my book. A technician came in and drew my blood. Shortly before 11 A.M. a nurse came in and gave me my first-ever IV drip, along with a shot that she claimed would help relax me. Then an orderly came and wheeled me on a gurney to the operating room. On the way, we passed a room where I saw a mother cradling her newborn.

The surgery room was freezing.

"Would you like a warm blanket?" a nurse asked.

"Yes," I said. I couldn't believe how cold it was. I felt like I was in a meat-market refrigerator. I wouldn't have been surprised to see slabs of meat, curing and hanging from the ceiling's corners.

Dr. Whitfield came in and sat on a stool as a nurse positioned my feet into stirrups. "Honey, I need you to scoot down just a bit to the edge of the table," the nurse said. I edged my rump to the table's end.

Dr. Whitfield wheeled his seat over so he could look me in the eyes. "We're going to give you something to put you to sleep in just a minute," he said. "You might hear a loud noise. Don't be frightened. This machine is like a vacuum." He pointed to a large, round canister at the foot of the table. "We use it to clean out your uterus. This won't take long. You're going to be just fine."

Too terrified to say anything in response, I simply nodded.

Dr. Whitfield reached up and patted my forearm. "You okay, Karen?"

"Yes, sir," I lied.

The anesthesiologist asked me to lift my head so he could wrap a mask over face.

"How long will it take for me to fall asleep?" I asked.

"Not long," he replied as he slipped the mask over my face. "Start counting to one hundred."

I don't remember anything after twenty-five.

I slept most of the rest of the day. The next day, around noon, Dr. Whitfield released me. He told me to expect bleeding and cramping for the next couple of weeks. He told Mama to call him immediately if I ran a temperature or had any clotting.

We drove home in silence. I stayed out of school the rest of that week. Wesley didn't send flowers or come by the house to check on me, and neither did his mother.

MANY YEARS LATER I felt compelled to tell my brother that I was wrong not to heed his advice. I've never enjoyed admitting that Frank is right about anything, but time had passed, and my attitude about my own abortion changed when I cradled my firstborn and realized what it meant to give life to another.

Frank was bouncing Konnie, the youngest of my four children, on his lap. I laughed as my eight-month-old daughter yanked on his fuzzy beard. Later, as he walked me to my car and helped load Konnie into her car seat, I turned to my brother. "I need to ask your forgiveness for something," I said.

Frank leaned up against the door to my Toyota and crossed his arms over his barrel chest. "I'm listening," he said.

"I'm sorry I had that abortion," I said. "I wish I'd listened to you.

But I was angry with you. I didn't think you had any right to tell me what to do with my life. I was wrong. You were right."

"I made mistakes, too, Karen," Frank said. "I messed a lot of things up. I understand why you were angry with me. I don't blame you for being mad."

Then he reached over and wrapped me up in a big bear hug. Forgiveness is something our family has learned to embrace. We've had to.

looking
for a fresh start

1 WENT BACK TO SCHOOL THE WEEK AFTER THE ABORTION AND ACTED AS IF NOTHING HAD HAPPENED. I FINISHED reading *How Green Was My Valley* and handed in my book report. My peers at CHS were reading *In Cold Blood* and *The Exorcist*. I started Truman Capote's book but I couldn't finish it. It scared me too much. The last thing I wanted to worry about was some crazed killer lurking outside our bedroom window. And I didn't even trouble myself with Blatty's demons. I had enough of my own to worry about without hunting up some more.

The bickering between Mama and me increased. We just didn't know how to be civil to each other. She resented me because she wanted to move to Oregon, and I despised everything about her. We fought all the time.

My pregnancy convinced Mama that I couldn't be trusted. She instituted a curfew. Be home by 11 P.M. school nights, midnight on the weekends. I scoffed at her demands. "Who's gonna make me? You and who else?" She wanted me to go on the pill or quit seeing Wesley. The relationship between us had cooled significantly, but I was still seeing Wes and occasionally still having sex with him. I told Mama to mind her own business.

Linda never said much of anything. She'd go to our room, close the door, and sit quietly on her bed, books open, doing her homework.

One morning, a few weeks after the abortion, Mama suggested that maybe it was time I move out. "Perhaps you ought to get out on your own if you can't show me any more respect than you do," she said.

Finally she'd done it—thrown me out, the way I'd always feared she would. I refused to cry in front of her. Grabbing a handful of hanging clothes from my closet, I tossed them into the back of my car. I was late for school. A hard rain had been falling all morning long. "I'll come back for the rest of my stuff this evening," I said as I stormed out the door and slammed it behind me.

As soon as I got behind the wheel, angry tears rushed forth. With cold rain pelting my windshield and hot tears stinging my eyes, I whipped my car around in the middle of Fifty-second Street.

Condensation on the windows obscured my view as I ran a corner stop sign. The front end of my Dodge nearly clipped a young girl crossing the street. The crossing guard reached out and pulled her to safety. I saw it all in slow motion from the corner of my eye, but I was crying too hard. I wasn't about to stop and get another lecture.

A city police officer showed up at school looking for me during third period that day. The minute I saw him in the counselor's office, I knew why he was there. "Let's go somewhere else so we can talk," he said.

We walked across the street, to Lakebottom, the city park where Karen and I would sometimes go to knock around a few tennis balls. Karen was a decent player, but I hadn't improved any over the years. I was still using my wooden Billie Jean King racket.

"I guess you know what I want to talk to you about," the officer said.

"I suppose it's that little girl I hit this morning," I said.

"You didn't hit her," the officer said, correcting me. "But it appears you came pretty close."

I didn't respond.

"I checked with your counselor," the officer continued. "She said you've never really been any trouble at school. She said you're a pretty decent kid." The officer wasn't much taller than me. He had dark, close-cropped hair. His smile was generous, and he seemed genuinely concerned. I looked away from his steady gaze. "So you want to tell me what happened this morning?" he asked.

"Mama and I had a fight," I replied not looking up. "I was crying. It was raining. I didn't see the girl until it was too late."

"Do you and your mama fight a lot?" he asked.

"Seems like it," I said. "This morning she told me I needed to get out."

"Do you have someplace to go?" he asked.

"I dunno," I replied. "Maybe."

"I think it might be a good idea for you to go elsewhere for a while," the officer said. "Until things between you and your mama calm down."

"Yeah, probably," I said. "I have a friend whose mama is an attorney. I'm going to go talk with her this afternoon."

"Who's that?" he asked.

"Rufe McCombs."

"She's a good woman," he said. "I think that's a good idea. You know, Karen, you don't have that much longer until you graduate. You need to finish up."

"I know," I said.

"You need to get things figured out at home," he said.

"I know," I replied. "I'm going to see Mrs. McCombs as soon as school's out today."

"I think that's a terrific idea," he said. "Meanwhile, stay out of trouble."

"Yes, sir."

RUFE MCCOMBS WELCOMED ME into her office that afternoon. "To what do I owe this honor?" she asked. "Please, please, sit down."

"I have a favor to ask, Mrs. McCombs," I said. As calmly as I could, I told her how Mama and I were fighting all the time. I told her about the abortion; about how I almost ran over a kid that morning; about the police officer coming to see me at school. And then I asked her if it would be okay if I moved in with their family for a while. Until things between Mama and me cooled off.

Rufe studied me carefully, her chin resting in her hand. "Well, I don't have a problem with it," she said. "But I'll have to check with Mac, of course."

Mac was Rufe's husband. He was like a father to me. I was confident he wasn't going to turn me out into the streets.

"And I'll want to talk with your mother, first," Rufe added.

That troubled me. Mama had never had anything to do with any of my friends' parents. I knew she felt inferior to Rufe McCombs in all sorts of ways. Whenever Rufe and Mac invited me to join them for dinner at the country club, Mama said I was putting on airs. Trying to live a life I wasn't born to. Mama measured everything with material terms, and she always came up short. I knew Mama wouldn't like the idea of me moving in with the McCombs family. But honestly, I didn't know where else to go.

I moved in that very night and stayed gone until the end of winter term. I went weeks without talking to or seeing Mama. If I needed something from my room, I made sure to go by the house when I knew Mama wouldn't be there.

Mac and Rufe never pressured me to repair my relationship with Mama. Each morning Mac would wake Beth and me with a cheery "Hello, darlings!" Before we could crawl out of bed, he would carry in bowls of cornflakes for us to eat and glasses of Tab for us to drink. The only time he yelled at me was when I went to bed with wet hair: "You'll catch pneumonia!" In many ways Mac mothered me more than any woman ever did. He would wash my clothes, fix me dinner, fill my car up with gas, and make sure I had lunch money. What girl in her right mind would want to give up that kind of attention?

But in those days a parent had to sign your report card, so at the end of winter term when I received mine, Rufe suggested that perhaps it was time I moved back home. The cooling-off period had helped, and Mama and I did our best to be civil to each other. We even started to actually talk, rather than just yelling all the time.

While I was at the McCombs's, Wes quit coming around altogether. I got word he was seeing some other gal. I caught a glimpse of him and his new girlfriend heading downtown one afternoon as I was driving to Rose Hill, and I realized again how foolish I had been to take up with him in the first place. We had nothing in common. I abhorred drug use of any sort. Frank's experiences gave me all the reasons I ever needed to just say no to drugs. Despite Wes's pleas for me to just take one toke, I never did—not then, not ever.

Before he started seeing another gal, Wes had agreed to be my prom date. Mama didn't want me seeing Wesley for any reason, but she did take me shopping at a fabric store to pick out material for my dress. We settled on a dotted-Swiss organza with tiny blue flowers, and I'd found a seamstress in Bibb City who could make the dress.

It turned out perfect. When I put it on, I felt like Julie Andrews in *The Sound of Music.* I wanted to twirl and sing at the top of my lungs. I cut my hair short that spring, and I'd been steadily dropping weight. Beth and I would go on these crazy fad diets where we'd see how many days we could fast. Diet cola was our only nourishment. We once went three days in a row without a thing to eat.

I didn't particularly want to go to the prom with Wes, but there wasn't a line of beaus waiting to take me. I suppose I could have asked one of my friends from church, but that never really occurred to me, even after Wes told me he couldn't escort me. He had been caught smoking pot at Pacelli. The administrators decided that the appropriate punishment for him was a weekend at a monastery. It was the very same weekend as prom.

I didn't believe Wes when he told me. Nobody sends a kid to a monastery for smoking pot, but when Pauline Skibbey called me to apologize, I knew it was true. I spent my senior prom sprawled across my bed, crying and envisioning slicing my wrists. Mama would find

me in the morning, dressed in a prom gown covered in blood. My
relationship with Wes had continually caused me to think and act
recklessly. I probably would have carried out my vision if Linda
hadn't been home. I knew she'd find me before Mama. The thought
of doing that to Linda was enough to stop me. I'd already caused her
enough trouble. I did find an occasion to wear my prom dress—to
Angie Skibbey's wedding. Wesley's jaw dropped to his chest when I
arrived at the church in Mike Garcia's spiffy MG.

Mike was a Columbus High graduate and one of the best-looking
guys in town. His father was a professor at Columbus College, and his
brother, Rick, was a classmate of mine. Mike worked at the Medical
Center. I worked afternoons and weekends at the uniform shop near
the hospital. Mike offered to escort me to the wedding because he was
just a great guy. He'd listened to some of my travails with Wes, and
I think he relished the thought of making Wesley jealous as much as
I did. Walking into that church on Mike's arm was the closest thing to
a Cinderella moment I'd ever experienced. He was dressed in a white
tux coat, black pants, and black cummerbund. All the Garcia boys
owned their own tuxes. Pauline Skibbey was so taken with Mike Garcia that she remarked, "Oh, Karen! What a handsome man. He looks
like he could be the groom. Do you want to have a double wedding?"

After the ceremony Mike and I drove off in a fit of laughter. And
then, just for fun, Mike took me to his home in Green Island Hills, long
considered the town's best real estate for palatial homes. Mike wanted
to parade me around in front of his brother, as if to say, "See what you
missed, Buddy?" It was the same message he'd delivered to Wes.

Mike's friendship was invaluable to me during a time when I had
little, if any, self-confidence. He treated me with respect and kindness, something that Wes never did. Mike helped me set a standard for
myself and for the guys I would later date. He never took advantage
of me in any sense of the word.

And the really good thing about Mike was that Mama absolutely
adored him. Mike was known about town as a lady's man—and

apparently it didn't matter what age the lady was. Mama was thrilled to see me out with someone like him. Being with Mike made me feel as if I had done something worthy in Mama's eyes. I knew it wouldn't last—Mike was just being big-brotherly to me, that's all—but as long as he was around, Mama seemed to warm up to me.

I suspected a thawing on Mama's behalf when she asked me to go with her to the movies one night to see Mia Farrow and Robert Redford. Mama didn't go to very many picture shows. Sometimes she'd go to the drive-in where she could sit in her car and smoke and watch *Billy Jack,* but *The Great Gatsby* is the only movie I recall watching with Mama at the theater. The show itself was magical, but being there together, like I was one of her friends and not just her tag-along daughter, made the evening all the more mystical to me. To this day, I count that night as about the best one Mama and I have had since Daddy died.

There is only one other day that I cherish more—May 31, 1974—the day I graduated from Columbus High School. Frank flew home for the event, and the week before he arrived, Mama had us carry all the living and dining room furniture out onto the front lawn. She said it was time for spring cleaning. Then she grabbed the Kirby and sucked up all the dust balls, while Linda and I took Lemon Pledge to every stick of furniture in the house and on the lawn. After we put everything back in its rightful place, Mama started in on the yard. You would've thought Jimmy Carter was coming to visit, the way Mama was carrying on. I don't remember Frank walking through the front door and exclaiming, "Wow! Girls! This place is spic-and-span," but it was.

Frank was the nicest he had been in years to both Linda and me. He didn't boss us around even once, and he didn't mention the abortion or how disappointed he was in me. He took me out for a Coke and ran around with me getting stuff ready for graduation.

The ceremony was at 4:30 P.M. at the downtown coliseum. I was up early because we had a practice session before noon. Mama was in the kitchen dumping coffee granules into the top of the coffeepot. I loved the coffee's pungent smell, and I liked to watch it percolate, *blurp-blurp*, into the glass crown atop the pot. But I didn't care for its bitter taste. I opened the refrigerator and poured myself a glass of iced tea.

"Good morning," Mama said. "Ready for the big day?"

"I reckon so, ma'am," I said.

"It's going to be hot as blazes this afternoon," she noted.

I stood at the kitchen sink and looked at the sky. A cloud of steam lay trapped between the tops of the pine trees and the aquamarine sky beyond. It was if God had tucked a sheet of Saran Wrap over our section of the earth. There was a milky white film everywhere I looked.

"Some of the boys said they're going to wear shorts underneath their gowns," I said.

"Don't you even think about it."

"I wouldn't, Mama."

The doorbell rang. "I'll get it," I said. I walked out of the kitchen and through the dining room. I didn't really need to rush. Frank and Linda were still sleeping. They weren't about to race me to the door.

It was the neighbors from across the street dropping off a gift-wrapped box and wishing me well on my graduation day. For weeks now people from all over town had been leaving presents on my doorstep or sending money in the mail. This graduation business was more lucrative than any Christmas or birthday that I could remember. Certainly much better than my last birthday. Boxes were piled three and four deep around my bed. Embroidered pillowcases, four pair of panties, size six; a silver-plated hairbrush and matching mirror; a couple of gold-plated pen sets from V. V. Vick Jewelers, charms for my fourteen-karat-gold bracelet, including the tiniest Volkswagen Bug you ever saw from Beth McCombs; photo frames of every sort; half a dozen plump towels; and four sets of sheets—pink, white, blue gingham, and one with tiny yellow daisies.

I think every elderly person at Rose Hill Baptist must've mailed me a check. I had nearly three hundred dollars in the bank from all the folks who'd sent me ten and twenty dollars in the mail. I was beginning to see how those television evangelists could rake in the dough. If one hundred people sent in five dollars, a fellow could make five hundred dollars pretty swiftly. I reminded myself to do those calculations for Granny Leona. She'd send in five or ten bucks to the television preachers every time she cashed her Social Security check. Then by the end of the month she didn't have enough money left to buy a dozen of those Little Debbie oatmeal cakes she loved so much.

I took a quick shower, towel-dried my hair, and rushed off to practice. There were about four hundred of us graduating, and it took an hour to line us up, two by two. I had a deeper appreciation for Noah after watching our class advisors herd us around.

When I got back home, Mama was sitting on the front stoop drinking a cup of coffee and smoking a cigarette. I eased Old Blue up next to the curb and walked across the lawn. I noticed the milky film from the morning had burnt off. Parched pinesap scented the air. Mama was dressed in shorts and a white, sleeveless top. Her arms and legs were lightly bronzed, like the skin of a rightly roasted marshmallow. "How was practice?" she asked.

"Boring," I said. I sat down next to her on the brick steps.

"Mary Sue will be here in a bit," Mama said.

"Is she bringing the kids?"

"I think she got a sitter for them."

Mary Sue had finally tired of Uncle Joe. She left him shortly after Baby Joe was born. I kept Melissa and Joe quite a bit while Mary Sue studied to be a licensed practical nurse, like Mama had years before. She had lived in the projects at Peabody while she finished up her schooling. But once she got done, she bought a ranch-style house out past Edgewood Elementary. Melissa and Joe were attending the same elementary school where I'd started my education—back before we went to Hawaii, back before anybody we knew had heard of Vietnam.

I was trying hard not to think of Daddy right now. I had missed him something fierce during the sixth-grade graduation ceremony at

Tillinghurst Elementary. Mama didn't really care for school activities after Daddy died. I think she felt out of place among all those other mothers who had their husbands still. But she'd picked a folded chair right down front in the school cafeteria so I could see her from the stage while we sang the songs we'd memorized. And she smiled real big when I got a reading award. I knew in my heart then that Mama was missing Daddy, too. Just like now.

I picked up a handful of pine straw and started building a house between my feet, like the ones my girlfriends and I used to construct during our elementary recesses. Mama watched. Then she stood up, brushed off her butt, and said, "Wait right here, I've got something for you."

I kept my head down. I didn't want Mama to see the puddle of tears in my eyes. I'd learned that the best way to stop myself from crying was to stop thinking about whatever was making me sad. But it's hard not to think of your dead daddy on special days like birthdays, Christmas, Easter, and Father's Day. On those really big occasions like high school or college graduations, weddings or when your own babies are born, it's best just to pull out the towel. There's no possible way to get through those days without a big old crying jag.

Mama sat back down and handed me a tiny box. It was wrapped in gold paper and sealed with a big gold bow. "Your graduation gift," she said, smiling. Mama loves to give presents better than anything in the world. Well, almost. She may like getting them even more.

I unwrapped it, taking care not to rip the paper or the bow. I lifted the lid off the white box, and resting there on a bed of cotton was a watch, an exquisite timepiece crafted from diamonds and gold.

"Oh, Mama!" I exclaimed. "It's so beautiful!" I put my arms around her neck and gave her a big smooch on the cheek.

"I'm glad you like it," she said, patting my arm, which was still firmly planted around her neck. "I wanted to get you something special."

"Here, help me put it on," I said, sticking out my wrist. Mama unclasped the watch and slipped it over my left hand, taking care to cinch the clasp up tight. The early-afternoon sun bounced off the diamonds and made tiny rainbows of light. I sat still, mesmerized by my new treasure.

Mama studied me for a minute or two, then she lit another cigarette and took a deep drag. "Karen, there's a couple of things I want to tell you."

I went back to building my pine-straw house. Mama doesn't like to make eye contact when she's talking all serious like.

"Yes, ma'am?" I said.

"Your daddy, he'd be so proud of you today. He was always so proud of you. I don't know if you remember or not, but when you were really little, he'd have me dress you up so he could take you out to the base to show all his buddies his little girl. Your daddy loved your blond hair. I could never get it to do anything. It was always sticking out every which way. But he thought you were such a pretty thing with that white blond hair."

Tears, salty and hot, streamed down my cheeks. I didn't dare look at her or say anything. I didn't know what had caused Mama to lift the veil of silence that had shrouded her since the day Daddy died, but I didn't want to give her any reason to stop talking now. I had waited umpteen thousand days to hear Mama speak Daddy's name again. She could've told me a zillion stories of "Dave this" and "Dave that," and I would never have tired of them.

Trouble was, Mama had quit saying Daddy's name once he died. It simply pained her too much to tell us kids the stories we longed to hear. And because we all loved Mama so, we couldn't bear to ask about the things that would surely stir her to sadness. So I'd never asked Mama how she and Daddy met, or when he proposed, or why he wanted to be a soldier or was there something else he longed to do, if only he'd lived. I didn't know where his favorite fishing hole was or what kind of cake he liked best. I wasn't sure if he read books or if he had an author he liked most. Or if he took Mama to the picture show. And I didn't know if my soldier daddy was afraid he'd never live to see any of his children graduate from high school— something he never got the chance to do himself. I really wanted to ask Mama, do you think Daddy was afraid to die?

But I didn't ask her any of the million questions running through my head. I just listened respectfully the way I might if Pastor Smitty was trying to instruct me, as Mama told me about the ways Daddy loved me.

She recalled the night I fell off the bed and busted my chin open. "Dave put you in the car and drove you to the hospital by himself," she said.

"I remember I was hollering for you all the way to Martin Army."

"I bet you did," Mama said. A grin crept across her face. She took a sip from her coffee cup. "When your daddy died, I was lost, Karen. It was like somebody had thrown me out in the middle of an ocean without a life jacket or anything. I was grabbing onto anything that came my way."

Yep, I thought. A lot of bad shit floats around in the sea of despair.

Mama took another drag on her cigarette and continued. "I know I made a lot of mistakes. I did a lot of foolish things. I'm sorry about that. I'm sorry for the way I hurt you. I wish I'd been a better mother for you kids."

I was wiping away the tears as fast as I could, but quick thaws are never easily managed. My emotions were rushing forward, carrying me along. "You're a good mama," I muttered. But she had tuned me out. She had set a course for herself with this mother-daughter talk, and nothing was going to distract her until she spit out whatever it was she had to say.

"Don't you see, that's why I have got to get out of here? I need a fresh start, someplace new. Someplace where I can make new friends. The only friends I have here are the girls I used to barhop with. I'm tired of that. But if I don't get out of here, I will never get away from it."

I didn't have to ask what Mama was talking about. I knew good and well where the conversation was headed now. We'd fought about it all year long.

"Karen, I want you to go ahead and go on to Berry College with Lynn this fall, the way you've planned, but, honey, I can't stay here. I'm taking your sister and moving to Oregon."

What could I say? I'd asked Mama to let me graduate from the high school where I'd started, and she'd done that. I knew she wanted to get situated in Oregon before Linda started high school in the fall. I would be turning eighteen in November. There was nothing holding Mama to Columbus anymore.

She'd brought us back to this area because it connected us to Daddy in a way that only a military town could. Moving to Columbus was one sure way to keep in touch with the past, one we shared with Daddy. Now Mama needed a place to build a future for herself.

"You do what you have to do, Mama. I'll be okay."

I was lying about being okay. After Daddy died, losing Mama was always the thing I'd feared most.

FOLLOWING MY GRADUATION CEREMONY, I went out with Wes and some friends. I drank just enough rum to induce vomiting. Wes took me home before midnight, and we never went on another date.

Mama sold the house lickety-split. On Labor Day weekend she and Frank finished packing up the last of the mattresses into the U-Haul truck. I'd already boxed up most of my things and taken them to Beth McCombs's house on Lynda Lane. Daddy Mac and Rufe had offered to let me stay with them again. They promised Mama they'd make sure I got to Berry College in time for registration in late September.

Linda cried all the way to the Tennessee border and beyond, and Mama never once told her to knock it off. And I cried nearly every night for the next four months. Nobody told me to knock it off, either. Desolate without my family, I packed my bags after one term at Berry and moved to Oregon in December 1974.

I decided to make the move west after Mama called me on the pay phone in my college dorm to wish me a happy eighteenth birthday. We talked about her new job and the apartment she'd found near Linda's school in Aloha, Oregon. I told her how much I liked my sociology professor and how wretched my English literature professor was. Shortly before we hung up, Mama said, "I love you, Karen."

I couldn't remember Mama ever saying "I love you" before that night. She didn't even say it that day in September when she pulled the car away from the curb and drove off.

Leaving Georgia proved to be nearly as hard on me as being left behind. Columbus is home to some of the fondest memories I have of Daddy. Even today, as I drive past Edgewood Park and our old home, I think of the afternoons spent playing catch with Daddy. I remember Frankie walking me to school. And the times we kids woke up early on Saturday mornings so we could swing from the lever of the refrigerator door without Mama catching us. I remember standing at the picture window as a little girl and screaming at the thunder and lightning.

I recall with a grin the sheer panic Daddy must've felt when he found me sprawled out on the hardwood floor, my chin busted open as blood spurted on the ceiling. Daddy made me giggle through my tears as he rushed me to Martin Army Hospital. And I remember the way he laughed at me one evening when he found me curled up on the couch with a mirror, combing my eyelashes. To this day, the friends I made in Columbus continue to be some of my most cherished companions.

Karen Mendenhall was only a junior at Columbus High when I decided to leave. We sat on her bed with all the lights out and wept for hours the night I told her I was moving to Oregon. Finally, her mom put an end to our crying jag by yelling at us: "Girls! Too late for chitchat. Go to sleep now!"

We burst into a fit of giggles and eventually fell asleep, still muttering about our mamas and all the grief they'd given us throughout our growing-up years. Daddies might hold the key to a daughter's heart, but it's our mamas who hold the key to the ball and chain trailing a young girl's spirit.

Part IV • 1975 — 2003

the years of
apricot skies,
rushing winds,
and journey's end

crayons
and pencil nubs

Rufe, Mac, and Beth helped me pack up my dorm room at Berry and prepare my stuff to be shipped to Oregon. The night before I flew out, I got so sick, Mac worried that I might not be able to make my flight. "You aren't going to have to worry about dying if your plane crashes," he said. "You're going to shit yourself to death." Beth and Rufe laughed while I groaned and made another dash for the bathroom.

The previous week Donna and Karen Mendenhall had hosted a going-away party for me. Mac made me my favorite chocolate pound cake. Donna set the table with linen and silver. My many friends from Rose Hill Baptist turned out to bid me farewell. The Burke boys, Jimmy and Jerry, were there. Jimmy was dating Lynn at the time. I had learned from Mrs. Burke that her son had a crush on me while I was a freshman at Columbus High. She had found a stash of love letters he'd written to me but never given me. I couldn't help but wonder, if he had, how would my life have been different? Would I have ever returned to the trailer court to strike up a doomed relationship? Jimmy and Lynn were great friends. I wanted things to work out between them, so there was no jealousy, no remorse, just a lot of what-ifs in my mind.

Also at the farewell party were Ed Hendrix, Patsy Ward, Andy Kelley, David Toney, Debbie and Dee Jo Baker, Buddy and Lynn

Wilkes, and a host of others who dropped in. Many who showed up for the party also came by the Columbus airport to wave me off. I didn't know it then, but I wouldn't see some of them until decades later. Wesley Skibbey was not among the crowd. We hadn't spoken since graduation night. I didn't bother telling him that I was moving across the country.

Of course, I didn't really realize how far across the country Oregon was. Mama had tried to talk me into staying at Berry for the full year. "It's the rainy season in Portland," she said. "Why don't you stay until summer?"

I wish I'd listened to her. But as usual, I was led by my heart, not reason. It was almost Christmas. I wanted to be with my family.

Mama forgot to mention that the rainy season in Portland could last until mid-June. There were a lot of other things she forgot to tell me, too. Important things about how when a girl falls in love, it can alter her destination in life.

Within four years of moving to Oregon, I had earned a B.S. degree in communication and education from Oregon State University (Mama always said the B.S. part came natural, I didn't really need to earn it), and I'd met and married a native Oregonian.

During the summer of 1978, I'd called Granny Leona in Tennessee to tell her I was getting married.

"What's the boy's name?" Granny asked.

"Timothy Zacharias," I said. "He's from Joseph, Oregon."

"Well, you couldn't get any more biblical than that," she replied. I laughed.

Tim was everything Wesley had not been. He was intelligent and kind and patient. And best of all, he was one of the most godly men I'd ever met. His parents, Gene and Gwen, had raised him in the jungles of Ecuador, where they were serving as missionaries with Wickliffe Bible Translators. Tim had spent much of his formative years reading books, over and over again, by flashlight, eating alligator for dinner, and playing with his pet, a monkey named Judy. By the time we met, Tim was a graduate of Judson Baptist College, where he'd been a member of the basketball and soccer teams. He was at OSU working on his degree in history when a mutual friend introduced us.

We didn't take to each other right way. He thought I was a flirt. I thought he was a nerd. At the time I was dating a member of OSU's crew team. Tim didn't attract me. But over the course of the next four months, we grew to be friends, and from that friendship a romance sprouted. We had our first date in February 1978. I called Karen Mendenhall when I got home that night. It was about 1 A.M. Georgia time. "I've met the man I'm going to marry," I said.

"How do you know?" Karen asked, trying to sound awake.

"I don't know," I said. "I just know it."

Tim and I were engaged by the end of March. We married in August. Karen and Lynn flew out to Oregon to be my attendants. We had not seen one another in three and a half years, but our friendship didn't skip a beat. We spent the week traveling to the Oregon coast and Willamette valley, laughing and telling stories about our mamas and the Rose Hill gang, just like we always did. Lynn and Jimmy had broken up, and Karen had called off her relationship with Andy Kelley and was dating a fellow I didn't know—Philip Clark, a Hardaway boy.

Mama spared no expense at my wedding. She paid for everything— the dress, the flowers, the cake, the reception—without complaint. She did it for me and for Daddy. It was the sort of wedding he would've wanted to give me himself, had he lived.

Uncle James, who was living in Colorado at the time, flew out for the event. I think it was his way of trying to fulfill his promise to Daddy. James had turned his life around and was working a respectable job as a maintenance supervisor for several buildings in downtown Denver. He was very sweet to me. James would have probably escorted me down the aisle if I'd asked, but I had asked Frank do it.

Moments before he walked me down the aisle, Frank lifted my veil, bent over, and kissed me on the cheek.

"I wish Daddy were here," I said, wiping away a tear.

"Me, too," he said.

After a brief honeymoon to the Oregon coast, Tim and I returned to OSU to complete our senior year. Three months later I was pregnant with the first of our four children. Our son, Stephan, was born in August 1979. He was followed in close succession by identical twin sisters, Ashley and Shelby, and then Konnie.

When the nurse at the college infirmary confirmed that I was pregnant, I was distraught. Tim had planned on going to seminary. I wanted to teach high school. This put a definite kink in our plans. But when the nurse suggested an abortion would fix everything, I knew better. "No, thanks," I said. "It's really not an option for me."

That was the same answer I gave another nurse at the Wallowa County Health Department in December 1983, when I discovered I was pregnant for the fourth time. Ashley and Shelby were only seventeen months old. I'd just barely got them weaned.

We were living in the very remote town of Enterprise, where Tim was working as a history teacher. His family lived nearby, but mine had moved far off. Linda and her husband, Greg, were living in Washington. Mama and Frank and his family were in Alaska. Not long after moving to Oregon, Frank had joined the Army and was making a career of it. He was stationed in Anchorage with his wife, Janet, when my son was born.

Despite his religious conversion, Frank's drug habit continued to plague him. In 1981 his drug dealing earned him an all-expenses-paid trip to one of the best drug-treatment programs in the nation, the Army's disciplinary barracks in Fort Leavenworth, Kansas. Janet was pregnant with their second child. His daughter Amy was a preschooler.

Mama moved to Alaska to support Janet and the kids while Frank served out his prison term. David Paul Spears II, my brother's son, was nearly a year old before his daddy laid eyes on him for the first time. Frank walked out of that Kansas prison and into a degree program at the University of Alaska, where he earned his engineering degree and his self-respect. Mama stayed in Alaska because she liked her job and the rivers.

She kept trying to get me up there, but I refused. "I've gone as far north as I'm going," I said.

Mama had come back to Oregon for a brief stint while I was pregnant with the twins. But when they were a week old, she sat with me on the front steps and told me once more why she needed to move another three thousand miles away. She had her reasons: better job, better opportunities. She felt guilty about leaving me again. "It seems I'm always taking off during the times when you need me most," Mama said.

"You do seem to have that habit," I replied.

I tried hard to mask my hurt over Mama's leaving. Being a mother myself had helped me see Mama in a new way. I understood how easy it was for a girl to forget who she used to be in an effort to be the mother her children need her to be. I was beginning to recognize, in very small ways, how my father's death had affected Mama.

When *People* magazine came out with its 10th anniversary of the fall of Saigon issue in March 1985, I sat in my home in Enterprise and wept. I had lost touch with all things military. I felt cut off from Daddy and Mama and from all things familiar. My days were consumed with laundry, naps, coloring books, and Cheerios.

I scrounged around the house for a pen and paper. The only writing utensil I could find was a broken crayon and the nub of a number-two pencil. Taking the paring knife from the kitchen drawer, I sharpened what was left of the pencil and wrote a letter to *People*. The unlined paper was stained with bitter tears when I put it in the mail. *People* published the letter in its April 1, 1985, issue.

I was 9 when my father was killed in Vietnam. He received the Purple Heart, many other medals and the traditional military funeral. Although I loved him and wish that war had never happened, the real hero in my life was the woman he left behind. My mother was 29 when my father was killed. She had three children and a 9th-grade education. She could have lived off the government, or being young and attractive, she could have married again. Instead, she got her high school equivalency, then her L.P.N. and worked for several years as a licensed practical nurse at night while going to college during the day to get her R.N. (making the dean's list, I might add). My mom was liberated before anyone ever heard of it. She, not my dad, bought the only two homes we ever had. She never remarried because no one could match up to the man she lost to Vietnam. She continues to work as a nurse in Anchorage, and as I grow older my love and re- spect for her grow deeper. I am sure my father is pleased that his death brought out the best in her.

This was my very first published piece. Vietnam made me a writer. I had to find some way to structure the chaos; writing gave me the ability to do that.

WHEN I LEFT GEORGIA, it never occurred to me it would be a permanent move. I'd been so busy getting grown up, finishing school, and having kids that I was simply too worn out to consider anything except the immediate, which was usually a toddler crying. I'd given birth to four kids in five years.

Granny Leona died when Stephan was a toddler. I didn't have the money to attend her funeral. I hadn't been back to see my kin in Tennessee in years. In 1985 I grew terribly homesick. We didn't have any money, but Tim promised to take me south as soon as possible. That summer we loaded the kids, all preschoolers, into a Volkswagen van and drove south.

Mama thought the trip would disappoint me. She expected me to feel disconnected from the land of my youth, and she was hoping I would no longer feel like an immigrant to the Great Northwest. "You can never go home, you know," she warned me. "It won't ever be the same again."

Mama was wrong. Columbus, Georgia, always feels like home to me. I'm tied to its landscape and its people in a way that Mama can't understand. I suspect it's because it's where I best remember us as a family.

IT HAD BEEN ten years since I'd left Georgia. I vowed to never let that much time elapse between visits again. I might not be able to raise my children as Georgians, but I was determined to make sure that they knew the South of my childhood. So I took them to the park on Morris Road and showed them the house where I tumbled willy-nilly off the bunk bed and Daddy rushed me to Martin Army Hospital. I took them to the park where Daddy, Frank, and I played catch. And I bought them Krystal hamburgers and told them Mama used to buy a bagful for five dollars. I took them to visit Kadie the Kinnett cow. They giggled at one another as they stood under Kadie's giant udder.

Then Tim and I took the kids to Nashville and Rogersville to meet Papaw David's people and to visit his gravesite in Greeneville. We stayed with Uncle Hugh Lee and Aunt Nina. When we left, Hugh Lee was sad for days. "I've never missed so many people at once in my entire life before," he said.

We visited Uncle Woody and Aunt Gertie and Uncle Carl and Aunt Blanche. We ate snap beans and fresh tomatoes from Carl's garden and drank the sweet tea Blanche fixed earlier that day. And at each stop, I hugged my kinfolk and told them how much I loved and missed them. I returned to Oregon feeling more disconnected and distraught than ever. I was weary of chasing after Mama. I'd moved to Oregon to be near my family, and all my family had moved elsewhere. I didn't know who I was or where I belonged.

That following spring our daughter Ashley was diagnosed with syringomyelia, a rare spinal disorder whose origins are still undetermined. The disorder can be crippling, as sacs within the spine fill with fluid and put pressure on the nerves. In Ashley's case, it resulted in a spinal curvature of thirty degrees and nerve damage to her right leg.

In March 1986 Ashley underwent hours of surgery at the University of Southern California San Francisco Medical Center. She was three years old and had never been away from her twin sister for even a night. Mama did not come down for the surgery. Tim and I were in San Francisco alone with Ashley. Tim's parents were caring for the other three children. Ashley spent ten grueling days in the hospital, mostly doped up on morphine.

It was a full week before we knew if she could walk. Earlier attempts to get her on her feet had failed. She would either throw up or cry out in pain. Doctors had skillfully inserted a shunt that drained the fluid from the sacs in her spine into her abdomen. But that had left her with two major wounds, one in the spine, one in the stomach. We finally coaxed her to walk across the room by telling her that if she would walk over to the phone, she could talk to Shelby. Their friendship was sealed in cement even then. Her gray eyes were lit with desire and determination. Ashley gingerly slid her slippered feet across the linoleum floor. It took her nearly twenty minutes, but she finally reached the phone and cried as she spoke to her sister for the first time in nearly two weeks. Tim and I wept with them.

After that family crisis, Mama and Frank reconsidered their decision to live in Alaska. Deciding it was too far away, they returned to Washington, near Linda. Mama got a job working as a prison nurse in Shelton, and Frank opened up his own engineering business in Auburn.

Before the twins started school, Tim and I relocated to Pendleton, Oregon. It wasn't nearly so remote as Enterprise and put me a little closer to my family—now it was only a six-hour drive to Mama's, instead of eight.

Ashley's medical condition continued to improve. I continued to write. Lynn and Karen flew out for visits. Beth took the train (she's afraid of flying). Some summers, I would load the kids in the van and drive south again. Sometimes Tim went, sometimes I went alone with the kids.

When Rufe McCombs got ready to retire, Beth called and ask if I would write her mother's memoirs. I told Beth I didn't know a thing about writing a book, but Rufe insisted. I was in graduate school at Eastern Oregon University at the time, trying to update my teaching certificate. My professor, George Venn, assured me that I was up to the task. "I'll show you how," he said. And he did.

Mercer University Press published *Benched: The Memoirs of Judge Rufe McCombs* in 1997, and in 1998 it was nominated for Georgia Author of the Year award.

It was during the summer of 1996, while I was in Georgia working on Rufe's book, that I began to search for the men who had served with my father. I only knew the names of two men—Sergeant Hank Thorne and Sergeant Erwin Naylor. I hadn't heard from either of them since 1966. Thirty years had passed since Daddy died. Yet, his death was still as raw as to me as if it had happened the day before yesterday.

third man down

f INDING THE MEN WHO SERVED WITH MY FATHER MIGHT HAVE BEEN EASIER IF I HAD STARTED EARLIER. But even if I'd tried as a teenager, it would've been a difficult task. Mama had long cut herself and us off from Daddy's Army buddies. She didn't stay in touch with Nita Thorne or Shirley Naylor or any of the other military wives she'd hung around with almost daily in Hawaii.

The Naylors invited us up to their place several times, but Mama never did take us to visit them. She and Shirley had been best friends when we lived in Hawaii. After Daddy died, we made a couple of trips to Alabama to visit the Thorne family, but not after Hank returned from Vietnam. Mama simply could not bear seeing other military wives with their husbands and kids. It reminded her of all that she was missing.

I finally tracked down John Osborne, the man who was serving as my father's commanding officer at the time of his death. Osborne had written the letter to Mama explaining Daddy's death in full detail. He had described Daddy as "a close and dear personal friend."

My brother was the only family member who had spoken directly with Osborne following our father's death. Sometime during those teenage years when his angst over Daddy's death was reaching a fever pitch, Frank had called Captain Osborne. "It was right after I graduated from Lyman Ward," my brother told me. "Mama said that Dad's commanding officer had written her a letter sometime after Dad died. She didn't have his phone number, but she remembered that he lived in Kentucky."

It took several phone calls before Frank connected with Osborne. "I told him I was David Spears's son and that I was trying to find out more information about my father and his last days. He was very nice, and he told me what he could remember, but I came away feeling frustrated. Like I had more questions than I did answers. It was definitely a feeling of being unsatisfied."

After that, Frank never tried to find out anything more about our father's death or his last days in Vietnam.

Unlike me, Frank has never felt that Daddy died in vain.

"Dad knew exactly what he was doing," he said. "He knew he was fighting in Vietnam for all the right reasons. He was fighting to make people free, but the people of America didn't think we needed to be there, and they were too damn self-centered to care about our fathers. That's why the Vietnam veterans came home to empty airports or to people spitting on them. There were several times I wanted to go over there and kill every North Vietnamese I could find."

Frank's eldest son is named after our father, and like the grandfather he never knew, my nephew is a military man who was trained at Fort Benning, Georgia. Frank's not troubled that his son volunteered to serve. "I'm proud to have my son carry my father's name. And if being a soldier costs him his life, I'll be proud of that, too. And I make damn sure he knows it.

"At least now people are giving soldiers respect for what they and their families have sacrificed," he said. "The only respect Dad ever got was from the other soldiers at the time. Soldiers always respect each other because they know why they are doing what they do."

Frank remembers that during our father's funeral procession, older gentlemen alongside the roadways paused from their work to salute

Daddy's hearse. "They were probably World War II veterans," Frank said. "As the funeral procession passed by, they stopped what they were doing on the sidewalks and in their lawns and solemnly saluted as Dad's hearse went by. But that was the total of the thanks given to him by strangers for the sacrifice he made in giving his life for his country."

It's awfully sad, really, that even though my brother and I grew up in the same household, missing the same father, we never talked about Daddy or about our sorrows. I wish we could have, but the attitude of the day just didn't allow for such discussions, not even behind closed doors.

CAPTAIN OSBORNE DID NOT seek out our family after he returned from his tour in Vietnam the way Sergeant Naylor had. He had his own set of troubles to deal with—a divorce on the horizon, a couple of kids of his own to tend to, and the recurring nightmares that plagued him.

I understand how the pressures of daily living and the grief over an unpopular war may have kept him from coming alongside our family, but the little girl in me wishes he'd been there to tell me tales of my daddy, to take me fishing in a boat the way Daddy might have. Or simply to have watched out for us and given us a safe shelter from time to time. Most of all, I've longed to hear a firsthand account of how my father died.

I found Captain Osborne via a letter he'd sent to Mama. It was one of the few items from Daddy that she'd held on to over the years. Dated September 1, 1966, the lined notebook paper it's written on has yellowed, and the young man who wrote it has lived long enough to see his dark hair turn white. Osborne recounts the story of my father's death and at the end extends an invitation:

Incidentally, my home is in Russell Springs, Kentucky. And my wife and children reside there now. I will be returning there in late March

*of next year. You and your children are certainly invited to my home
and I would welcome the opportunity to talk with you personally. Sgt.
Spears and I had talked about such a trip and you will always be welcome there.*

Osborne included his phone number and the wish that his letter
might enable Mama to "face the new life that you must now face."

On a lark, I picked up the phone and punched in the 1966 phone
number of Osborne's Russell Springs home. A young woman answered the phone and said she was Captain Osborne's daughter-in-
law. She gave me his home address and phone number. Osborne is a
practicing accountant, as well as a retired professor of economics at
Morehead State University in Morehead, Kentucky, and I caught him
in his office one afternoon, between clients.

Our first conversation was disjointed. Osborne asked what I
wanted to know about my father. I was unprepared and he was short
on time. I managed to obtain his e-mail address and we began corre-
sponding.

I've never been sure how happy Osborne was to hear from me,
but his reaction didn't surprise me. Why should he be willing to re-
visit a difficult time of his life just because I wanted some answers?
Yet, as a daughter, I felt confused by his arm's-length approach to me.

From time to time, veterans I don't know will pick up the phone
and call me about some article I've written about Vietnam and our
family's experiences. Many times they tell me things they don't even
tell their buddies. I like to think that by talking about our family's
loss I've given permission to the veterans to talk freely about their
heartaches and memories.

"There aren't too many women out there who are as interested in
Vietnam as you are," Willie Norman remarked to me over coffee at
the Macon Road Denny's in Columbus, Georgia. Norman, a Vietnam veteran who served at An Khe during 1968, is just one of hundreds of veterans whom I've met because he read something I wrote.

I met Mayor Bob Poydasheff of Columbus in the same fashion. Poydasheff called me after one of my articles appeared in the *Columbus Ledger-Enquirer.* He told me it had moved him deeply. We talked about his tours in Vietnam, and he told me a story about when he was running for mayor. "One woman wrote to the *Ledger* and said she didn't care at all about my military service, she had no intentions of voting for me," Poydasheff recalled.

While it's true that military service shouldn't automatically qualify anyone for political office, I think Poydasheff was more frustrated over this woman's total disregard for his years of service to his country than he was about losing her vote. He said his tour of duty in Vietnam had taught him the skills he needed to be a city leader.

Why could veterans like Willie Norman and Bob Poydasheff feel perfectly at ease talking to me, a complete stranger, about Vietnam, while my father's commanding officer seemed reticent to discuss his experiences? I suspect he has a harder time because when he looks at me he sees my father's ghost. Osborne's reserve might have caused others to back away, but it drew me in. I accepted the invitation that he extended to Mama in his letter of 1966 and arrived on his Kentucky doorstep nearly thirty-six years to the day after my father died.

Osborne greeted me with a firm handshake. I commented on the sparkling bass boat, the color of merlot, that sat in the drive. It was the sort of boat Daddy would have loved. Osborne led Konnie, my youngest daughter, and me into his home office. Konnie had come along to videotape the interview so I could share it with Mama when I returned.

Osborne is a handsome man, big-boned and tall enough to make me feel petite. He has a fluff of white hair and a golfer's tan. This day he wore a blue polo shirt and khaki shorts. A bronzed elk, the outdoorsman's talisman, was perched atop the bookshelf. He sipped from a glass of iced tea as we talked. Osborne spoke with a Southern drawl as thick as sorghum.

I asked if he remembered writing the letters to Mama.

"I remember the first one because your Mama chewed my butt for it," he said. "It was the first one I ever had to do, and I was torn all to pieces about it. Your dad and I had gotten really close."

Osborne said rank and file doesn't mean a thing when you are sharing a tent in the midst of war, night after night after night. The two country boys had become tight.

"When Dave got killed, I had to write my first letter. I wound up having to write a bunch, but I don't know whether you knew it or not, but your daddy was the first one (from the battery) killed. So trying to sit down and write that letter out in the field, I just couldn't do it."

The first sergeant noticed the struggle Osborne was having and suggested he just copy a form letter from a soldier's handbook. So that's what Osborne did. "I took the easy way out," he said, chuckling. "But then your mom wrote and kinda chewed my butt and said she knew we were close and she expected more than that. So then I sat down at Duc Co, which was the next place we went after your dad got killed, and wrote her that letter."

I reached over his desk and handed Captain Osborne the letter he wrote that day near a schoolyard in Duc Co. Silence settled around us as he read the words he'd written decades before:

Sgt. Spears was the acting chief of firing battery and was sleeping in my tent, along with myself and my medic, a Sp. 4 Riddle. At about 5:30 a.m. there was a single explosion which woke me up. Sp. 4 Riddle informed me that he was hit, and as Sgt. Spears was not yet awake, I immediately checked him. He was, of course, hit and unconscious. Sp. 4 Riddle, although wounded in the hip, and myself, both immediately rendered first aid to your husband and within five minutes there was also a doctor and three senior medics in attendance to him.

My ExO, Lt. Duffy and at least nine other men in my battery gave blood for immediate transfusions. In all everything humanly possible was done but your husband's wounds were too great and he died

*shortly without having ever regained consciousness . . . I don't think
he ever knew what hit him.*

*After a complete check, it is my opinion and the opinion of the
Army that he was killed by a single, incoming, enemy mortar round.
It was thought at first that it could have been a muzzle burst from one
of our own guns. But after a complete investigation, I am firmly convinced that it was not.*

Osborne paused and looked up at me; he said he'd nearly forgotten
what he'd written. A battle injury he received that December after
Daddy died had put him in a coma for forty-five days. As he contin-
ued reading the letter, Osborne commented that he'd lied to Mama.
Daddy did not die peacefully in his sleep as he had initially reported.
Nobody sleeps while fiery mortar sears through tender flesh.

"Your dad had been sound asleep," he said. "But he did wake up.
I lied about that. There was no sense at the time to talk about the suffering and wounds he had. It wouldn't accomplish anything. I hope
you can forgive me that lie."

I asked Osborne to tell me how much my father had suffered.

"At first a lot. But then we got him some pain medication and he
was better."

I wasn't surprised by his confession. I'd obtained a copy of my father's autopsy report, nearly a year after I'd made the official request
for his personnel file. I carefully read through the Certificate of
Death and the Record of Preparation and Disposition of Remains
form signed by Bruce E. Means, the licensed embalmer from New
Jersey who'd helped prepare Daddy's body for shipment. I took note
of several things that differed from the stories we'd been told about
Daddy's death. First was the time difference. Means's report stated
it had taken Daddy at least an hour to die. The report listed cause of
death as "shrapnel wound of the abdomen and chest." Common
sense told me that a person wouldn't sleep through such an event and
that Daddy likely died from blood loss caused by his wounds.

Osborne continued: "It was just before daylight. We were all sound asleep. It was pitch-dark. It was rainy. Raining hard. It was during the monsoon season. I did not hear the round go off. You get so accustomed to the noise. We fired off what is called harassing and interdictory fire. One of the gun sections fired every fifteen to twenty minutes, all night long. It was just to harass the enemy and to keep them awake. Well, we learned to sleep through it, and I'm sure they did, too.

"This round went off and I wasn't even conscious of it. I was still asleep. But your dad started hollering, 'Doc! Doc! Doc! I'm hit! I'm hit!' Well, I started to turn over and I felt a good pain and knew I was hit with something. I immediately grabbed my rifle, thinking there was somebody in the tent. We'd had that happen before. I shined the light around but there was nothing.

"And the medic said, 'I've been hit, too, sir.' But your dad had taken on the worst. I needed the medic's help, so I asked, 'How bad are you hit?' and he said, 'I'm all right. I was just hit in the butt.' He was hit right square in the butt. It was a pretty deep wound, too.

"Anyway, we got over to your dad and got him calmed down so we could talk to him. You could see on his right side that he had some small intestines that were coming out. Well, you're taught how to treat that. We put some bandages over it and checked him out hastily. And, fortunately, there was a doctor in the LZ [landing zone] with us. So we got on the radio, he came up, and they took him then."

Osborne had caught some shrapnel across the top of his legs. He said it looked as though he'd been running through a briar patch. When shrapnel hits, it's hot; you might feel the burn, but if you're excited, as he was, you don't really feel the pain so much.

Osborne said my father's intestinal wounds were not enough to have killed him. Rather, Daddy's death was the result of a multitude of blunders, the sort that happen in war zones when people are careless or excited or trying to tend to the wounded and fend off the enemy at the same time.

"We didn't know [how badly he was injured] because the doctor had got there and we didn't do a real good check on Dave. What happened was, one [shrapnel] had come up through the cot and hit him in the back and entered his lung. He had severe bleeding in his lungs. The doctor found this. But we couldn't get a dust-off out there because it was dark. And it was raining pretty hard."

A dust-off is the insider term for medical evacuation chopper. With the help of Senator Gordon Smith (R-Ore), I obtained a copy of the duty officer's report for that day. The report is an hour-by-hour account of troop movement, any crashes that might have occurred, any casualties sustained, any dust-offs requested.

The call for a dust-off was the tenth entry on the log that day but the first communication from the troops. All previous entries simply recorded which units the journal was tracking, with a notation that things were pretty quiet until then. At 5:35 A.M. a call came from the 2nd Battalion, 9th Artillery. It reads: "B/2/9 req. DUSTOFF. Short rd or burst from frd H & I mort resulting in 3 casualties: 1 litter, 1 walking, and 3rd man down, has injuries: ext. unk. DUSTOFF ASAP when weather clears."

Translated, H&I is that harassing and interdictory fire that Osborne referred to. The initial report stated that Daddy was struck by a mortar round from one of the U.S. Army's own cannons. This was likely the source of the news reports that said my father, the gun chief, had been killed by one of his own shells. The log also indicated that the rescue helicopter was unable to get to him due to bad weather. Further reports blamed bad weather for a plane crash on a hillside near Qui Nhon. And it was noted that two more aircraft were grounded at Duc Co as a result of the rains.

But Osborne told me there were other problems with the dust-off that day. "They were taking too long to get down there. I was really pissed. And you don't piss off somebody who has five big guns," Osborne said, chuckling.

He decided he'd give the pilot a wake-up call himself.

"I dropped a round in the middle of the LZ," Osborne said. "That got their attention. They came, finally, after we dropped that short round. But on the way out, they ran out of fuel and had to go back. They'd failed to refuel the night before. The pilot got court-martialed over it."

That moment of carelessness—the oversight of not refueling the night before—may have cost my father his life. Daddy was twenty minutes' flying time from an evacuation hospital. If the dust-off had reached him in a timely fashion, if the care he'd received had been thorough, he likely could have survived his wounds.

Osborne has debated the what-ifs of that day for decades. "As it turns out, I don't know whether it would have done any good or not," Osborne said. He folded his thick forearms over each other and contemplated his answer. "The doctor did a real good job. And I've never seen so many people line up to give blood in my life. I almost didn't have enough people to function because everybody was in line, wanting to give blood."

Osborne said Daddy was receiving direct transfusions from other men in Battery B. I asked if my father was awake at the time.

"He was unconscious most of the time," Osborne said. "He stayed conscious for about thirty to forty-five minutes, but then he started losing so much blood."

It had taken the doctor awhile to locate the bleeder. "The doctor realized there was a lot of internal bleeding that he couldn't do anything about. So we had to start trying to keep him alive with transfusions. Had a dust-off come out immediately and got him back to the field hospital where they could've done surgery, I don't know if he would've made it or not."

Osborne was so busy trying to tend to others and get organized that morning that he was unaware of how much time had elapsed.

"You have to realize," he explained, "this was the first casualty [in Battery B, 2nd/9th Artillery] we had in the big buildup in Vietnam, and so nobody knew what the hell was going on. We'd never been faced with this. We didn't know until I did an investigation that morning what hit us."

Daddy had left for Vietnam from Hickam Air Force Base in December 1965, as part of Operation Blue Light, known as one of the largest and longest airlifts of personnel and cargo into a combat zone in military history. As part of the 3rd Brigade, he had been one of four thousand soldiers deployed to Vietnam's Central Highlands. They established base camp near Pleiku, a town of about twenty thousand people at the time. The 25th Infantry brought in nine thousand tons of equipment.

The 3rd Brigade was the first from the 25th Infantry called to action. Battery B, 2nd Battalion, 9th Artillery provided direct support for the infantry. Since arriving in Vietnam, Daddy had spent very few days at base camp. Captain Osborne did not arrive until March. Battery B spent most of their time in the field, engaging the North Vietnamese who patrolled the Cambodian border.

The June 5, 1966, issue of the *Bronco Bugle,* the troops newspaper, noted that "the 2nd Battalion, 9th Artillery, boasted one of the most charged up batteries in Vietnam." The *Bugle*'s report on the Operation Paul Revere Campaign under way in the Central Highlands stated that the artillery unit "fired for 24 hours without a break. All the while, small arms and mortar fire were falling on the battery. Most of the men didn't sleep for 48 hours."

The June 6, 1966, issue of the *Bronco Bugle* praised the medical team attached to the 3rd Brigade:

> On the brigades present Operation Paul Revere, southwest of Pleiku, the medical company was able to show its efficiency in treating injured personnel of the brigade. On Saturday an element of the task force met heavy contact with what they know to have been a North Vietnamese regiment. Naturally, there were some friendly casualties. "Every wounded man who reached our hospital alive, reached the next higher echelon alive, thanks to the finest doctors I have ever worked with," said Doctor (Captain) William

Gardner, the Bronco Brigade surgeon. All patients suffering head or eye injuries were immediately evacuated to Pleiku or Qui Nhon. Other patients requiring major surgery are evacuated to either Pleiku or An Khe. "A seriously wounded man can be on an operating table in Pleiku within half an hour after he reaches us," stated Doctor (Captain) Edward Denison, the B Company Commander.

Yet, despite the claims regarding the efficiency of the dust-off pilots and the boasts about the low mortality rate of the Vietnam War, on July, 24, 1966, Daddy died shortly before daybreak in a muddy LZ in the Ia Drang Valley.

Osborne conducted an immediate investigation. "I found the shrapnel. I sent it off to be investigated, and it came back 'unknown.' "

So, Osborne argued, the mortar couldn't possibly have been from their own guns. Taking a piece of pink notebook paper, he drew a circle representing the camp and marked Xes to show the placement of the five guns in the circle. The circle was about two hundred meters in diameter. Sergeant Hank Thorne, daddy's best buddy, was reportedly operating the howitzer that night.

"That's one of the other reasons I conducted an investigation," Osborne said. "I never wanted him to ever think he pulled the shell that killed your dad."

Osborne said that when he first arrived in Vietnam, Daddy had warned him that Hank Thorne had a drinking problem. Because of things he wrote in a letter to Mama, I knew Sergeant Thorne did feel responsible for Daddy's death.

Dated August 29, 1966, the letter is twelve pages long and is written with an unsteady hand and a faltering heart. The family declined to allow me to quote from it. But in essence, Thorne said he was hurting so badly over Daddy's death that he couldn't sleep, eat, or think straight. He said that he put off writing the letter because he lacked the nerve. His befuddled state of mind is evident by his remark that Mama couldn't possible understand his pain over Daddy's death. Thorne said he and Daddy were already good buddies, but they had become even better friends in Vietnam. And that's why Osborne had put off telling him about Daddy's death. He reiterated the story Osborne had initially told Mama—that Daddy was asleep in his tent when an incoming mortar round struck and that my father never woke up and didn't have any idea what hit him.

Thorne repeated himself in a rambling monologue over the next few pages, telling Mama that he is hurting bad and that he just doesn't know what to say. He said Daddy didn't have any last words for us, his family. But then Thorne admitted that he wasn't with Daddy after he got hit, so he couldn't really be sure about that.

He made reference to the discrepancy surrounding the mortar blast. Thorne said at first everyone thought it was fire from one of their own guns, but he knew better because he'd heard the mortar round when it came in. At no point did Thorne say that the round might have come from his gun.

He repeated again how close he and Daddy and Osborne were and how grieved he was over Daddy's death. He said he and his men were exhausted after being in the jungle for one hundred days. But, he added, they still had a job to do.

Thorne said he would be home on December 7, and he encouraged Mama to be at the airport with his wife, Nita, for his arrival. Then he asked Mama to continue to write to him because letters are the best thing a soldier can get in Vietnam. Thorne added that Osborne was giving him pep talks on a daily basis, telling him not to lose hope, but survivor's guilt was eating away at him.

Then Thorne made an outlandish remark, one that proves just how distraught he was over Daddy's death. He told Mama he wished he could come home, marry her, and take care of her and us kids for the rest of his life. That remark alone was enough to scare Mama away. She did not answer his letter, and she never discussed the contents of it with Nita. I'm convinced Sergeant Thorne was just so overcome with grief that he was talking out of his head when he told Mama he wanted to marry her. But I'm equally convinced that he suspected that it was a blast from his gun that killed my father and not an incoming mortar round.

Hank Thorne died before I began searching for him. Nita told me that her husband never spoke of Vietnam but woke up often in the middle of the night, yelling out my father's name. If Sergeant Thorne ever mentioned the discrepancy over the mortar round to his family, they never said. I'm still not sure if he told them that the Army brass had determined that the shrapnel came from a howitzer he was firing that morning. They made that decision about a month after my father's death. Osborne said some of the brass came out and conducted an investigation. The official Army report concluded that the shell from Thorne's gun had hit a tree near the middle of the camp and exploded and it was shrapnel from that explosion that killed my father.

But according to Osborne, "It ain't what happened, and I'll argue that until after I'm dead. The wounds all of us had came from ground level. If the round had hit this tree and went off prematurely, the shrapnel would have been coming toward us at a downward angle. This can't be what happened."

Osborne believes without question that the mortar round that exploded that morning was incoming fire. Two other mortar rounds had exploded in the base camp that morning, he explained. "This round went off at the same time and confused people. They didn't know if it was incoming or outgoing." Moreover, Osborne said the distance from Thorne's gun to the tree in question was less than sixty meters, not far enough for the shell's safety features to release and its inertia functions to kick into place. "The setback on an artillery shell precluded it from going off before it traveled over one hundred meters," Osborne explained. "It can't. You could take one and hit it with a hammer, and it's not going to go off.

"They can call it official, whatever they want to," Osborne said. "I'll never believe that's what happened. Because the way the wounds were and where it landed. Your dad's had come in through his back into his lungs and through his back into his intestines. His intestines were protruding from the front out. If he'd been hit from the top down, they would have gone the other way. So it had to come from the ground."

Later on, sandbags around the tents would prevent that sort of injury from occurring, Osborne said. But up until my father's death, Osborne said the company's practice had not been to sandbag around their tents.

"Your dad's death saved a lot of lives in Vietnam," Osborne said, noting that the subsequent investigation had included a report of what they could do to prevent further casualties. Osborne had been lying on a cot less than four feet from my father when the incident occurred. He knows how fortunate he was to escape the fate my father met that day.

I asked Osborne if he thought my father knew he was going to die.

"He knew he was hit bad," Osborne said. "I don't think any of us knew, except the doctor, how bad. We were all just in shock when he died. We didn't think he'd been hit that bad. I knew he had an intestinal wound, but I'd seen enough of that. But I didn't know about the wound in the lungs.

"I was kind of ticked at the doctor. With no more major wounds than Dave had, I didn't understand why he couldn't keep your dad alive. That's when the doctor said, 'Wait a minute. There are two wounds, one in his back y'all didn't know about. That's what killed him.'"

Osborne said prior to my father's death, the artillery unit had considered themselves invincible. "We thought, 'We're back here where it's safe. They're not going to mess with us.' Well, we found out after that they did mess with us . . . a lot."

A second Army report confirmed Osborne's account. The report stated, without any further explanation, that my father's death had been the result of enemy fire.

I'D BEEN AT Osborne's home for nearly three hours, and I had questions still unanswered. But before I could ask them, Osborne asked a question of his own. "Something I want to know is did your mother get the money I sent?"

"I don't know anything about it," I replied.

"There was about six thousand dollars, in Vietnamese currency, in a safe of your dad's," Osborne said. "We bought one-hundred-dollar money orders in her name and sent a damn stack of them to her." As he spoke he stretched out his fingers six inches wide to show the depth of the stack.

I told him I didn't think Mama had ever received the money.

"I had to send it through channels because it was an estate thing, and I just wondered whatever happened," Osborne said. "I was in the boonies where I couldn't follow up on it."

Later I learned that Mama didn't receive that stack of money orders from Osborne. She said the only personal effects of my father's she received were his wedding band, his watch, a few pictures, and his wallet, which contained only one dollar. She gave that dollar to Aunt Mary Sue, who kept it in her Bible.

Mama knew Daddy had a stash of money somewhere—money he made playing poker or saved back from his pay. He had written to her about it shortly before he died. The letter is postmarked July 16, just eight days prior to his death:

> *I will be sending you that big bank account that you have been looking forward to. When I send it let me know how much you get so that I will know that you got all of it. For I will have to send it in hundred dollars money orders.*
>
> *You know how we used to sit down on payday and wish that we could put all that money in the bank? Well this is our chance to do just that. You will be getting almost $2,000 with my back pay and what I have got playing poker. Yes, I still play poker. Now don't get*

too pissed off because I only get $50 a month so I can't loose all our money playing poker. That is about all we have to do with what we get paid over here.

The Army had some concerns about my father's personal items being returned because his records contained numerous references to a tracer ordered by someone. Mama knew nothing about that. A letter dated Feburary 16, 1967, and addressed to Oren Womack, chief of Support Services in Washington, D.C., notes that a thorough investigation was conducted by headquarters and that there didn't appear to be any documents regarding an inventory of my father's belongings. That letter calls for further investigation by the Army's inspector general.

On May 25, 1967, another letter was added to my father's file that ultimately resolved the matter for the Army. It stated that Mama hadn't made any inquiries about Daddy's belongings, so it was assumed that she received everything and no further action was necessary.

I suspect someone fraudulently cashed the money orders Osborne sent to Mama. It was Mama's responsibility to put a tracer on anything of Daddy's that wasn't returned. If she had known that Captain Osborne had sent her that stack of money orders, Mama would have done just that. She didn't know about it, and Captain Osborne never followed up to ensure that Daddy's money was delivered safely to Mama.

I hoped Captain Osborne could help me resolve the question of whether my father had been decapitated, as some of my kinfolk had claimed, so I asked him about it. I showed him a picture of my father in his casket. The photo disturbed him immensely.

"You know, I don't understand this picture," he said.

"Why?" I asked.

"Well, he's swollen very, very badly. His face is very full. And his hair is too long. That bothers me. That's the first time I've seen that."

Then he expressed the same reaction that I had as a child. "It doesn't look anything like him to me. Not forty years later. It doesn't. I wouldn't have known who that was."

Moreover, looking at the photo, Osborne said he could understand why someone would think my father might have been decapitated. "I can see why someone might say that," he said. "But we all stood there and saluted your dad before they put him on the helicopter. The only incision on his neck was from where they had put the trach tube in."

After Daddy's lungs had filled with fluid, the doctor sliced his throat and inserted a trach tube. The autopsy report supports Osborne's statements. There are notations on the drawing, and the report refers to the incision. Contrary to what some of the kinfolk suggested, Daddy had not been decapitated. His head wasn't rolling around in the casket.

It's true, he looked all hinky-kinky squeezed into that casket. But it was a military casket, and Daddy was a broad-shouldered man; it was too narrow for him. And once a person is embalmed, he's hard as marble. There was no way for the funeral-home folks tending to him in Rogersville to situate Daddy's head differently, to center his chin over his tie. It was what it was, but it was not a decapitation, not according to the evidence or the eyewitness accounts.

Osborne also explained a troubling notation on Daddy's autopsy report. Under a box titled "condition of remains," someone had marked "apparent GSW to back from abdomen." This was the same autopsy report signed by Bruce Means, the embalmer. Means had identified the cause of death as "shrapnel wounds of abdomen and chest."

I knew "GSW" meant "gunshot wound." Could it be that someone had intentionally shot my father in the back? And if so, who? Why? And, if so, why would Daddy's buddies try to cover it up?

Osborne referred again to how the mortar hit the ground outside the tent. He is convinced that a hot piece of shrapnel, not a bullet, shot upward through my father's cot and into his back, piercing his lung. "When the shrapnel goes in, it cauterizes itself because it's so hot," Osborne explained. "So there's no surface bleeding." A small piece of shrapnel could give the appearance of a gunshot wound, he said.

I struggled with Osborne's explanation. While the daughter in me wanted to believe his story, the documentation, specifically the autopsy report's reference to an "apparent gunshot wound," bothered me.

If I could obtain them, the court-martial records might help eradicate any lingering doubts. But even with help from Senator Gordon Smith and others, I haven't tracked down any such records. In fact, none of the men that I've encountered from B Battery remember anything about an investigation into my father's death or the subsequent court-martial that Osborne referred to. They also disagree about whether it was an incoming round or a bad round from Thorne's gun that killed Dad.

John Nash lives in Albany, Georgia. He has a baritone voice that's as thick as milk gravy. He described himself as an independent and hardheaded fellow. Age doesn't seem to have mellowed him much. He's a "like me or leave me alone" sort of guy. Plain-spoken, he has little tolerance for bullshit. "I was there when your dad got hit," he told me. "It was early in the morning when the mortar rounds came in. I was awakened by the rounds and a loud scream. It was a really loud scream. It sounded like a wildcat. That was followed by a lot of confusion. Then somebody said Sergeant Spears had been hit."

Nash was a private first class at the time. He said he helped transfer the radio call for the dust-off. "But the fog was too heavy. By the time the chopper got there, your dad was dead."

I asked Nash if it's possible that somebody had shot Daddy.

"I believe if that kind of talk was going around, I'd remember that. I remember that I was in a truck, sleeping on the mortar rounds, when we got incoming fire. I was awakened by your dad hollering. Then everybody around us started scrambling around. We all hit our foxholes."

Nash said Daddy had spent a lot of time trying to mentor him. "I was young, twenty, at the time," Nash said. "I was a good soldier, but I drank too much. Got into trouble sometimes. Your dad looked out for me a lot. He tried to keep me out of trouble. I thought a lot of him, and I believed he liked me. Sergeant Spears had a real good personality. I didn't know anybody who didn't like him. He was real understanding."

Nash couldn't imagine anyone taking aim at Daddy for any reason. "I was a kid with an attitude," he said. "I thought I knew more than anybody over there. I hated for somebody to tell me what to do. But your dad would talk to me. He was always trying to keep me from doing stupid things. I never hurt anyone else, but I hurt myself. If he seen something coming on, he'd try to stop me."

Like Osborne, Nash was stunned by my father's death. "I couldn't believe it. The whole time we was there, we only got incoming like that five or six times. We moved around pretty extensively, from Kontum Province to the rubber plantation to the Ia Drang Valley. I don't think you will ever find the spot where your father died. Our places were never marked as fire bases. And probably them places are so growed over by now, it's as if nobody was ever there."

MANY MONTHS AFTER I traveled to Kentucky to meet Captain Osborne, I received a phone call from another veteran who had been with my father that day. His story convinced me that I was as close to the truth as I'd likely ever get.

"Hello," a man's voice said. "Is this Karen Spears?"

"Yes," I said. I couldn't place the voice. There was a long pause. I heard a muffled sound.

"I'm sorry," he said.

When I heard his crying, I figured I had a veteran on the line. "It's okay," I said. "I understand."

"Give me a moment," he said, trying to gain his composure.

"It's all right," I said. Another long pause.

"My name is Pablo."

I knew his last name. "You are Pablo Gallegos?" I asked.

His weeping intensified. "I'm sorry," he said again. "I knew your dad."

"I know who you are," I said. "I've been looking for you. I'm so glad you called."

I had come across Pablo Gallegos's name hundreds of times in my father's files. If I closed my eyes, I could see the all-capital print of his signature on the Statement of Recognition form that I had received along with my father's autopsy report. I had asked both John Nash and John Osborne if they knew who this Gallegos guy was. Neither did. The roster of Dad's company did not list him as being a member of the 2nd Battalion. I had never heard my father mention him. At one point, in my frustration, I had scribbled a note across Gallegos's name: "Nobody knows this man."

But there was that troubling Statement of Recognition document, the one in which the individual signing the paper stated: "I recognize the remains because of the following facial features, scars, birthmark, and other unusual features." And there was the signature of Pablo Gallegos.

Gallegos was a senior medic at headquarters for the Ninth Artillery. Because my father was not wearing his dog tags at the time of the attack, Gallegos had to identify my father for the death records.

Gallegos had found me via a memorial page designed by the folks at the Virtual Wall (www.virtualwall.org). Veteran Jim Schueckler, known as Uncle Polecat, along with veterans Ken Davis and Channing Prothro, had taken several of the articles I'd written about my father and designed a tribute page to him. They did this without any financial remuneration. They design such tributes in order to help families get in touch with veterans who may have served with their loved ones.

Gallegos had gone to the site and typed in Dad's name and found those articles and my phone number. He said he'd been haunted for the past thirty-seven years, wondering what happened to Sergeant Spears's family. "It's been thirty-seven years, but some things you never forget," he said.

For Gallegos, the death of a man like my father was one of those memorable moments in a young man's life. As a career military man,

Daddy, thirty-five, was seemingly invincible to such a young fellow. Gallegos was only nineteen. He had been shaken by my father's death and remembered the day clearly.

"They were sleeping in the tent when they got mortared," Gallegos recalled. "The mortar tore up the tent. The other medic—I don't remember his name—had a shrapnel wound in the butt. It was deep. But he still took care of your dad. Your dad got the majority of the shrapnel. The medic did what he could, but by the time the medvac arrived your dad had passed way."

Gallegos said it wasn't rain that kept the dust-off from reaching Dad. It was fog. "The dust-off couldn't get in because of the fog and because the artillery unit was under heavy fire that day," Gallegos recalled. "It was unusual for the artillery to be under such heavy fire because the infantry is usually the ones who get all the fire. But that day there was a lot of fog and a lot of fire. I didn't know Sergeant Spears all that well, but I knew him. I'd been in Hawaii, at Schofield, before we arrived in Pleiku."

Gallegos left Vietnam in October 1966. He made it home safely, if not whole. He fathered five children and gave thirty-three years of his life to the U.S. Postal Service before retiring.

From time to time a replica of the Vietnam Veterans Memorial Wall comes through his neighborhood. When it does, Gallegos always goes and pays his respects to my father. "I make an etching of his name every time," he said. "And for the past thirty-seven years I've wondered what happened to Sgt. Spears' family."

I told him we'd turned out fine.

"Well, I know your dad would be proud of all of you," he said.

Then I wept.

Gallegos is a member of the Run for the Wall motorcycle group. Hundreds of veterans, and many others, travel from Los Angeles to D.C. every Memorial Day, but Gallegos said he had never been able to make the entire cross-country trip. He'd gone only part way.

When Gallegos made his first trip to the Vietnam Veterans

Memorial Wall, he invited me along. In May 2004, I flew to Los Angeles and joined Gallegos, his wife, Marie, and hundreds of other bikers and support vehicles for the sixteenth annual rumble across America. Before we rolled out of California, Pablo and Marie gave me a gift—a black vest, adorned with pins and patches, one of which was the 25th Infantry's insignia and one that read "In memory of David Spears. Vietnam 1966."

I was wearing that vest, a black mini skirt, and boots when we thundered into town that Memorial Day weekend. Gallegos made the trip specifically to honor my father. I went to honor them both. With Pablo's permission, I left my vest at the base of Panel 9 East of the Memorial Wall, directly below my father's name.

THE DAY AFTER Pablo Gallegos first called me, I received an e-mail from another veteran who had served with Daddy. Doug Johnson, of Nebraska, was an assistant gunner under Daddy. Johnson found me the same way Gallegos had, via the Virtual Wall. Johnson was not in touch with Gallegos and had no idea that the two of us had talked. Like Gallegos, he had not stayed in touch with the men from Battery B. He sent me the following e-mail, titled "Surprise":

> *Say, I have been wondering about Sgt. Spears' children for a long time. I was with him in Vietnam in the same gun section (2nd). He was quite the guy. When we did something it was done the best. Our gun pit was the sharpest, the personal bunker was the best.*

I was surprised all right. I asked Johnson to recount what he remembered of the day Daddy died. Here's his reply:

> *For some reason I never heard the explosion (as I must have been darn tired). Saylor came and got me saying Sgt. Spears has been hit. They need blood bad since I was Type O, we ran to the tent. Bob Kessler was giving blood (1 section trucker) at that time but I didn't have to be-*

cause he had expired. Our regular medic got hit at the same time (Rid-
dle) and headquarters was there with us at the time. I think that is how
medic Pablo Gallegos got in our battery because he had to take care of
both of them, and since we lost our regular medic he stayed with us.
I don't think medic Riddle wounds were life threatening. All of us
guys were in a state of shock over Sgt. Spears' death.

Johnson said it was not an incoming mortar but a short round
from Thorne's gun that killed Dad:

It was Sgt. Thorne's 3 section gun. This was at night so most people
were sleeping, as I was. You never know which way they are going to
fire these guns. You always set up your sleeping tent or canopy behind
the gun. But when they start to firing and it's over you, you just lay
there with your hands over your ears and bounce on the air mattress.
As you don't know if they are shooting right over you or how far
down the tube (barrel) it is. If it's possible, you are better off to get up
and help. Anyway, Saylor said it was a muzzle blast (where the pro-
jectile goes off a short distance from the tube).

With Johnson's help, I found several other men from B Battery—
Gary Smith of New Jersey, who plotted the coordinates for the gun;
Gary Catlett of California, my father's driver in Vietnam; and An-
drew Melick Jr. of Oregon, a gunner.

Smith didn't see the gun blast that killed my father. Like Daddy,
he was sleeping. He wasn't sure who was conducting the H&I fire
that day. He wondered if perhaps Daddy was operating the gun
when the muzzle blast happened. But the retired police officer is
sure of one thing—it wasn't incoming fire that killed my father. "The
ammo we were using was leftover from Korea stockpiles," Smith said.
"We'd all been worried about how stable those rounds were."

Smith, who was nineteen years old when he did his tour in Vietnam, said my father's death stunned him. "It shocked us all," he said.

Andrew Melick, Jr., was on R&R in Thailand when Daddy died. He learned of Daddy's death from the other guys in the camp. "Nobody ever said anything about it being incoming fire," he recalled. "I was told it was a misfire from one of our own guns. That your daddy had been hit be a piece of shrap metal."

Melick was one of the fellows who regularly played poker with Daddy. But during those games, neither man conversed much. Melick knew Sergeant Spears was married, but he had no idea that my father had three children. "I didn't make very many friends over there," Melick explained. "Your daddy and I didn't talk buddy, buddy."

Gary Catlett, my father's driver, spent a lot of time with Daddy, and he remembers one day in particular, when my father got pissed at him. "We were going into a hip shoot. I was driving along, out of nowhere. The information we got was that headquarters wanted us to shoot from the road. So I pulled off the road into this big open field. The engineers had gone in and cut down all these trees. But they left stumps about two feet high. Your dad was standing up, over the window. He was pointing in the direction he wanted me to go. I was watching his hand. The drive was really bumpy. I could feel the guys behind me. They were barely able to stay in the truck. The ammo was bouncing around. I'm surprised we didn't all get killed.

"I was watching your dad pointing, when *Wham!* We came to a dead stop. I hit one of those stumps. It tore the entire front end of the truck.

"Your dad was so mad. He screamed at me, 'Catlett, I ought to leave your ass here!' "

"I yelled back at him, 'I don't think so, sir!' "

Gary Catlett laughed as he related this story. Then he quickly added, "But your dad never stayed mad. Two minutes later, he was over it."

Dad was all business. "We talked a little, but your dad wasn't one to get too personal," Catlett recalled. "He was really good friends with Sergeant Thorne. But your father's first priority was to take care of us.

He was all soldier. Well-versed and straightforward. There's nobody I'd have rather have gone to war with; your dad was so confident. He had experience. He was the kind of guy that could walk through a minefield and have mines exploding all around him and he'd still be calm. He knew how to keep morale up. We respected him."

After Dad's death, Catlett withdrew to a quiet place. "When somebody gets hit, it numbs you. When we went to Vietnam, your dad told us that a lot of us wouldn't be coming back. I remember thinking I didn't know about anyone else, but I was coming back. I never had much fear over there. It wasn't like we were going into the tunnels, blood-hunting out the Viet Cong."

He tried to prepare for the inevitable loss of his fellow soldiers. "It's hard to get close to anyone. That's the way war is. You know they could be gone, so you prepare yourself for that. I was saddened by your father's death, but what can you do about it?"

All the fellows were worried about the aged mortars. "We could never depend on those rounds," Catlett explained. "I put one in a tube one time and the tip of the fuse hit the breech block and started sizzling. We slammed that thing up and shot it. That was scary. From that point on we started cutting the fuses."

Catlett said he was asleep on the ammo pile the morning Daddy got hit. "I used to sleep right on the ammo. I figured if I was going to go, I would go up in style. If that round had been incoming fire, everybody would've known it. I'm sure it was H&I fire. It went out of the tube and blew up. Faulty rounds weren't an unusual thing. But usually they'd get further away from camp before they exploded. The guns were sitting twenty-five meters apart. We staggered 'em, like a *W*. So when the round hit, it covered a big area."

Catlett said the round had come from the forward gun. Thorne's gun.

The eyewitness testimony from the men who were at the camp the day Daddy died—Osborne, Nash, Thorne, Johnson, Smith, Melick, and Catlett—is conflicting. But they all agree on one important fact—Daddy's wounds were caused by shrapnel, not a gunshot.

Daddy's autopsy report indicated he had a gunshot wound from his back through his abdomen, but I could not find one eyewitness of that day's event to support that finding. Nor could I find any evidence that he had been decapitated or that the mortar round detonated prematurely while he was operating his own howitzer.

A congressional investigation launched by Senator Gordon Smith resulted in the following analysis by researchers at the National Archives at College Park:

> Our staff searched all the records we have in our custody that might have contained information regarding the incident in which SSgt. David P. Spears was killed. There are not records of the 2/9th artillery for this time frame. The daily journal and the daily situation report for the 3rd Brigade/25th Infantry Task Force mention the accident. Copies are enclosed. The task force was attached to the 4th Infantry Division at this time. Their records provide no additional information, either in the division general staff or division artillery files. . . . The records of the next higher echelon, First Field Force Vietnam, reiterate the information that was passed to them by the brigade. The G-3 daily journal reads: "Fm 3/25 LT. Powell, to MAJ Cropper, 240525—B/2/9 had a 105 muzzle burst. Rslts: 3 wounded, 1 serious, 2 minor. Medvac requested but weathered in. No additional details." The records of the United States Army Vietnam Provost Marshal and the 18th Military Police brigade do not cover this time frame. Line of duty investigations and summary court martial are not included among our records.

I was never able to verify by documentation the story Osborne told me about the dereliction-of-duty charge against the helicopter pilot who failed to fuel up the night before the mortar attack. Nor was I able to track down any proof of the money orders Osborne said he sent to Mama. The copies of the situation report, sent from the National Archives and marked "confidential," provided no further information, other than that at 0530 "a muzzle burst occurred in B Btry area, resulting in two wounded and one killed."

Third man down.

None of this searching can change the outcome of what happened the morning of July 24, 1966. And certainly my search has done little to make Mama feel any better. Rehashing all this only reminds her of how much she's missed Daddy all these years.

Some days I don't know why I'm compelled to pursue this. I wonder how I might have reacted if I'd found out that my father had been shot in the back as the autopsy findings suggested. Or what if I had stumbled across evidence that he had indeed been decapitated? Would I really want to know that?

I'd like to think so. I'd like to think I have enough of my father in me to handle the toughest moments in the battle for truth. I know one thing: If my father had lived, I would have wanted to walk the grounds at the Vietnam Veterans Memorial in D.C. arm in arm with him and listen as he told me the stories of the buddies he lost. I would've wanted him to share the most intimate details of the battles they waged and the bravery they displayed. And I would've told him what I tell every Vietnam veteran: I'm so glad you made it home safely.

So I guess in a sense this search is a way to have that conversation with my father. He's not around to tell me what happened that day, or in the days leading up to that moment the 9th Artillery came under fire on a rainy, foggy morning in a muddy LZ, somewhere in the Ia Drang Valley. By seeking out these men who served with my father and obtaining as much documentation as I can find, I've been able to craft the story my father might have told me had the chopper gotten to him in time that morning.

I also hope that through this process I'm able to relate to others, perhaps even some decision makers, the true cost of war.

In honor of his sacrifice, my father was awarded the Purple Heart, the Bronze Medal, the Gallantry Cross with Palm, and the Vietnamese Military Merit Medal.

Perhaps even more precious than these, he earned the respect, love, and admiration of the men who served alongside him. Staff Sergeant David Paul Spears had the highest distinction of all—the honor of being a soldier's soldier.

In the weeks following his death, one of the men in B Battery wrote the following words and sent them to Mama, unsigned:

HE'S GONE NOW

He's gone now, the buddy I once knew
His voice I'll hear no more
We traveled long and distant miles to a strange and foreign shore

We shared our rations, shared our fun
And shared our sorrow, too.
He often spoke of folks back home and the things he'd like to do.

He wanted so to see again the hills of Tennessee.
To roam them with his dog and gun, as free as free could be.
To take again his rod and reel, and find a place to fish.
To while away a lazy day, but he'll never have his wish.

He had a wife and kids back home, two girls and one young lad.
I know they wonder why he's gone, this man they called their Dad.
So when their tears of woe are done and every cheek is dry,
I'll visit them someday I hope and try to tell them why.

A man lays down his precious life for what he feels is right
And pray so hard they'll understand. Somehow, I feel they might.

I never knew myself before, of what such men were made.
But having known his friendship now, for nothing would I trade.

He died, that buddy of mine, to help save freedom's cause,
In a land so far away. A land he'd hoped like all of us
To leave some sunny day.

But he's gone now, this buddy I once knew. His smile I'll no
    more see,
Except locked up deep inside my soul as a treasured memory.

As a buddy is laid to rest may his family remember he was in a
    far away land
Fighting against his will that all the world may be a better place
    to live.

trekking in country

L INDA REACHED INTO HER PURSE AND PULLED OUT TWO PHOTOS. ONE WAS A SNAPSHOT OF ALL OUR KIDS, TAKEN the previous Christmas. Only Amy, Frank's oldest, was missing. Married and with a family of her own now, Amy wasn't able to make it to Mama's home in Shelton, Washington, where for the past decade we'd all gathered each year to celebrate the holidays.

Dave and Shelby Spears have a total of thirteen grandkids. Frank and his wife, Janet, were blessed with six—Amy, David, John, Jessica, Robert, and Rebecca. Tim and I have four. And Linda and her husband, Greg, have three—Mannie, Taylor, and Gabe.

The kids have all grown up hearing the stories about Papaw David. They know he went off to war during the Christmas season of 1965 and that he returned that next August in a shiny silver casket, as our family's, a hometown's, and the nation's military hero. In their own ways, the grandkids have each missed having Papaw David around. They are the new generation of freedom's children.

The price of freedom is extremely high, and it cannot be paid by one generation. It cuts across four, including a soldier's wife or girlfriend, siblings or children, parents and grandparents, aunts and uncles, nephews and nieces, in-laws and outlaws, comrades and friends. The last generation to mourn a hero is the grandchildren. After that the sacrifice is only remembered distantly.

The other snapshot my sister handed me was of Mama, Frank, Linda, and me.

"Hey, that's a good shot of the four of us," I said.

"You're supposed to leave these somewhere over there," she said.

"Where?" I asked.

"I don't know," she answered. "But you'll know it when you see it."

I put them inside my bag for safekeeping. This day, March 1, 2003, was just another overcast Saturday in Portland. My sister had driven two hours from her home in Westport, Washington, to Portland's International Airport, simply to bid me farewell on a journey she still could not believe I was making. "I could never do what you're doing," she said.

"Why?" I asked.

"Lots of reasons, but the twenty-five-hour plane flight is one of 'em," she said. Linda's dark hair fell in layers around her shoulders as she laughed.

Linda has been graced with the dark skin and the dark eyes of Mama's Cherokee ancestors. All the kinfolk say she resembles Granny Ruth. Frank and I both have the blue eyes and the freckles our father had when he was young. The only resemblance Linda and I share is our smiles. People who remember Daddy best tell us our smiles are just like his. We both like hearing that.

The other thing Linda and I share isn't as noticeable, but we got it from Mama: our fear of flying. Mama won't get on a plane to save her life. And, honest to Pete, between 1978, the summer Elvis died, and 1994, I not only refused to fly, but the very thought of it made me sick to my stomach. I'd wake up in the middle of the night in near convulsions, just thinking about boarding a plane. Not that I was going anywhere, mind you. I was a stay-at-home mom to four kids. I could barely get to the bathroom alone, much less take a plane trip anywhere.

Now I fly more than ever. Mostly it's because this search has demanded it, but partly because it's a display of victory to me. A way to demonstrate that my decisions in life are not ruled by fear. That doesn't mean I don't have fears, it just means that, like Mama, I've learned to press on in spite of them.

Still, even I had to admit, the prospect of a twenty-five-hour flight was terrifying, especially considering where I was headed—Vietnam.

On Sunday, March 2, a group of people from twenty-four states, the bulk of them the adult children of soldiers killed in the Vietnam War, departed Los Angeles's LAX for Vietnam. The goal? To return to the battlefields where our fathers died.

I didn't ask Linda to go with me. I knew better. In November 2002 I'd tried to get her to go with me to Washington, D.C., for the twentieth-anniversary ceremonies of the Vietnam Veterans Memorial. I even offered to help pay her way, but she said no. The recent sniper shootings around the D.C. area had contributed to her concerns about the trip. But mainly she was afraid of her own grief. "I'm afraid if I start crying, I might never stop," she said.

I understand Linda's fears about the power of grief. But sometimes I wish my brother and sister would join me in this journey. I know in some ways it's a compliment. They think that I'm strong enough emotionally and spiritually to do the things that they shy away from, such as going to the Wall. But I think they sometimes fail to realize that I hurt every bit as much as they do.

Thankfully, God has sent others alongside me who understand that my grief is what compels me to do these things. Charlie Harootunian is such a man. I met Charlie, a Vietnam veteran, while I was in D.C. A volunteer with the National Parks Service, he performs his duties with unfailing devotion. He makes it a point to stay in contact with the families he meets at the Wall, and he has become a dear friend who constantly encourages me to find ways to keep my father's memory alive. When I complained to him about how lonely this journey is at times, Charlie reminded me that the past is too painful for my family, especially Mama. He encouraged me to give her more time to work through her grief. He also told me how proud he was of me and that he knew Mama was, too. I draw my courage and strength from veterans like Charlie. These men and women enable me to pick up the razor blade and slice slowly through all the sorrow, to get at my father's marrow.

In 2002 I went to D.C. at the invitation of my friend Pauline Laurent, a Vietnam widow and author of the book *Grief Denied: A Vietnam Widow's Story.* Pauline had been instrumental in helping me obtain my father's personnel and death records. And she encouraged me to connect with Sons and Daughters in Touch, a national organization that seeks to bring together the adult children of American servicemen killed or missing in action as a result of the Vietnam War. At her urging, I joined SDIT.

On Wednesday, November 6, Terry McGregor walked into the lobby of Washington, D.C.'s Key Bridge Marriott, his hands stuffed into the pockets of a tan overcoat and a broad grin across his face, and welcomed me to town.

Previously, our only contact had been e-mails. Terry lives in Los Angeles and I live in Oregon, but we both belong to Sons and Daughters in Touch. Our fathers paid our dues to this exclusive club. Their names—Donald V. McGregor and David P. Spears—are just two of more than 58,000 etched in black granite and embedded in the earth at D.C.'s Vietnam Veterans Memorial. We are children of the Wall.

Terry was six years old when his father was killed. Captain Donald McGregor, twenty-nine, was a military advisor assigned to the 1st Battalion, 51st Army of the Republic of South Vietnam. He was slain by sniper fire on August 13, 1963, near the village of An Hoa. He'd been in country six weeks and was on his first mission in the field. Captain McGregor left behind two other sons, Jerry, nine, and Charles, three, and his beloved bride, Leola, twenty-nine.

Terry told me about his family as we walked in darkness, searching with a flashlight for Panel 1 East, Line 26, and Panel 9 East, Line 71, scanning the Wall for our fathers' names. Terry's last memory of his father is not of a sober father-to-young-son talk about war. He does not recall a lingering hug or tearful good-byes. Instead, what he remembers of those last moments is the timbre of his father's laughter and the buzzing motor of hair clippers. "I remember him standing on the sidewalk outside our little house in Idaho and someone was shearing his hair. I don't remember who it was, but they were shaving his head and the two of them were laughing, having a good time. That's my last memory of Dad."

Other than my own siblings, Terry was the first person I met face-to-face whose father died in Vietnam. Meeting him was like finding a childhood pal after decades of separation, or finding out that you aren't the only green Martian on planet Earth. Terry and I share a history of similar sorrows because our fathers share a history as slain soldiers.

At Terry's urging, I'd signed up with the National Park Service to read my father's name for the commemorative service of the twentieth anniversary of the Wall. There had been only two other occasions at which all the names on the Wall were read—at the Wall's dedication and at the tenth anniversary.

It takes four days to read through all the names. Since both our fathers died in the early years, we were among the first readers scheduled. Jan Scruggs, president of the Vietnam Veterans Memorial Fund, introduced Terry on Thursday afternoon.

It was ten-thirty Thursday night when I approached the podium. Puddles of rain made the stage slippery, so I walked across it gingerly. Behind me the ground lights cast an eerie glow on the black surface. My father's name was almost directly behind my back. I'd asked Terry if I could say something besides my father's name. We'd discussed this matter at some length over dinner. He'd encouraged me to say whatever was on my heart.

Thanks to an elaborate sound system, the names of soldiers, dead and gone but not forgotten, reverberated throughout the grounds. I took a deep breath and began reading the list of thirty names before

me: James Kevin O'Leary, Richard Norman Payne, Thomas Frank
Presby, Ronda Lee Raglin. I paused between each name. Finally, I
came to Dad's name: "And my father—you were a hero to me long
before Vietnam—David Paul Spears."

When I walked off the stage, Terry wrapped me in a bear hug.

While we were in D.C., Terry bugged me constantly about joining Sons and Daughters in Touch on their journey to Vietnam. I
knew about the trip from the SDIT newsletter. It had been in the
planning/fund-raising stages for three years. But I couldn't imagine
going. Where would I come up with the money? Besides, I didn't
have much of a desire to go. Most of my life I'd harbored a deep-
seated resentment against the Vietnamese. Weren't they the ones responsible for my father's death?

But something happened there in D.C. on Veterans Day that totally broke me. My friend Kathy Crisp Webb was with me when it
happened.

A self-described "Daddy's girl," Kathy was the second of four
children born to Master Sergeant William "Bill" Crisp and his wife,
Peggy Lou. Kathy was nine when her father was killed in action in
Vietnam. Her sister, Linda, was twelve and her brothers, Billy and
Mark, were six years old and twenty months. Like me, Kathy has
vivid memories of her father.

She and I were talking about our fathers as we entered the east
end of the memorial grounds. Despite the hard rains that fell earlier
that morning, thousands of people were gathering for the afternoon
ceremony. Up until that point, I had not collapsed in tears as Linda
had feared she might if she'd been there. Oh, sure, I'd been emotional reading Daddy's name. And I'd teared up standing there in
front of the Number 9 East Panel looking at my father's name. It felt
great to finally be able to see Daddy eye-to-eye. Still, I had not experienced that overwhelming grief that frightened Linda away. But as
Kathy and I passed under a maple tree dripping with gold, I looked
off to my left and noticed a group of Vietnamese soldiers, dressed in

tan uniforms, holding flags. An American flag and a flag from the Army of the Republic of South Vietnam (ARVN). When I saw those Vietnamese veterans standing in honor of their comrades-in-arms, our fathers, my spirit collapsed.

I cried for the entire day. Nothing I did could ebb the flow. Kathy tried her best to console me, but it wasn't consolation I needed. I wasn't weeping tears of anger. I was weeping over the humility and honor of those men, and for the great losses both our nations had suffered. Nothing, not even Senator John Kerry's tremendous speech that day, moved me nearly as much as that Vietnamese honor guard. I knew then that I would join Sons and Daughter in Touch on that journey to Vietnam.

THE DECISION TO GO to Vietnam came at a great cost to me, personally and professionally, and to our family, financially and emotionally. At the time, I was working a full-time job as a reporter and columnist for a Washington newspaper. I enjoyed what I did, and it showed. I'd won numerous awards and had a good rapport with readers, many of whom wrote to tell me how much they looked forward to my weekly column.

But when I approached my boss about taking the trip to Vietnam and offered to write stories about the trip, he said, "I'm not interested in any stories about children returning to the battlefields where their fathers died, and I don't think our readers will be, either."

I was stunned. I thought it was the cruelest thing anyone has ever said to me, bar none. It was callous, cold, and simply mean. I felt that way then; I feel the same way now.

My boss continued, "Your vacation is denied. If you make this trip to Vietnam, we will consider it job abandonment and that you have voluntarily resigned. Choose the job or choose the trip."

My decision to give up a full-time job and half our family's annual income didn't trouble my husband one bit, even though we both knew I could not stay in eastern Oregon and expect to work as a journalist at that level again. Tim didn't care about the money, or how the lack of it might hurt us with four kids in college. He just shrugged his shoulders and said, "So what? Go. You have to go."

And now he was here, beside me at Portland's International Airport, making sure my bags were properly tagged, my tickets and passport in hand. I knew he would love and miss me but that I had his blessings and his prayers. His love humbles me every single day.

As Tim and Linda hugged and kissed me good-bye, we all fought back tears. I knew they understood how frightened I really was, and not because of the long plane flight. A friend had once said that if the Vietnam War doesn't confuse you, it's because you don't understand all the issues. Our family had long considered Vietnam a terrifying place. For many families like ours, the country represented nothing but crushing grief and oppressive sorrows.

While our nation debated a possible war in Iraq, my mother dropped to her knees and asked the good Lord to bring her daughter safely back home again. It was the same thing she'd prayed for Daddy more than thirty-five years before. Mama was worried sick. The last time she'd sent a loved one off to Vietnam, he didn't come home alive.

"You be careful over there," she'd said when we spoke shortly before I left. "War is breaking out all over the world."

"I'll be all right, Mama," I replied. "Don't you worry." I managed to spit it out with a lot more confidence than I really felt.

vietnam 2003:

in honor, peace, and understanding

JOINING US FOR THE TREK IN COUNTRY WERE A DOZEN OR SO VIETNAM VETERANS, A COUPLE OF PRIESTS, several widows, and a handful of nurses who had served in regional hospitals near the battlefields of Da Nang, Bien Hoa, and Quang Tri. Even a few dignitaries—Tom Corey, president of Vietnam Veterans of America, and Rich Sanders, president of VietNow.

But for most of us, this was our first trip to Vietnam. The plane flight included pit stops in Taiwan and Singapore. Strong headwinds created such a choppy ride that it was akin to navigating the Columbia River in a motorboat on a very windy day. You couldn't help but feel a bit queasy at times. And without some very powerful drugs, catching some shut-eye was nearly impossible. I'd spent most of the night chatting with veteran Ned Devereaux, of Portland, and fellow SDIT member Rob Wilde, of Bend, Oregon. My incessant questioning was probably driving them both crazy.

Morning found nearly everyone milling about the plane's cabin. Only Mokie Porter, editor of Vietnam Veterans of America magazine, *The Veteran*, remained unconscious. Yet, even Mokie awoke when the plane started its descent into Ho Chi Minh City at around 4:30 P.M.

As the plane dropped within sight of the Mekong Delta, I elbowed my way to a window, half expecting to see the Viet Cong wielding guns and shouting unintelligibly. Instead, I saw a quilted agricultural landscape, similar to farmland I'd viewed from American skies. Other sons and daughters, widows and veterans rushed to the windows as the plane continued its descent. Crowds formed around the windows on the left side of the plane. Given our collective weight, I'm surprised the pilot didn't start veering right in an effort to correct. We were leaning over one another, three and four to a seat, our noses pressed up against the panes, like kids gathering around Macy's windows at Christmastime. We were oohhing and ahhhing and laughing as salty tears trickled down our cheeks. Vietnam didn't look so scary after all. Relieved in so many untold ways, we gleefully hugged one another, sat back down, and buckled up for the landing.

Our tour guides from Global Spectrum, the Virginia-based tour company that specializes in such trips for veterans, had prepared us for all the rigmarole at customs. Have passports ready. Don't fool around. Stay with your group. Don't wander off. Hang on to your bags. I felt like a kid at church camp.

Tan Son Nhat Airport in Ho Chi Minh City didn't look like it could have changed much in the past thirty years. Having never been there before I can't be certain, but there's none of the bright chrome, neon lighting, or automated machinery found in our nation's airports, and security didn't seem to be much of a problem because of all those military police with their red-and-gold badges tacked on the sleeves of their green uniforms. One wiry fellow stood up from his seat at the customs desk and gestured angrily, indicating that we weren't in a straight-enough line and that we'd best form one as soon as possible.

Yanking on my bag, I turned and smiled at Treva Whichard, widow of Captain James Atchison, who was with her daughter, Agnes. Treva returned my smile. I marveled silently as the afternoon sun streamed in through the grime-streaked windows, forming an ethereal glow around Treva and her daughter. Then Treva made a comment that I would find myself pondering repeatedly for the rest of the trip. "I feel like I've finally come home," she said.

That stunned me. I couldn't imagine how a Vietnam war widow could feel at home in Vietnam. I understood that our grief bound us to this strange and distant shore. It bound us together the way only death can, the way it had bound our fathers to one another, the way it binds our countries still. But hanging around Tan Son Nhat airport, I didn't feel one bit at home, especially not with all those armed guards standing post.

Our first few days were spent at the Rex Hotel in Ho Chi Minh City. According to local lore, or maybe more aptly, tourist legend, the hotel's rooftop was used each night by the U.S. Army brass to map out the next day's maneuvers. The hotel retains a certain 1950s charm. Bamboo chairs are scattered about. Crystal chandeliers drip from the ceiling. An hourlong massage costs 75,000 dong, the equivalent of five dollars. The hotel staff even changes the carpets in the elevators daily. In the morning the rugs read: GOOD MORNING, REX HOTEL. And later in the day the rugs read: GOOD AFTERNOON, REX HOTEL.

We spent the first couple of days touring, but on the third day, as most of the group shimmied into the dank, dark tunnels at Cu Chi and marveled at the bravery of the men designated as tunnel rats, I begged off the trip, along with two of my teammates, Kelly Rihn and Cammie Geoghegan Olson. I tried to explain to our team leader, veteran Dick Schonberger, that we were weary of sight-seeing. We just wanted a day to hang out, to poke around the shops in Ho Chi Minh City, to have a relaxing lunch, get a manicure, and be pampered before we embarked upon a grueling trip to the country's interior. "What are you? A bunch of candyasses?" Dick bellowed, when we broke the news that we wouldn't be joining the rest of the team. Cammie cowered. Kelly and I laughed. From that moment on, we three girls were affectionately called the Candyass Team.

Cammie Geoghegan Olson of Virginia was only five months old when her father was killed. Lieutenant John Lance "Jack" Geoghegan, twenty-four, was depicted in the book *We Were Soldiers Once . . . and Young,* by Lieutenant General Harold G. Moore and war correspondent Joseph Galloway. Geoghegan and all but three of his men were slaughtered in the Ia Drang Valley on November 15, 1965. Jack Geoghegan was helping a wounded soldier named Willie Godboldt when they were both gunned down. The two soldiers' names are next to each other on the Vietnam Veterans Memorial.

Kelly was seven months old when her father, Specialist Joel Coleman, died. He received his orders for Vietnam in November 1965 and was assigned to Alpha Company, 2nd Battalion, 7th Cavalry Regiment, 1st Cavalry Division. He shipped out to Vietnam on December 22, 1965. In early May 1966, Alpha Company was sent up the coast to Bong Son for Operation Davy Crockett. On May 5, 1966, after a day of searching villages, a bone-tired Alpha Company dug in for the night near a green rice paddy bordered by a thin wood line. Shortly after they settled in, thirty rounds of machine-gun fire popped out from the tree line. Joel Coleman, twenty-one, was killed by hostile ground fire. Neither Kelly nor Cammie have any memories of their fathers. For them and many others, going to Vietnam was a way to make a memory out of something their fathers knew.

I'm pretty certain Cammie will never take another *cyclo* ride again in her life. As the noon hour approached, we girls bartered rides from three fellows pedaling their three-wheel bikes to carry us from the Ho Chi Minh City market to the Caravelle Hotel, about five blocks away. The deal was we'd pay two U.S. dollars each. But the *cyclo* drivers decided after we arrived that they wanted 200,000 dong, more than ten dollars each. After I paid the sum we'd previously agreed upon, the drivers began to yell at us. The three men circled Cammie and demanded more money. Frightened, she started pulling out every wad of dong she had stuffed in her pocket. Kelly and I grabbed her by the elbows and herded her away. If Cammie lived in Ho Chi Minh City, she'd be out on the streets handing out every last penny she could scour up. Kelly and I voted her captain of the Candyass Team.

Because the Rex Hotel maintains computers with Internet connections, I was able to post a letter to the Virtual Wall so that veterans and loved ones, particularly Mama, could log on and read about the journey as it was happening. This was my journal entry for Friday, March 7:

As brother Mark Pitts and I walked back to the hotel from the Saigon bar last night, a boy approached me. (Can you walk on these streets without someone somewhere approaching you to buy something?)

"Jerry's my American name," he said, in the best English I've heard from a Vietnamese person yet. Jerry proceeded to tell me that he needed to sell $20 worth of goods before he could go home. It was already 10:30 p.m. "I have to pay for my school and my brother's school. I only have a mom. Dad left us for another woman," Jerry explained. "In my school I have the best English, but my writing is bad." I know how he feels some days.

Jerry, 14, took my hand and led me across the streets near the Rex Hotel. Not an easy feat. It's kind of like bungee jumping into early morning rush hour. Stop, go, bounce, dodge, OHMYGOD THERE'S 1,500 motorbikes headed straight for me! "Don't look. Follow me," Jerry said. Jerry was able to weasel a couple of bucks from Mark, who said as he handed over the dough, "Jerry, you've got game. Now go away."

Our group started out at the Apocalypse Now bar but had to change plans when a fellow took a special liking to our great leader, Tony Cordero (son of MAJ William E. Cordero). Wrong crowd at that bar, we decided. But Brother Terry McGregor could not escape the clutches of the most cunning 8-year old girl who wrapped her arms around his waist outside the bar. She pleaded with McGregor to buy her wares. When he refused, she cast slurs his way. "Charlie! I no like you!" Beggars are on every street corner in every place we've been so far. Outside the Rex last night, in a red and white dress with a peter-pan collar, stood a girl, about 7, begging folks to buy her flowers. There was no parent in sight. Nothing. She was absolutely beautiful, with her big almond eyes, pleading and holding flowers up to the bus windows or in front of pedestrians. "Please, madam. Please, sir," she begged. But even her poverty didn't compare to what we saw along the Mekong Delta on Thursday.

A three-hour drive from the Rex, the Mekong is flecked with banana, pod and palm trees. But everywhere we went there were people. In the most rural, remote areas, people squat and eat *pho* from ceramic bowls, or sit on plastic chairs. People pedal bikes loaded with straw, or balloons or baskets, three and five bikes deep as buses and vans, and cars whiz past, blowing horns. No one flinches. Not ever. There is a motorbike repair shop in every block, even in the country. And graves, likes those in Louisiana sitting above ground, are scattered randomly about. Stuck in between the rice paddies or the bike shops. They are brightly decorated and often have miniature temples built into them. A place for sacrifice and incense.

The Mekong River reminded me much of my beloved Chattahoochee River in Georgia. It was muddy and wide and surrounded by thick vegetation. Flowers, scarlet, ivory, and lavender, grew among the wildest brambles. We ate a lunch of elephant fish, pork, chicken, rice, rice, and did I mention rice, at this far-out-of-the-way place, which was a nursery of some sort. Lots of potted flowers about. Instead of kids begging for stuff, however, a group of children handed us purple and pink roses as we disembarked from the boat. We toasted our dinner with rice whiskey. I shared a shot with a friend. Have you ever tossed back a shot of diesel fuel? Then, you understand. My head was spinning within seconds. I kept eating, hoping that would help me center myself once more. Geeish! Then, after dinner, the dessert. No, not passion fruit. But the delight of holding a 50-pound python in my very own hands. A truly spiritual experience for me. If you haven't read it, you should read Dennis Covington's *Salvation on Sand Mountain*. The story of a journalist who, while on assignment, gets caught up in the spirit and ends up taking up the rattler like those faith-based southern folks he's writing about. I love that book. Not because I've been a member of those churches, but because I think being able to grasp in our hands the things we fear most is a powerful thing. Even if we can only hang on for a moment.

I lived my early life in fear after Daddy died. He was the center of what made me feel safe. I've spent much of my adult life trying to regain that sense of security and safety and to not feel so threatened by the powers of this world that are beyond my control. So it seemed only spiritual that I should come to Vietnam and pick up the python. The place where my fears began and now the place where I have held those fears in my hand, if only for a moment. Brother Mark Pitts didn't have quite the same spiritual experience with his snake-handling moment. . . . Yes, us fatherless children of 'Nam have all sorts of fears. But we are here facing them. The way our fathers did before us. Today we split up for the first time, to head to the sites where our fathers fought their battles. Keep us in your prayers. Courage is not the absence of fear but the ability to press on in spite of it. You veterans taught us that. Thank you for that.

ON SATURDAY, MARCH 8, we split up into smaller, color-coded teams, to begin our trek in country to visit our fathers' death sites. I was part of the Orange Team, which all the veterans agreed had the most grueling itinerary.

We were headed into one of the most remote areas of Vietnam, the Central Highlands. Our team boarded a bus at o'dark-thirty for a ride through Ho Chi Minh City. We stared bleary-eyed as people clustered like starlings in parking lots and grassy knolls, contorting their bodies into tai chi pretzels as part of their morning exercise regime, and buzzing into markets with baskets of fish and fruit, and baskets of baskets. Heavy-equipment trucks, a rare sight, roared by us. They are allowed on the streets only during the dark, Viet, our guide, explained, because it's too dangerous during daylight when the city's fifteen million people are hustling about on mopeds, bikes, and *cyclos.*

At Tan Son Nhat Airport, we boarded a turboprop plane and headed into Pleiku, in the Central Highlands. The plane was cramped; a national soccer team filled up most of it. Our group of ten sat near the back, and the turboprop engines were so loud we couldn't hear one another over their roar.

Most of the way, I studied a Vietnamese family sitting just ahead of me. The young mother nestled down on the inside seat as the father tended to three girls. The youngest was a dark-eyed cherub obviously proud of her new walking shoes, which she kept untying and her daddy kept retying. The toddler ambled about the aisle the entire trip.

The mountain range stretching out beneath the plane reminded me of the Great Smoky Mountains that Daddy loved so well. I wondered if Granny Leona knew where I was at that moment. Could she look down from heaven and see me? Could Daddy?

I pulled a pair of plastic heart-shaped sunglasses from my pack and handed them to the toddler. Her nose was too pug to hold them up, so the glasses fell sideways across her cheeks. While her father laughed at the silly sight, I fought back hot tears. I was thinking about Cammie and Kelly. Their fathers hadn't lived long enough to see them strut about in their first new pair of shoes or put on their first pair of plastic sunglasses.

At Pleiku's airport, as a warm wind billowed, I stood on the tarmac and made a 360-degree turn. I couldn't get over the mountains. I had never pictured Vietnam as a country with mountains. I thought only of blood-soaked jungles. I was glad for the ridges that rose up out of the valley. I knew Daddy would have felt some safety, hedged in on all sides by mountains. After all, he was a son of Appalachia.

Our veteran guide, Dick Schonberger, informed us that we would have a full day. We had thirty minutes to clean up at the Pleiku Hotel, the town's best hotel, before heading out for Dragon Mountain and the Ia Drang Valley.

A snappy wind blew across the fields of brittle grasses at the base of Dragon Mountain, just outside Pleiku. Shortly before he died, my father had sent a picture to Granny Leona. In the photo, Daddy and his Army buddies posed with a couple of dozen Montagnard children. The Montagnards are a mix of tribal people, including Banar and Jarrai. They supported the American efforts during the war and continue to suffer under Vietnam's Communist rule. In the picture Daddy sent Granny, the kids' clothes are ragged. Each child stands barefoot in a muddy gully. Behind them is a sturdy howitzer and the slope of Dragon Mountain. I wore a copy of that photo about my neck throughout the trip.

As we drove past Dragon Mountain, our guides, Hai and Viet, began chattering excitedly. Viet explained that they felt we had found the gully where Dad had posed for that photo thirty-seven years past. Directing the van drivers to pull over, they climbed out of the vehicles and began passing copies of the picture to local villagers. The villagers concurred with Viet and Hai. That was good enough for me.

My teammates asked what they could do to help. I asked them to gather rocks with me. I was constructing a rock monument, a cairn. Half a dozen local children from the nearby village joined us. Two of the girls dashed home to put on their best dresses. I handed copies of my father's picture to the kids as they formed a crescent behind me.

Then I reached for the family photos that my sister had given me days earlier as she said good-bye at Portland's airport. She'd told me that God would show me where to leave the photos. She was right. I placed them in front of the makeshift monument, propping them against the cairn with smaller rocks.

Opening the lid on a plastic jar I'd brought with me, I began to pour the contents out. "Inside this jar is dirt from Fort Benning, the place where my father trained troops for years," I said. "And sand from the North Shore of Hawaii, where he loved to fish." Then, scraping it with a rock, I scooped up the red clay soil of Vietnam and mixed it into the jar.

"When Native Americans were a nomadic tribe, they would build rock monuments before leaving camp," I explained. "These monuments were a way for them to mark their journey—to see how far they had traveled and in which direction."

I looked up at my teammates who had formed a half-circle in front of me. I saw the tears streaming down the faces of my sisters, Cammie and Kelly. I recognized how fortunate I'd been. I was nine when my father died. I could remember the way Daddy walked and the way he talked. I remembered how he smelled of sun-dried T-shirts and Old Spice. And I recalled how his laughter made a room rumble. Daddy laughed a lot. It troubled me deeply that Cammie and Kelly lacked such memories of their fathers. Tears streamed down my own face. "As military children we were a nomadic tribe," I said. "And for those of us who lost fathers here, Vietnam is our rock monument. My prayer is that when we look back we will realize how far we've come in our love and appreciation for the Vietnamese people."

I've walked the streets where my father roamed as a boy. I've sat in the pews of the church where he was baptized. Over the years, I've made several trips to my father's grave at Andrew Johnson National Cemetery in Tennessee. And trips to the Vietnam Veterans Memorial in Washington, D.C. But I've never felt my father's presence more strongly than I did there in that dusty red-dirt gully at the base of Dragon Mountain, in a land full of people whose language I couldn't speak and whose customs I didn't know. Finally I knew what it felt like to come home. This was the place where my father had been waiting for me all these years.

It was then that I understood what widow Treva Whichard had meant on that first day in country when we were standing in the customs line at Tan Son Nhat Airport.

I bowed my head and uttered a prayer of thanks: "Thank you, God, for taking care of our family all these years. Thank you for Mom, and Frank and Linda. And for all the mercy and grace that got us through all the hard times. We still miss Daddy, but it's okay.

I know he's been right there with you, watching over us all these years."

ANOTHER SEVERAL HOURS passed before we reached the remote village of Plei Me, site of a special forces camp, and our only access to the Ia Drang Valley, where both Cammie's father and my father bled to death. The Ia Drang Valley was one of the more violent regions of the war.

In a manioc field just outside Plei Me we found the untouched remnants of our fathers' presence—rusted hinges from ammunition boxes, chunks of mortar, and shards of shell casings. At the base of a bush, I placed a bouquet of flowers, alongside those Cammie left in honor of her father. Even though Cammie was blessed with a devoted stepfather who honored the memory of her dad, she is still haunted by her father's absence.

"It's that not knowing, not knowing anything. Not knowing what his voice sounds like. Not knowing how he walked. It's hard. It's not fair," Cammie said, her voice breaking with emotion. Kelly and I wrapped her in a hug.

Like the kudzu vines common throughout America's Southeast, dense overgrowth covers the Ia Drang Valley as far as the eye can see. Because of continued unrest among the dozens of bickering minority peoples in that region, visitors are not allowed into the valley. Historically, the minority groups have tried to separate themselves from one another, and from the Communist regime. Cammie and I made a vow in that field; we vowed we'd make it into the Ia Drang Valley someday, to our fathers' death sites.

Then, as our teammates waited in vans, Cammie, Kelly, and I walked through the village of Plei Me, passing out colorful balloons to the children. Mothers covered their mouths and giggled at the spectacle—three prissy white girls strolling down the red-dirt road of a Third World village. We wondered if they had seen Americans since the soldiers pulled out. We might have been the first white women some of them had ever seen.

A boy and a man drove by us in a wagon with wooden wheels, pulled along by a water buffalo. Kelly stopped suddenly. "Do you hear that?" she asked.

Cammie and I stood still as gateposts. "Hear what?" I asked.

"That music," Kelly said. "It's the Beatles."

Sure enough, in one of the most surreal moments of our trip, a Beatles refrain echoed from a nearby hut: "Yesterday, all my troubles seemed so far away."

We burst out in laughter. Was it possible our fathers were serenading us from the heavens above?

I MET PETER in a marketplace, but Peter is not his real name. Because he lives in a Communist country, under an oppressive regime, Peter asked me not to use his real name. On the day we met he asked me why I was in his country. I told him all about Sons and Daughters in Touch and our historic return to the battlefields where our fathers were slain.

"I am like you," he said.

"In what way?" I asked.

"My father, too, was killed during the American War," he said. "He was an ARVN soldier."

I invited Peter to drop by my hotel room after dinner for a visit. When he arrived, he pointed out the rules posted near the phone: "No guests allowed in hotel rooms." Another sign that Big Brother is watching, Peter said. His almond-shaped eyes lit up as he laughed.

Peter wore a short-sleeved cotton shirt and black pants. His dark hair was cropped close on the sides, longer on top. His laugh was a deep bellow, something you'd expect from a much bigger man. Delicate of frame, he weighed about 135 pounds and was only about five feet eight inches tall. But his spirit was overpowering; it filled the room.

He wanted to share his story of growing up fatherless in Vietnam. I admired his bravery; this one indulgence could have landed him in jail and gotten me a swift boot home, or worse.

The youngest of seven children, Peter was three years old when his father was slain. An ARVN lieutenant, he was killed at Quang Tri in 1972, during what the Vietnamese refer to as the Summer of the Red Fire. "There was very terrible fighting there for three months between the North and South Vietnamese," Peter said. "Only you can guess the South was naturally all blown away."

Peter's last memory with his father was a surprise trip to Quang Tri. "I remember it was two weeks before he died," he said. "He took me and an older brother in a jeep to his base camp. It was the first and only time. We were very excited. He took us to a munitions-storage room. He let us play with the ammunition. I don't know why. There was guns, bullets, everything."

A short time later, when Peter's mother heard her husband had died, she took her older sons and went in search of the body. But the North Vietnamese had piled the dead ARVN in heaps alongside the roads in Quang Tri, Peter explained. "It was impossible for my mother to find him."

So she returned to their home in Hue without a body to bury. She wasn't the only distraught widow in the neighborhood to do so.

"In my village between 1972 through 1975, I could say everyone's house lost someone," Peter said. "There were so many."

After the Summer of the Red Fire, Peter and his family had to flee Hue when the North Vietnamese drove them out. Peter remembers his mother handing him a basket of household items and telling him to run quickly for his life. "She tells me, 'Run. Be safe. Run to Da Nang,'" Peter recalled.

Throngs of people were fleeing the city. Along with dozens of refugees, Peter and his family climbed into a military van. There were forty people crammed one on top of the other when the rig rolled on an *S* curve at the top of Cloudy Mountain and down a

steep ravine. Peter and his family escaped mostly unharmed, save for
bruises. Sixteen others died in the crash.

For a while Peter was forced to head into the jungles to find work.
That was the worst time, he said. I asked him to write down the story
as he told it to me that night. Here is what he wrote:

> After finishing my high school, being unable to go to university, to
> find any job, I had to go to the jungle to work as a gold prospector to
> earn my life and to support my mom. So many dangers in the jun-
> gle: dangerous animals such as tigers, leopards; high and slippery
> mountain sides; tunnel collapse, disease such as malaria, yellow fever
> and so on. Many young men died there forever. There were so many
> threats that it's necessary to go in a group. Truong Son range lies
> along the western side of Vietnam, so we just headed west, some-
> times from our hometown, sometimes from the DMZ or further
> north. The first time I did it I was nearly 18 and I worked that field
> for a year, each journey lasted around one month.
>
> I witnessed so many broken-heart stories there and I can never
> forget. But the death of my friend who I tried to save his life has
> been haunting me all the time. I don't remember how long he had
> fell sick of malaria until I tried to bring him out of the jungle, but
> I'm sure we had been in the jungle rather long, everybody got ex-
> hausted. I was the youngest and strongest (!) that time, so it's only me
> who could take care of him. The journey from the town (about
> 20–30 km north of DMZ) to the place we worked took us over two
> days. Of course, it took me more with him on my shoulder. We had
> to cross over streams, mountains . . . and he seemed to be heavier,
> hour by hour. After one and a half days I could not stand anymore. I
> laid him down on a top of a small hill, asking him not to move any-
> where and trying to find someone else to help. I finally found a tribal
> village and some tribesmen followed me immediately. It was about 9
> a.m. when I left him, and I could get there around 4 or 5 p.m. It was
> too long with him, I knew, but much, much longer with me. We

soon found the hill where I laid him, but found nothing. We spread over the area and finally found him dead by a stream (around 200 yards away) with his head in the water. He was so thirsty with the fever I knew, but I wondered if he got some water before he died or still being thirsty . . . I felt like something inside me broke, and it's still hurting me now when I am typing these lines. But you know, it's not the hardest thing I suffered. I only faced with the worst thing when I brought his corpse to his mother. I didn't know how and what to tell her. . . . Sorry Karen, I cannot go on.

Many American soldiers wanted to marry Peter's mother, to take her to the land of the brave and the free. "She was young, thirty-five," Peter said. "And very beautiful. Americans liked her." But she was not interested in moving to America with any of the strong soldiers who offered to take care of her and her children.

Peter's mother kept a picture of his father, decked out in his ARVN uniform, above the home altar, and the mandatory photo of Ho Chi Minh, or as the nationalists call him, "Uncle Ho."

One day the provincial police came into Peter's home. When they saw the altar, they became enraged and screamed at his mother. "'Who is this enemy soldier?'" Peter recalled them demanding. "'Why you hang this enemy above Ho Chi Minh?'"

Peter's brothers told the soldiers, "This is our father."

The soldiers yelled back, "'I don't care he's your father! He's an enemy! Throw him away!'"

So Peter's mother took their father's picture down. Along with that of Ho Chi Minh, he noted with a chuckle. She threw the picture of Ho Chi Minh away. But she hid his father's picture.

I asked Peter if he blames Americans for his father's death, the way I had blamed the Vietnamese for the loss of my father.

No, he said. He blames the Communists. They mistreated so many after the Americans left Saigon in 1975. Those who served with the

Army of the Republic of South Vietnam were considered traitors. Their families were despised by the North Vietnamese.

"In spite of what people think of me and of my family—that we are losers, traitors—I'm proud of my father," he said.

Peter appreciated the Americans and the Vietnamese who fought to free his country from oppressive rule. His father's death strengthened his desire to be a free man himself.

Three times Peter tried to find passage to America. The first time was in 1990, when he bribed his way aboard a boat, but after a week drifting about the South China Sea, a fierce storm arose and tossed the boat back to Vietnamese shores. Peter was devastated. "When we came to the shore there was a flag," he recalled. "A North Vietnamese flag. A red flag with a yellow star. The police were waiting for us."

In 1992 Peter tried again to escape his motherland.

"I was working as a carpenter," he said. "I paid for a place on the boat to escape. But I missed the boat."

Perhaps it was God's way of watching over him. "Everybody on the boat was killed."

No matter how hard I tried, I could not imagine wanting to live in another country so badly that I would be willing to risk life, limb, and livelihood for that chance the way Peter and thousands of other Vietnamese had done.

As a small child, with a basket full of family treasures clutched to his chest, Peter had fled his hometown of Hue while North Vietnamese dropped fiery bombs in the streets. As a teen, he had worked in malaria-infested jungles to help support his war-ragged family. As a young adult, he had risked his life in an ill-equipped boat for passage to America. Peter had suffered so much for freedom's sake. Not only had he lost his father, this courageous young man was willing to lose his own life for a chance to live as a free man. Peter said we should both be proud of our fathers—they died fighting so all Vietnamese people could live in a nation free from oppression.

Sitting there in that hotel room, listening to Peter's stories, I was overcome with grief. Not just grief over the loss of our childhoods and the continual absence of our fathers, but for all the suffering his family and thousands of other Vietnamese families had endured. I knew losing Daddy would've been easier emotionally for me if such a sacrifice had ensured a life of freedom for men like Peter.

Thanks to a lot of political mangling and military mismanagement, American troops and the soldiers for the Army of the Republic of South Vietnam failed in their mission, but did that diminish the sacrifices these men made? Or our families' sacrifices?

Of course not. If anything, the suffering of Peter's family and, yes, the suffering my family endured are greater because our fathers did not succeed in their mission. Peter grew up fearing a retaliatory Communist regime. I grew up fearing men and ghosts I could not name. In those terrifying moments, we both wanted the same thing—our fathers to rescue us from war's poverty and pain.

We'd grown up halfway across the world from each other, but under the same cloud of confusion. The North Vietnamese had labeled all the ARVN soldiers traitors. American antiwar protestors berated Vietnam veterans as murderers. In both instances, fathers like ours were spit upon and cursed. And as kids, we'd grown up in societies that didn't allow us to talk about our fears or our fathers. That silence had stewed for a long time. I asked Peter to explain how he'd reached a peace about his father's death:

The "sorrow of war" is what I have wanted to share with you personally, and all Americans commonly. You are right when believing that Vietnamese seem to be "happier." Some things seem to be forgotten so quickly by Vietnamese.

In fact, as you know, suffering from fighting, starving and losing someone's dear would never be easy for everyone. But, historically, wars took place in Vietnam so many times that we say "1,000 years of Chinese domination, 100 years of French domination and 20 years of civil war" and that people think of Vietnam as a war not a country!

It seems that we did not have any time to recover, to build our country and, bitterly, we did not have enough tears for the dead. Take my mom as an example, when my father died, undoubtedly, she cried so many tears, but I'm sure it didn't last long. She must not have wanted to live anymore, but she couldn't do it. He went away and left behind him 7 kids. Who would look after them if not her? Working hard to raise all her children has helped her to forget everything. No time for her to think of the reason why he died, who killed him. Now all she could do was to save all her energy to support the children. Time passed by and one day she's suddenly found her kids grow well and they love each other and love her. She would sometimes cry only happy tears when looking back and feel pleased with somethings she had done for her kids, and thinking she's just completed a great mission that her passed-away husband gave to her.

Moreover, it's Vietnamese nature to forgive and forget. On the battlefields we fought the enemy bravely, we were willing to sacrifice ourselves to protect our country. But if the day after they came back not in military uniform we would take them as friends. We could only survive by doing that. We could never live with the pains and hatreds inside. Yes, Vietnamese are very religious. Catholi[ci]sm has taught us to forget and Buddhism [has taught us] to set our minds free from the hatred, the greed. Life and others could only be seen beautiful and nice with a peaceful mind.

Instead of living with the bad memories of the past, we should look forward to live a better life, to treat each other well and everything would be very easy with love and peace in our heart.

Peter gave me the precious gift of grace that night when he taught me why our fathers had risked and, indeed, given their lives. It was so that men like Peter might one day live in a free country, one that promises its people economic opportunity and the freedom to hang their dead father's picture wherever they like, a nation that grants people the freedom to invite whomever they wish into their homes or hotel rooms, and to use their given names without fear of retribution. The freedom to read a book of their own choosing, or to worship in a church of their choice. The sort of freedoms I've enjoyed every single day of my life and taken for granted for far too many of them.

I wished somebody had explained all this to me when I was a young girl.

Peter had his own wish: "Why could I not have met you ten years ago?"

The last time Peter tried to flee Vietnam was in 1995.

"I bought two sets of bones of American soldiers," he said. "One set had 30 percent of the body. The other had 90 percent. They had the dog tags with them. We made a photograph of the dog tags, and we sent them to Thailand to be examined. We thought with these bones we could get permission to go to America."

He said the bones were certified to be those of American soldiers, enabling him to broker a deal. "American officials said they would get me out if I would show them where the bones were found," he said.

But the deal was spoiled by a raid from the provincial police, who confiscated the bones.

"The Vietnamese government wanted to return the soldiers bones themselves, not through the Vietnamese people," Peter said. "A fleet of police cars surrounded our home and took the American bones away. The Vietnamese government took credit for returning them."

He was not penalized by the police for hoarding the bones. "No. No punishment. That's a good thing," he said, chuckling.

And now, Peter said, it was too late to leave. "I don't want to leave my mother. You know we have a saying in Vietnam, 'A mother can raise ten children but ten children cannot care for one mother.'

Sometimes my older brothers are a little bit careless. Our mother is ill and they don't check on her. I feel I must stay. I have obligations to my mother."

Then, Peter told me about the towering statue in the center of Da Nang. As tall as a three-story building, the carved statue is a woman donned in traditional Vietnamese peasant garb. She stands with her right arm outstretched and her left hand over her breast, near her heart. She carries several bags, perhaps the sum total of her family's possessions. Her face is stoic, resigned to fate. She looks strong, powerful, but there's a tenderness around her eyes. As if they have seen the future and fear its sorrows. "This is Hero Mother," Peter said.

She represents the women who grieved the loss of their sons, their brothers, their husbands in the American War in Vietnam. "One by one, these mothers saw their husbands and kids off to battles and never met them again," Peter said. Just as his mother had done.

"Some mothers lost seven sons or more. Men died for the country. They are actual heroes. But it's the mothers, the wives, who suffered at home, who are the real heroes. That is what I think."

The North Vietnamese built this memorial to honor women who lost so much during the war. Peter said the Vietnamese people try to find other ways to honor these women as well. "We build them houses, give them money and gifts very often."

Peter recalled that when he was attending university he worked part-time in a hotel that was caring for a hero mother. He and his coworkers would often ask her to tell the story of her loss.

"She told us, 'I lost seven men of mine, my husband and six sons. My husband and the first son left for the battle almost at the same time in the early 1960s. I sometimes received their letters that first year, rather late, three or four months after the sending day. Then the letters were less and less.

"'I also sent them some, but they could not receive any, I guess, because they moved very often. I received the bad news from my husband's unit first and then the son's. In the same month. Bitterly, their letters still came when they had been dead. My other sons gradually went and never came back. I was waiting for them, at least one of them, coming back to me the next few years after the war, but then no one.' "

Peter and his coworkers were always surprised whenever they heard this hero mother's tale. "She told her story in a very calm tone of voice," Peter said. "No tears. No emotion. Not at all. Why?"

But having witnessed his own mother's grief, Peter knew the answer. "She had cried so much tears when receiving the bad news, when unhopefully waiting for someone to come back. There is no more tears to cry now," he said. "That is what I think."

THE PAIN OF WAR does not end when the bombing stops. Despite the decades that have passed, many of my fellow SDIT friends are still waiting for their fathers' remains to be returned home for burial. There are over 1,800 American soldiers still missing in action in Vietnam, Cambodia, and Laos. There is no getting over the Vietnam War for those families. Not for any of us, really. The Vietnam War, as all wars do, forever altered the landscape of our nation and our families, causing us to fight our way through some tough terrain.

I have come to terms with a harsh history, as a daughter and as a citizen of a free nation. I don't miss my father any less with each passing year. I am simply more aware of all the life he's missed. I did not go to Vietnam seeking closure. Grief is a journey with a beginning, but it does not have an end, not in this life anyway. But my trip helped me realize that Vietnam isn't the scary jungle I'd always imagined it to be.

"For the first time in my thirty-seven years of life, I believe I will think of the country first, not the war, when I hear the word *Vietnam*," Cammie said during our long flight home.

Moments before we'd boarded a plane in Singapore, bound for Los Angeles, our group gathered around big-screen televisions and listened as President Bush announced that American troops would soon invade Iraq. My heart sank into my gut. I said a prayer for the families that would soon be thrust into an inevitable lifelong journey of grief and reconciliation.

The search for honor, peace, and understanding is, ultimately, up to each one of us.

"The art is to ransom sacred moments—the message of the past— and to deposit them in the bank of eternity," Rabbi Marshall Meyer once said while commenting on the death of Martin Luther King, Jr.

Our journey in country allowed us sons and daughters the chance to ransom the sacred moments of our fathers' lives so we can carry them to eternity's shores. We're sure our soldier fathers will have camp set up by the time we arrive.

hero mama

THE CORRECTIONAL OFFICER STUDIED ME WITH A WARY EYE AS I EMPTIED MY POCKETS OF CAR KEYS AND COINS and placed them in a bowl she handed me. I paused when she said, "Remove your shoes, ma'am."

"My shoes?" I replied, looking at the stain-ridden carpet beneath my feet. "Not unless you give me a pair of slippers to put on."

Standing behind me, Linda cried out, "I'm not taking off my shoes!"

"You're going to have leave that camera here," the officer said, ignoring Linda's protests.

Frustrated, I glanced out the glass doors Linda and I had, of our own free will, walked through into the Washington Corrections Center in Shelton, Washington.

Rain pounded the glass, sounding like a barrage of BB shot. It was the kind of ruckus that Frank and his childhood buddy Joe Kirkland used to fire off, sending squirrels and birds helter-skelter, seeking refuge in the tallest Georgia pines.

I put up a fuss when the officer tried to take away my camera. Finally, she gave in about the camera, not the shoes. "Okay, as long as you don't take any pictures of the facility," she ordered.

"Sure, no problem," I replied.

I handed my driver's license to another officer and signed in as a guest. Linda did the same.

It was Monday, March 31, 2003. I'd been back from Vietnam for nearly two weeks, barely long enough to recoup from the extreme jet lag that had me waking at two every morning and sleeping at three every afternoon.

Gates clinked and rattled as Linda and I were led from one section of the facility to another. Frank and I had been in prison before—him for drug use, me for my job as a reporter—but this was Linda's first look at the bowels of a maximum-security prison, and she didn't like it one bit. Her dark eyes were cast downward, and a frown creased her forehead. Her thick, dark hair cascaded past her shoulders and partially hid her face, like an exquisite shawl.

Mama's coworkers had planned a surprise retirement party for her last day. Sneaking Linda, Frank, and me into the prison was the biggest surprise of all. Frank hadn't arrived yet. Fearing that Mama would show up for work early, as was her custom, her coworkers intended to lock Linda and me away in an office at the infirmary until they got Mama situated.

We were walking between the administrative building and the infirmary when a man stepping onto a prison bus stopped to greet us. "I knew your Mama and Daddy at Fort Benning," he said.

Linda and I looked at each other.

"You knew our daddy?" I asked.

"Yes, ma'am. And your mama, too," he replied. "I used to see her hanging out at the NCO Club on base."

"And now you work with her?" Linda asked. We were both stunned. Mama had never said a word about working with someone who'd known her in Georgia.

"Yes, ma'am," he said.

"Nice to meet you, sir," I said as the man took another step onto the bus. Prison officials were scurrying around us, rushing us off before

Mama arrived. They locked us in the office of the supervisory nurse. The small window in the door had been covered with a sign that said DO NOT DISTURB. A desk cluttered with files and loose paper stood in one corner. A clock ticked away.

Mama worked the swing shift. It was nearly 2:30 P.M. Frank still hadn't arrived, but Linda and I could hear Mama talking outside in the hall.

"What do we do if she comes in here?" I asked.

"She won't," said Beth, the supervisory nurse. "She never comes in here if I have that sign up."

Mama had been a prison nurse at Shelton for eighteen years. She had first worked in a prison while living in Alaska. She claimed it wasn't as hard on her physically as working in a hospital's intensive care units.

It always struck me as odd that Mama had been drawn to the most difficult jobs. Much of her early career was spent tending to heart attack and stroke victims, most of whom died in those years. In her later career, Mama cared for some of the most god-awful folks in the entire nation. Murderers. Rapists. Just plain mean and evil people. I could never figure out if growing up the only sister of all those brothers had toughened Mama or if Daddy's death had scarred her so badly that the only pain she could feel was so sharp that others naturally recoiled from it. Whichever it was, Mama never shied away from tough jobs.

The door opened and finally Frank slipped in, laughing. "Can you believe they let me in this place?" he said.

"I can't believe they ever let you out of prison in the first place," I teased.

Frank hadn't been behind bars since he was released from Fort Leavenworth. "The great thing about this visit is knowing I get to leave when I want," Frank said, laughing again.

Linda rolled her eyes at the two of us. Our baby sister can be the most pious person in the world. Sometimes she acts as if God dropped her off with the wrong family. Nothing about prison hu-mors her in the least. "You look nice," Linda said to him, changing the subject.

Frank was wearing dress slacks and a plaid-print shirt with a tie. He'd dropped about thirty pounds since I'd last seen him at Christmas. He'd been diagnosed with diabetes since then and was working to control it with diet and exercise. He'd also quit smoking a year earlier.

I was wearing a pink shirt I had made for me at the silk market in Hoi An and a pair of black silk pants. Linda was dressed in black slacks and top. We all looked festive.

None of us had ever expected Mama to retire. She'd worked since Daddy died. It was hard to imagine her rolling around the country in a recreational vehicle. She had friends, but most of them were people she worked with. She had given up any hopes of a sustainable love life once she moved west at age thirty-seven. She'd dated sporadically over the years, but nothing of any consequence. If she was lonely, she never let on, at least not to us.

Beth opened the door and motioned for us to follow her down the hallway. Mama was already there with most of the infirmary staff, from all shifts. The break room was narrow, so people were spilling out into the hall. Beth squeezed by them, followed by Linda, Frank, and me.

Mama was across the room, holding a Ritz cracker with a slice of deli meat in one hand and a napkin in the other, talking to a coworker. She wore a blue wool blazer, a pair of jeans, and high-heeled boots. In December she'd shocked us all by bleaching her dark brunette hair a golden hue, the color of harvest wheat. Mama didn't need a man in her life to make her feel desirable. The right clothes could always do that for her. These days she buys her padded bras at Victoria's Secret.

Linda walked up to Mama and gave her a hug.

"What are you doing here?" Mama asked. Then she saw Frank and me. "How'd you get in?"

I hadn't seen Mama since Christmas, since my trip to Vietnam, but she's simply not the kind of gal who whoops and hollers. Her smile and the moistness in her dark eyes told me more than any words ever could. We hugged. "I can't believe you drove all the way up here," Mama said.

"I wouldn't miss this for anything," I replied.

For the next hour or so we lingered in that room, picking at the melons and deli foods spread across a banquet table underneath the sign that read HAPPY RETIREMENT, SHELBY.

Person after person welcomed me to the prison and told me what a wonderful mother I had.

"She's one of the best," one lady said. "Tough, but smart. She taught me a lot."

"Are you the writer?" another woman asked.

"Yes," I replied.

"I feel like I've known you for years," she said. "Your mother is so proud of you. She brings your articles to work for all of us to read."

"She does?" I asked, blinking back hot tears. It had never occurred to me that Mama talked about me or my work to her coworkers.

"Didn't you just go to Vietnam?"

"Yes," I said.

"That must've been some trip," she replied.

"The trip of a lifetime," I answered.

Later that night Mama and I sat in the den of her home watching the videos I'd taken during my trip. I thought about how our relationship had been changed by the events surrounding this book.

When I began this search in 1996, I just wanted to find the men who served with Daddy. Somebody who could tell me what happened the day he died. Somebody who could tell me what kind of soldier and man he'd been. The sorts of stories Mama couldn't or simply hadn't shared with me over the years.

Granny was the only person I'd ever felt I could freely discuss my father with, and she was dead. Sometimes Linda and I talked about

Daddy, but not as much as we talked about raising kids. Frank and I had never really discussed our growing-up years, Mama, or how Daddy's death had devastated us.

Mama had mailed me all of Daddy's letters in December 2001. I had not asked for them. I knew about them, of course. As a teenager I had snuck into her bedroom and pulled down the box where she stored them. I would hold my breath as I opened the red-white-and-blue-striped envelopes. And I would invariably weep as I read the words my father wrote to the woman he loved. I would cry not only because I missed my father but because I missed the woman my mother was before his death. The mother I lost to America's most unpopular war.

When Mama mailed me those letters, she and I were not on the best of terms. She'd left my house in a huff in June following my twin daughters' graduation. The long days of summer had passed without either of us uttering a word to each other. There wasn't any one thing that had caused the rift between us. It was a pile of discarded rubbish, the sort that sits in a heap for years in the backyard while everyone ignores it.

Finally, I relented and called her shortly before the girls and I went to Hawaii. I had not been back to the island since 1966. Our last years with Daddy were spent enjoying the paradise that is Oahu. I looked forward to sharing my memories of Daddy with my daughters. I wanted them to visualize their grandpa as a young father, playing horseshoes in the mud, riding a moped through the pineapple fields, fishing the surf of Oahu's North Shore, marching around cannons at Schofield, and hiding Easter eggs under banana trees. I urged Mama to make the trip with us. She flatly refused.

Mama simply didn't understand why I was going back to Hawaii. Or why as a writer I wanted to poke around such a sorrowful story. She was certain it was just my way of making her look bad. All that condemnation I'd directed toward her as a teen had taken root and embedded itself into her psyche.

I tried to explain that that wasn't it, that I felt that this story was something God was directing me to write, for whatever reason. I told her that my feelings toward her as a teenager had long since been resolved. I understood things as a woman that I could not understand as a child. Like why a woman might confuse sex for love, the way I had with Wesley Skibbey, the way she had with countless men. I told her that I looked at her and our past with different eyes now—eyes more level with her own.

But she didn't believe me. Mama had never gotten over the feeling that she didn't measure up. In her quiet moments she saw herself as the timid young girl who used to deliver laundry to the back door of the big houses of Rogersville's wealthy families. Or as the sassy young widow who wore red hot pants and embraced "Harper Valley PTA" as her theme song.

Things had softened greatly between us. That change was the result not of any one pivotal moment but rather of the little, day-by-day communiqués. I had to know things only she could answer. We talked by phone several times a week and e-mailed more often. Mama was still reluctant to talk about Daddy and his death, her hurt, and the longings she'd suffered, but she knew that I wasn't going to give up and go away. I could be just as mule-headed as Mama, and I was determined to get this story down.

Even so, she wasn't making it easy for me. When Mama mailed me Daddy's letters, she sent them along with a warning. In a handwritten letter, she told me she expected two things from me in return—that I make copies of Daddy's letters for Frank and Linda, and that I not use them to shame her because "your father loved me very much, Karen. And he would be very disappointed if you used his letters to hurt your family."

While I was grateful for the letters, Mama's warning didn't faze me. Nobody could make me any more aware of the responsibility I had as a daughter and a writer to get our family's story straight. For me, writing is like being a mother, hoping to bring life to a child. I hold in my hands this miracle of beauty, awe, and wonder. Along with it is a burdensome responsibility.

It's a terrifying role, one I approach completely aware that it's going to take a power beyond me—a power I don't control and can't manufacture by sheer will. All life is a precious gift, even the life of words.

In retrospect, my search to reclaim my father did parallel that of Meg in the fictional tale *A Wrinkle in Time*.

"If you want to help your father you must learn patience," Mrs. Whoo had warned Meg. "To stake one's life for the truth. That is what we must do."

This search demanded that I risk my career and my relationship with my siblings and my mother. During that summer of silence, when Mama and I weren't speaking to each other, I asked Linda why she thought Mama was so upset with me.

"She doesn't understand why you keep bringing up all this stuff, why you feel like you need to write about it," Linda said. Linda isn't keen on revisiting the trailer park days herself.

"Sometimes I'm not sure why I need to do this myself," I replied. "But I'm not trying to hurt you or Mama or anyone else. I just know in my bones this is something I'm supposed to do."

This journey has taught me that my greatest flaws, and yes, Mama's too, could be a source of unfailing strength. "What were her greatest faults? Anger, impatience, stubbornness. Yes, it was Meg's faults that she turned to to save herself."

Mama could be mad at me all she wanted, but she couldn't deny that the reason I wouldn't let go of this is because I'd inherited her lockjaw grit and determination. She couldn't turn me away as she had when I was a child with her usual flippant rhetorical remark, "Why do you want to know all that for? You writing a book?"

Yes, ma'am. As it turns out, I am.

My incessant questions gave Mama the thing that had been denied her and the thousands of women like her—permission to talk about how difficult her life had been as a war widow.

As world news focused on the war in Iraq, Mama finally began to open up about how abandoned she'd felt by her country and her family.

"I didn't know what to do after your Daddy died," Mama told me. "Once he was buried, the Army was gone. Their whole attitude was 'We've done our duty.' I didn't know what to do. I'd been an Army wife since I was sixteen. I didn't know how to be a civilian. Where do you go? Where do you live? Where do you take three children to grow up? I didn't have a home. Hell, I'm surprised we survived at all. Shit, why didn't somebody help me through all of that?"

I'm glad Mama didn't expect any answers from me because I certainly didn't have any.

"I just don't know how everything got so screwed up," she added.

It was in that same conversation—the one we had there in her living room shortly after I returned from Vietnam and following her retirement party—that Mama revealed to me a long-held secret. "When your Daddy went to Vietnam I'd had a dream that your father was going to be killed. I knew from that moment on that it was going to happen. I wanted to stop it. But I couldn't."

Mama said she had been around the Army long enough to know that once Daddy was dead, she was on her own, completely.

"Once your sponsor's dead, you're not part of the Army anymore. Once he's dead, you're totally cut off. I wanted to tell the Army: But you killed my sponsor! I think about that all the time. Especially now, what's going to happen to all these guys who are coming back to Fort Benning from Iraq now and those who aren't? And their families?"

There's simply no way for a family to prepare themselves for the enduring loss war creates. Grief counseling might help some, but it can't erase the pain.

"I've always felt some loss," she said. "Even now."

Several times that night Mama commented on how surprised and glad she was to see me at her retirement party. We laughed over and over about Frank being back behind bars again. We talked about her plans to move to a beach house, in Westport, near Linda. And I told her about how I had sensed Daddy's presence at the base of Dragon Mountain and again as I stood looking over the Ia Drang Valley in Vietnam's Central Highlands.

Before we turned in that night, Mama told me that she thought I favored Daddy the most. "You have your daddy's eyes," she said.

Captain Osborne told me the same thing. But I suspect Mama's comment was motivated more by the way I view the world now than by the blue of my eyes.

When I visited Mama that summer in her new beach house, she whipped up a batch of banana pudding with a golden meringue topping. It's a treat she's made only a half dozen times since Daddy died. Daddy loved banana pudding, black coffee, and peaches with cream. He enjoyed fishing with Frank and speeding through the pineapple fields on a moped he'd restored, with Linda perched between his legs and me holding on from the back. And from the letters he wrote to her from Vietnam, I know Daddy missed making love to Mama under a tin roof on a rainy night. It rains a lot at the beach.

While she gave me a tour of the house, I thought of all the times as a teenager I'd begged God to send Mama a good man to take care of her. As I walked through her home, admiring the gleaming planters perched in an alcove above the stairwell and the spacious master suite off the dining room, I thought how far she'd come from trailer life. Then I realized that God had answered those long-ago prayers of mine.

No. He hadn't sent Mama a man to take care of her. Instead he allowed her to learn to take care of herself. And with one glance around her home today, it's easy to see that Mama took that lesson to heart.

Mama finds ways to fill her life, tending to flowers in her garden or taking long walks on the beach with her dog, or painting. Sometimes, when Frank or Linda drop in, Mama cooks up a mess of beans and rolls out some biscuits. Daddy always loved Mama's beans. And she is always happy when one of the grandchildren drops by.

Family pictures, framed in glass and silver, litter coffee tables and bedside tables throughout Mama's home. There are photos of Uncle Carl and Uncle Charlie. Of Frank, Linda, and me and our families, and of Grandpa Harve, Granny Ruth, and Aunt Cil. Mama displays pictures of everyone in her house but Daddy. Even though nearly four decades have passed, Shelby Jean Mayes Spears just can't bear a constant talisman of the love she lost.

During my visit to the Wall for the twentieth-anniversary ceremonies, a news reporter stopped me and asked about the picture I was wearing around my neck. So I showed her my father's name, David P. Spears, on the East Panel.

"I was blessed to have two heroes in my family," I told her: "my father and my mother."

The reporter wept when I said that. Afterward she sent me a note that said: "I just wanted to say how touched I was (and still am) by your story. It really puts the effects of the Vietnam War into perspective."

Long before I met Peter, before I laid eyes on that towering statue of Hero Mother in Da Nang, I knew my mother was every bit the hero my father had been.

Mama didn't always handle things with grace. She made her fair share of mistakes and then some. We all did. But for all Mama's faults, for all of mine, I realized that the best decision Daddy ever made was asking Shelby Jean Mayes to marry him and to have his babies.

I suspect Daddy had a premonition about that, too. I figure he knew that no matter what came our way, Mama would never give up the battle. Come hell or high water, she'd hold the line of defense. She would soldier on. And she'd teach each of us to do the same. She may not have slept on any pillow long enough to fashion a crown of chicken feathers, but I suspect someday God will give her a glistening diamond-and-ruby crown of her own.

Mama's steadfast love for Daddy is a reminder to me that the men who went to Vietnam were some of our nation's finest. They were professional soldiers who served their country honorably. Each one was someone's beloved son, someone's brother, another's faithful husband or friend. And thousands were devoted daddies to an untold number of children.

I am blessed to be the child of such a soldier. I am proud to be the daughter of a Vietnam veteran. And I'm equally proud to be the daughter of Shelby Jean Mayes Spears, my very own Hero Mama.

The Shelby Spears "Hero Mama" Scholarship Fund provides financial aid to single moms seeking to obtain a nursing degree at Columbus State University in Columbus, Georgia. Tax-deductible contributions can be made to the "Hero Mama" Scholarship Fund, Columbus State University Foundation, 4225 University Avenue, Columbus, GA 31907-3645. Or visit www.heromama.org

Sons and Daughters in Touch is a national organization designed to provide support to the adult children of American servicemen killed or missing in action as a result of the Vietnam War. For more information about SDIT, please call (800) 984-9994 or log on to the website at www.sdit.org

The Virtual Wall® Vietnam Veterans Memorial contains personal remembrances of letters, photographs, poetry, and citations honoring those women and men named on the Vietnam Veterans Memorial in Washington, D.C. For more information contact The Virtual Wall at www.virtualwall.org or by e-mail at The VirtualWall@FrontierNet.net

Vietnam Veterans of America, Inc. is dedicated exclusively to serving Vietnam-era veterans and their families. VVA relies totally on private contributions, which are tax-deductible to the donor. For more information, contact VVA at 8605 Cameron Street, Suite 400 Silver Spring, Maryland 20910-3710, by phone at (301) 585-4000, or on the web at www.vva.org

author's note
and acknowledgments

During the summer of 1966, I spent a good deal of time in a Tennessee holler at Aunt Cil's. Her house is gone now, but the barn where my cousin Lon used to slop the pigs is still standing. It's weathered quite a bit, just like me. But up around the bend is the church where Aunt Cil used to sing praise songs to the God she loved so well.

I recently returned to that church graveyard. I plucked a handful of wild roses growing beneath the church's stained-glass window and carried those flowers to the spot where Aunt Cil rests. A faded certificate marked her burial spot. At the time of Cil's death, Mama could not afford to buy her beloved aunt a headstone.

The tears of heaven's children fell, soaking the ground that covered Cil's body. Oh, how I loved her body! Round and soft and always eager to comfort worn-out souls. I wanted to curl up beside Cil and feel her warmth one last time.

But the ground has grown cold and Cil has long been dead. I knelt down and muttered a prayer, and thanked Cil for all those afternoons she spent telling me stories.

Then, I drove to a monument company in Rogersville and bought my great-aunt a headstone. A pink marble slab. Cil loved all things pink. On it I had inscribed a favorite quote—Words rise up out of the country—because Cil was the first to tell me the stories of Jesus, of Mama, and of our people.

In 1966, I was too young to realize what precious treasures stories are. But after I had a family of my own, I began to hunger for tales of my dead daddy and my lonesome mama.

In 1996, I began searching for the men who served with Daddy in

Vietnam, and prodding Mama to release the memories she grasped ever so tightly. This story could not have been told without her cooperation. She wasn't always a willing participant, but she was always honest. Thank you, Mama.

The names of two families have been changed in this book – that of my high school boyfriend, who for obvious reasons I didn't want to track down. And the family of the sergeant, who had been my father's best bud and may have contributed to his death, declined to participate in the story.

Mama's honest ways taught me not to rely on my memories alone. Trauma eats at a person's mind, creating gaps. Details are often hard to recall. When mine were in dispute, I turned to family and friends for help. My thanks to Frank Spears, Linda Spears Barnes; Mary Sue Spears; Delmer Floyd; Hugh and Nina and Joel Spears; James Spears; Linda Mayes; Dode and Betty Price; Lynn Wilkes; Karen Mendenhall; Steve Smith; and Pastor Smitty and Betty.

I owe a big hug to the men of Battery B, 2/9th Artillery, 3rd Brigade, 25th Infantry Division. A special thanks to Captain John Osborne; Doug Johnson; Pablo Gallegos; Gary Smith; Gary Catlett; John Nash; and Andrew Melick. Thank you for the ways in which you continue to honor my father with your stories.

I relied heavily on the expertise of people ohsomuch smarter than me. Joe Galloway, your book served as a compass, pointing me to the place where Daddy served and died. Thanks for your gracious mentorship and big ol' Texas heart. Bob Welch, thanks for clearing the path for me. Doug Bates, thanks for being the first to see the value of this tale and for introducing me to David Kelly, who enabled me to get it down on paper.

Senator Gordon Smith, Pauline Laurent, Patty Lee, and Jeanette Chervony helped me obtain my father's military records; thank you. Jeanette also spent countless unpaid hours maintaining the *Hero Mama* website. Thank you, Jeanette, for all you do on behalf of our fathers. And to all my brothers and sisters at Sons and Daughters in Touch; the faithful volunteers at the Vietnam Veterans Memorial; Diane Carlson Evans; Xuan Nguyen; the Virtual Wall crew; my pals at Vietnam Veterans of America, VietNow, and Run for the Wall; and veterans the world over, thanks for sharing your stories and indulging mine.

To those who blanketed me with prayers, fed me, and gave me shelter, my deepest appreciation: Ed and Connie Henricks; Hunter Mendenhall; Ken and Sherri Callaway; Philip and Karen Clark; Norman and Rhonda Waller. And to my long-suffering beau, Tim, and our brood, Stephan, Ashley, Shelby, and Konnie—you all do me proud every day.

Thanks also to Cathy Fussell, director of the Columbus State University Carson McCullers Center, for inviting me to be the first writer in residence and making me feel right at home while hard at work. Thanks also to the helpful assistance provided by CSU archivist Reagan Grimsley, and those ever-helpful librarians at W. C. Bradley Memorial Library in Columbus, Georgia, and the Kingsport Public Library in Kingsport, Tennessee.

My agent, Carole Bidnick, and my editor, Henry Ferris, understood from the get-go that this story was more than just a personal memoir; it's a reflection of families torn asunder by war. Thank you, Carole and Henry, for gracing this story with your earnest devotion and uncompromising professionalism. You've done Mama and Daddy proud.

I share this story in hopes that all people, but in particular our nation's leaders, will carefully consider how one soldier's tragic death can alter a family's destiny for all time.

It was Daddy and Mama who taught me that bravery isn't the absence of fear but the ability to press on in spite of it. So remember, y'all, be strong and of good courage, always.